Hill 660, Cape Gloucester, the Solomons

Foot by foot, man by man, the hostilities persisted without letup through the afternoon. By 4 o'clock, we could see that the prospects of gaining the crest were dubious. Right then, Lieutenant Colonel Buse had to make another tough decision: either abandon the plan to capture the hill that day and swing around the south base to form a junction with the weapons company on the beach, or take the bolder, more dangerous course of trying to seize the hill before darkness fell.

Lieutenant Colonel Buse chose the audacious alternative. . . .

But to do so, the Marines had to overcome a number of obstacles. The angle of the slope was very high. The Japs had machine guns cunningly placed all over the ridgeline. And the leathernecks were dead tired after fighting for eighteen days. They had been pushed to their limits; they were going on raw nerves.

At that critical stage, the Marines rose spontaneously and, shouting defiance, charged up the near-vertical face of Hill 660, and surged over the Jap defenses like wild breakers over a coral reef. The Marines took Hill 660 at 6 P.M., one hour before darkness. The defenders ran before they could be completely encircled. . . .

MARINE COMBAT CORRESPONDENT

World War II in the Pacific

Samuel E. Stavisky

IVY BOOKS • NEW YORK

An Ivy Book
Published by The Ballantine Publishing Group
Copyright © 1999 by Samuel E. Stavisky

www.randomhouse.com/BB/

Library of Congress Catalog Card Number: 99-90437

ISBN 0-8041-1865-5

Manufactured in the United States of America

First Edition: August 1999

10 9 8 7 6 5 4 3 2 1

To Bernice,
my wife and best friend,
who listened to my war stories
for fifty years and then declared:
"Enough already. Go write a book!"

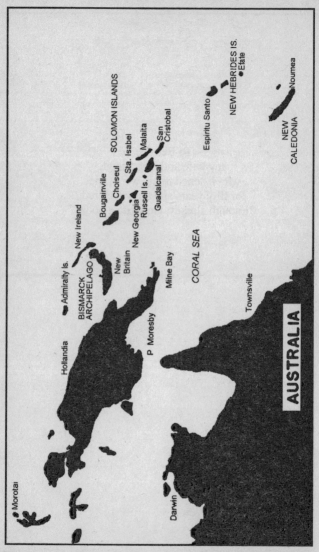

Overview of Pacific Key Points: Noumea (New Caledonia); Espiritu Santo (New Hebrides); Guadalcanal and Russell Islands, New Georgia Islands, New Britain (Solomon Islands); Hollandia (New Guinea); Coral Sea. *U.S. Marine Corps*

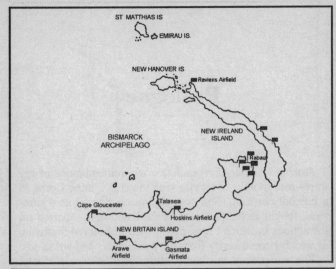

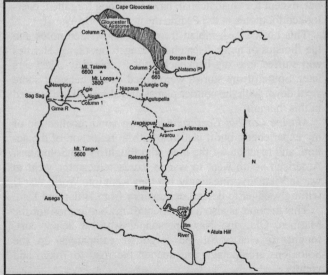

(A) New Britain Island (flags represent Japanese airfields). (B) Detail of western New Britain Island and of the Itni Patrol. *Cpls. James O. Harmon (Antigo, WI) and George A. Ward (Philadelphia, PA), U.S. Marine Corps*

Prologue

Marine Combat Correspondent is a remembrance of my thirty-four months of service with the U.S. Marine Corps as a combat correspondent who rigorously trained as a rifleman, fought in the Solomon Islands, and then reported on the actions in which I took part, which I observed firsthand, or which I could verify from the participants and witnesses.

The campaigns and battles described here were crucial but, except for Guadalcanal, have been long forgotten, overlooked footnotes in the Pacific theater of World War II.

This book is assembled from my handwritten notes and the flimsies of news dispatches I banged out on my Hermes and stuffed into my backpack, still legible fifty-odd years later. Some of my stories were killed by the censors; some went down with the courier planes and ships; all are revived in this memoir.

Marine Combat Correspondent is a vivid recollection of my experiences, but it is also a faithful reflection of the action, and reaction, of the men who fought in the Solomons. American youth went to war in Korea reluctantly, went to war in Vietnam protestingly, but they went into World War II willingly, eager to defend our country from Hitler and Tojo.

This memoir is also a testament of my admiration for the Marines, GIs, and Navy personnel who, at heavy cost, fought to victory in the forgotten campaigns up the Solomons archipelago and opened the road to Tokyo and victory.

CHAPTER 1

Washington

The Japanese bombers hit Pearl Harbor on Sunday, December 7, 1941.

I volunteered for the Army the next day.

Washington was savoring a cold, crisp Sunday morning, but inside the council chamber of the District Building the debate was sharp and heated.

Should the Newspaper Guild strike the *Washington Post*? The militants demanded that picket lines be drawn up at once, immediately after the meeting. I and other *Post* staffers tried to buy time, arguing for one more week of negotiations with management.

The *Post* had been rescued on the brink of dissolution only a few years before by Eugene Meyer, who had realized an ambition to crown his achievements in finance and government by operating a newspaper in the nation's capital. The *Post* had only recently begun to earn national recognition for fair reporting and liberal-view editorials, but it was still financially the weakest of the five dailies that saturated the Washington circulation area.

I had joined the *Post* in 1938 and liked the camaraderie of the small, dedicated staff. At twenty-seven and single, I could tolerate the paper's low salary scale, which had generated the walkout call. I was emphasizing my main arguments against an instant strike, when the double doors of the meeting room crashed open and a horrified voice cried out: "The Japs have bombed Pearl Harbor!"

As if one of the bombs had exploded among them, the startled staffers stampeded out of the chamber and through the long, slippery hallway, plunging down the twenty-odd

1

steps two or three at a time, and, ignoring the frantic honking, charged heedlessly through the traffic across the open triangle of Pennsylvania Avenue and E Street into the rundown building that shabbily housed the *Post* people, printing machines, and presses.

Militants and moderates alike rushed to their desks, phones, and typewriters, keyed up to write, edit, print, and produce the EXTRA! WAR! edition that would hit the streets in record time.

I slid into the seat at my rewrite desk and, with a nod from my adjacent city editor, began hammering out the local angles, weaving a seamless reaction story from the bits and pieces being phoned in by the reporters from their beats.

As more shocking details flashed over the news-service Teletype machines, clattering like washers filled with loose dishes, the newsroom was quickly inundated with reams of typed copy relayed to the editors, who made judgment calls on what information was to be shoved into the extra and what to be cut or penciled out. From copyboy to managing editor, the staff slid into a fast, steady rhythm without letup through the hectic night.

Meantime, as the stories and headlines were taking shape, the printers, pressmen, and delivery drivers raced to their stations. Harry Gladstein, the peripatetic circulation chief, bounced into the city room pleading with the writers and editors to hurry it up. Harry, bald pate perspiring, never removed his jacket and tie, as all the staffers did. Dapperly dressed, as was his everyday mode, Harry was itching to take to the streets himself, hawking the first fifty extras off the presses.

It was a long, exhilarating night that ran into Monday morning for me and the *Post* team. Even while banging out the endess copy for the several special editions, I had been mentally weighing the pros and cons, and had decided I would enlist in the Army and go off to war.

Early that very same Monday, the day after the sneak punch on Pearl Harbor, I joined the long, squirming line of volunteers striving to join the Army, but it was late afternoon before I reached the physical exam room of the recruiting station. The military medico fingered my thick spectacles and muttered to himself: "I can't believe it." Then he made a quick test of the lenses and exclaimed: "Three-twenty, five-twenty!"

The doc then looked directly into my pleading eyes and gravely pronounced his decision: "Son, when our country starts calling up widows and orphans, we'll send for you."

That was a downer, but I was determined to try again. The next day, after another arduous night at the *Post*, I tried again to enlist, this time with the Navy, even though the thought of riding a bucking destroyer in heavy seas induced a sensation of nausea. Again, after an exasperating day's queuing up, I was immediately and flatly turned down.

I was crushed. I was burning to get into combat, to defend the United States of America against Hitler and Tojo. I felt with a passion that every U.S. citizen should be bursting to fight, especially the first-generation offspring of immigrants, like myself. The attack on Pearl Harbor abruptly shook awake my childhood memory of Papa Zedel's joyful gratitude on reaching U.S. soil after fleeing from the brutal pogroms of his Ukrainian shtetl (village):

"I kissed the ground when I got off the boat," Zedel recalled in a rare moment of revelation.

The image of my dignified, black-bearded father, dressed in customary black suit and black derby, kissing the ground, left an indelible impression on me and made a lasting impact on my sense of patriotism.

I felt contempt for draft dodgers—loathed them—and later broke with two kin and a couple of newspaper colleagues who had manipulated the system to evade the draft. I never forgave them, or renewed ties of friendship.

John Riseling, the wispy, exuberant city editor, kept reassuring me that our home-front duty to get the news out was important, too, and was making an essential contribution to the war effort, but I was not to be consoled. I wanted in, and by in I meant in combat.

I became increasingly disconsolate as *Post* people departed to join the armed forces. In desperation, I even considered enlisting with the Canadian military, which had long been fighting overseas, but I learned that my poor eyesight would bar me there, too. I resigned myself to my fate—to be rejected—and began to put more enthusiasm into my rewrite slot.

In the spring of 1942, I got wind of a rumor that the Marine Corps was planning to create a Combat Correspondents Corps. Unable to see well without spectacles jammed to my nose, I had not even considered trying to enlist with the Marines. What little I knew about the Marine Corps, from a rare movie or magazine, had made it obvious to me that the sharpshooting amphibious branch of the armed forces would have nothing to do with an applicant whose shooting skill was limited to shooting the breeze and whose killer instinct was limited to hammering the typewriter keys.

As a newsman, I had had some contacts with the Army and Navy, but with the Marines? Oh, I did have one encounter with the Marines. It happened in 1938. The night of October 30, Orson Welles terrified the nation with his gripping radio drama, "War of the Worlds," in which creatures from Mars invaded our planet. The broadcast, mistaken for news, panicked the United States, as wild rumors quickly spread across the country.

That night the *Post* newsroom was thrown into a calculated frenzy of activity by the reports of emotional, extraordinary reactions to the invasion pouring in from the wire services and *Post* regional reporters.

Among the incidents passed on to me for the area roundup story was an item asserting that Marines at the Quantico, Virginia, base were seen on their knees praying. Ordinarily, as rewrite man I would have demanded that the reporter who called in the Marine bit assure me that his source was reliable. But there were too many other bizarre reactions streaming in, and I simply added it to the overall roundup.

The invasion from Mars proved to be an unintentional hoax, but we could not correct or call back all the silly stuff published in our early edition.

The following day, about 5 P.M., when the newsroom was starting to hum preparing the next morning's issue, and I was beating out my first rewrite, six husky Marines in dress uniform marched in, two abreast, and the leader, banging his beefy fist on the city desk, his thunderous voice threatening, barked: *"Freeze!"*

The newsroom froze. The city desk froze. My fingers froze on the typewriter keys. "Who wrote that shit about the Marines falling on their knees and praying?" the sergeant demanded, glaring around.

"We have something to say to that motherfucker!"

I glanced up at the imposing posse. Their powerful physiques would have been useful to the Redskins' first line. Their eyes were fastened on us—on me—steely, suspicious, hinting mayhem. My phone to the police reporter took that inauspicious moment to ring, and I automatically reached for it, when the massive mitt of a uniformed hunk slammed down on my fingers, smashing them. He didn't utter a word. He didn't have to.

Our bantam city editor, Riseling, slowly pushed his roller chair out from the desk, rose to his full height of five feet six inches, barely reaching the shoulders of the stupendous sergeant, and with a dry introductory cough, thrust his best honest-look face at the menacing Marine.

"Sergeant," John said, as if revealing a confidence, "the guy you want is not here. He's in New York. Works for the Amalgamated Press. He deserves a kick in the ass for reporting such a vicious canard about the Marines. I'll give you his address."

So saying, Riseling placed his thin hand on the brawny shoulder of the sergeant, and I could detect a tremor of appreciation down John's spine.

The leatherneck hesitated. Riseling rushed in soothingly. "Look, Sarge, my family loves the Marines. We've got two nephews in the Marines. Now, we wouldn't do anything to insult the Marines, would we?" He uttered the fib with the ring of conviction.

The avenger squad leader, confused, insisted Riseling give him the address of the vilifier. Then, fussing with the address, Riseling gave the sergeant the address of the New York City Hall.

The miffed Marines marched out, and the newsroom started humming again as staffers paid heartfelt tribute to our feisty city editor, a man renowned for his demand for the facts—the true facts—from his reporters.

Do I have to explain that the "Amalgamated News" didn't exist?

I always recalled that absurd incident whenever I later heard or read the word *Marine*.

This time, however, I investigated the combat correspondent report and found that, yes, the Marines were in the process of creating a unique adjunct of writer-fighters.

I promptly phoned Brig. Gen. Robert L. Denig, director of Marine public relations, and announced: "I'm assistant city editor of the *Washington Post*, and ready to join your new corps."

"You're in," Denig responded without hesitation. "I'm sending my sergeant major to sign you up."

I was ecstatic. Here I had been rejected by the Army and the Navy, and now I would get into the war with the Marines. Incredible!

Sgt. Maj. Joe Shipman, a China hand, tall and manly, the poster picture of a Marine, met me at Bassin's for coffee and explained that General Denig wanted newsmen with at least five years' experience. They would have to undergo the grueling make-or-break Marine Corps training course in order to fight in combat as Marines of the line. In brief: Fight, then write.

Just what I wanted to do. I was eager to get going.

Next day, I hurried to Arlington, Virginia, where the Corps had its headquarters, to meet the general, who surprisingly turned out to be shorter than my own height of 5'8½". I was unaware then that General Denig had the reputation of being the shortest Marine in World War I. Denig was a veteran of thirty-six years' service, his chest bemedaled for his combat service in France. His earnest face projected a firm jaw and a merry smile.

The general proved to be short on public relations knowhow but nonetheless keen on the combat correspondents concept.

As director of public relations for the Marine Corps, the little general's principal duty was to beef up recruitment, and he took on his unfamiliar assignment with zest, coming up with new ideas for the anachronistic PR department. When the war broke out, General Denig fell in love with the CC concept, purportedly first suggested by his deputy, Maj. George Van der Hoff, a reservist fresh out the Federal Housing Administration.

As General Denig saw it, the CCs would be good for the morale of the men in combat and for their families back home as well. He won over the commandant, and fought successfully to overcome the traditional resistance to any radical change in the Marine Corps establishment.

General Denig and I hit it off at our first meeting.

Reluctantly I had to inform the general that I had already been cast aside by the Army and Navy because of my substandard sight.

Denig chuckled. "No matter. I want you, Sam, and I can give you a waiver."

I was jubilant.

Two days later, the jubilation turned to desolation when I learned that the Navy, which had overriding jurisdiction and was disdainful of the combat correspondent concept, had overturned the waiver granted by the one-star Marine general. Rules are rules!

General Denig, however, was no pushover. He took the rebuff as an affront to his Marine rank and position. He appealed in person to the Commandant of the Marine Corps, three-star General Thomas Holcomb, who had recalled Denig from retirement to run the Corps's public affairs. The two had served as fellow battalion commanders in the campaigns through France in World War I and were fast friends.

General Holcomb had the reputation of being a tough, no-nonsense leader, and had been chosen by President Roosevelt to command the Marine Corps for a second four-year term. Holcomb was immersed in the pressing problems of reorganizing his scattered peacetime Marine units into an amphibious force capable of fighting the victorious Japanese army in the Pacific. Nonetheless, loyal to his trench-war buddy, the commandant—as confided to me by General Denig—took a puff of his ever-lit pipe and issued his own official waiver without even asking, "Who in the hell is Sam?"

Again, the Navy medical watchdogs were unimpressed, and refused to honor the commandant's imprimatur. It was to them a case of "No see. No go."

Now it was General Holcomb's turn to be offended. Furious, he stormed into U.S. Navy Headquarters and demanded of Secretary of the Navy Frank Knox—as Denig later told me—that the prerogatives of the Commandant, U.S. Marine Corps, be respected by the Navy's braided bureaucrats. The commandant's waiver—for what's his name—was absolutely undeniable, the Marine Corps chief declared.

The Secretary of the Navy, still reeling from the shock of losing the carrier *Lexington* a few days before in the Coral Sea, overwhelmed by the problems of dealing simultaneously with the predatory U-boats in the Atlantic and the marauding Japs in the Pacific, had no time for trivial matters, and simply waved Sam in, according to General Denig, who got the word from General Holcomb.

Apparently, the Secretary of the Navy not only didn't ask: "Who in the hell is Sam?" He didn't care. Why take on the Marines, too, when he already was up to his ears fighting Hitler and Tojo?

A trivial matter indeed!

To me, it was the Secretary of the Navy's most consequential decision of World War II.

I could scarcely believe the serendipitous ending of my roller-coaster ride. I thanked General Denig in person and my other two unknown patrons in absentia. I was not superstitious—not really—but I also thanked my lucky stars, and interpreted the extraordinary sequence of events as a good omen for my forthcoming service.

On May 25, 1942, with the prescribed regulations finally fulfilled, I was sworn into the Marine Corps . . . as a private.

I was a happy fellow. I was a happy Marine.

CHAPTER 2

Parris Island

We are the boots,
Most stupid of recruits;
We love to eat, but hate the chow;
We love to sleep, tonight or now;
We'd love to fight, but don't know how . . .
We are the boots . . .

Yes, we are the boots,
Dumb and despised brutes;
We can't learn how to make a sack,
We march for miles in heavy pack,
We need no brain, just use our back,
For we are the boots.

Oh, the sun is hot and the sand is deep,
Our aching feet can only creep;
We growl like wolves, but obey like sheep,
For we are the boots.

We "ride the range" and scrub latrines;
We loathe the sight of pork and beans;
We are the lowest of Marines . . .
We are the boots . . .

Poetaster Unknown

Among those sworn into the Marines with me that May 25, 1942, were Al Lewis, my Phi Alpha house roommate and *Washington Post* fellow newsman. A friendly grin on his round, rubicund face, effervescent as ever, Al stood beside me at the hand-raising rite, half an inch shorter, a year and a half older. Al was the ubiquitous police reporter of the *Post* and I was the rewrite man for the stream of stories he phoned in every evening in time to make the first edition. We wanted to serve together in the same Marine outfit.

A third *Washington Post* staffer, red-haired, gargoyle-faced, raucous-voiced Jack Gerrity, joined us, joking and restless as always despite the seriousness of the brief enrollment ritual.

We war-fevered fugitives from journalism were instructed, following induction, to board the 7 P.M. Washington train for Parris Island, South Carolina, that same day.

Al and I returned to the frat house for the last time as civilians. Then Jack took off for a bar, so as to depart from the nation's capital with a good taste in his mouth, he said. Al took off to see his girlfriend. I sat down to write my first war letter to Bernice, in Brooklyn, my love-at-first-sight whom I'd met on a blind date with Lewis.

At Union Station we fell in with a carload of noisy recruits from New York City, smoking and acting tough like "Dead End Kids," and a bewildered, befuddled gaggle of enlistees from the rural South. For a while it appeared certain the whizzing wisecracks would rekindle the Civil War, but once everyone had settled down in the hot, humid, cinder-strewn "cattle car," the locomotive heedlessly belching black smoke, the gibes soon sank harmlessly into the flowing cans of beer.

Spontaneously, we all broke into the pride-inspiring Marine Corps Hymn—"From the Halls of Montezuma"— again and again, as the train shook and shuddered through the night.

We red-eyed volunteers were empty of song and swagger when the train chugged into Port Royal, South Carolina, the following morning, backing in from Yemassee, to be greeted by a lobster-faced, big-bellied Marine sergeant, bellowing:

"Fall in! Fall in! From this minute on, you do what you're

told! Exactly what you're told! Don't even think of arguing . . . or you're dead!"

Since few of us at that befogged moment understood what the screaming sergeant wanted us to do, we bunched together, bumping and jostling one another. This reaction to his command infuriated lobster-face and, sputtering a string of four-letter epithets, he shoved us this way and that until we had formed a lineup of sorts. Satisfied, the sergeant called the roll, demanding "Yes, sir!" for each response.

Then he gave us blunt notice: "Remember this: You can't go back to mama! You joined of your free will! You stay here until we're finished with you! Don't you forget it!"

Immediately following his cordial welcome, the sleepless, stupefied recruits were herded onto trucks and packed off over the causeway to Parris Island, a dismal swampland that was to be our training camp for nine of the most miserable weeks in our lives.

At Parris Island the human cargo was unceremoniously dumped off into a sniggering pack of drill instructors panting like jackals to pounce upon their trapped prey.

Al, Jack, and I were randomly jerked into Platoon 388, formed on the spot, and which was immediately appraised by the designated DI to be the "dumbest-looking bunch of boots" he ever had seen. He reminded us of that plaudit at least once a week.

Limp, dazed, hungry, thirsty, the bedraggled column was hustled through the chow line into the miasmic heat of "The Rock," one of the more affectionate names for the training base. Without a pause, the wretched lot of us were forced to run a gauntlet of military dentists who gleefully yanked teeth as if their paychecks depended on the extraction count. I was lucky. I was marked down for a three-pull, but somehow was overlooked by the molar extermination squad.

As we staggered out of the jaw robbers' den, the stunned recruits were confronted by our impatient, wrathful drill instructor, who prodded his terrified wanna-bes into the mess hall at 2:15 P.M.—we had not eaten in eight hours—for a hasty lunch of cabbage, potatoes, hot dogs, bread and butter, and cold water—as much as we could wolf down in fifteen minutes.

Our DI next trooped us through the commissary to draw dungarees, blankets, and heavy field boots. The government issue was thrown at us by the disdainful supply clerks, who demanded of each: "What's your size?" and, snidely disregarding the reply, gave us whatever items of whatever size they had grabbed up from the clothing bins.

The field boots I drew were too large, and the festering blisters gave me fool's courage to raise the problem with the DI. He only snarled: "You'll have to get used to it, stupid," then, in a state of fury, he shrieked at his cowed charges: "The next fuckoff who complains will regret it forever."

Weighed down by our GI gear—which included heavy boots, six blankets, and three changes of clothing—we were marched off about a mile to the Quonset huts that were to be our barracks for the duration. We were glad to pull off our soggy civvies and don the dry khaki-green field uniforms.

The DI demonstrated to us just once how to make up the bunk, neatly, tightly, precisely so, and warned us to expect frequent inspections, with swift retribution to follow the slightest deviance from perfection.

He then confiscated all jackknives, cards, dice, condoms, and porn—in accordance with regulations, he told us. But later the scuttlebutt from more savvy boots insinuated that the seizure was not a rule but robbery.

Aroused the next morning at 5:30, we were hustled to a plentiful breakfast—no one dared to admit aloud that the bacon was too greasy, the coffee too weak. Immediately after, our DI ordered us to line up at attention, and, eyes glowering, he delivered a manifesto:

"I don't give a fuck about your religion, or how you pray, but in this platoon, I am GOD! Whatever I tell you to do, you do! And you do it pronto! Get that into your fat heads?"

How could any of us argue with that line of reasoning?

We dubbed him "Little Jeezus"—behind his back, of course.

Later, I came to suspect that Little Jeezus was aware of

the nom de guerre, and was pleased with the recognition accorded to the lord of Platoon 388 for the next nine weeks.

Wilted with exhaustion when evening chow call was sounded, several recruits, including myself, pleaded to skip that meal. Little Jeezus reacted as if hit by a shell fragment, and screeched:

"I don't care if you fuckers eat or not, but the manual says you make chow call three times a day. And unless you move your asses now, I'll break you out on double-time march tonight."

Little Jeezus demanded that we address him as "Sir," just as we addressed commissioned officers, and that when he stepped into our barracks, anytime, the first boot to see him was to sound off "Attention!" and all the others jump up and freeze. Once, when one of the recruits failed to rise instantly, he was forced to freeze at attention for twenty minutes.

Our DI issued new edicts and penalties daily. Forget the number of your rifle, and off you went to KP (kitchen policing). I inscribed my rifle number, #1472806, into my brain. Refer to a rifle as a "gun," and off you went to scrub the barracks floor. I fixated "rifle" in my head. My memory was never so quick and correct before.

One evening after a trying workout Little Jeezus read aloud to us, in a grave voice, *Rocks and Shoals,* the U.S. Navy's articles of governance, applicable as well to the U.S. Marine Corps. He stressed the fiat of strict obedience to superiors—he also stressed strict—adding at the end of his lecture that in his platoon the rules were what he said they were, and that there would be no appeal from his decisions.

To underscore this point, Little Jeezus often broke the platoon out on the double for any infraction of his rules, and sometimes for no reason at all. The most trifling error or failure to respond instantly to a command resulted in punishing full-pack marches through the boondocks at any hour of day or night.

Early on, the DI taught us our first lesson in covering ass. We had to wash our own soiled skivvies and other apparel, and hang them out to dry. The first time we did so, we discovered the next morning that our underwear had vanished.

We boots reported our losses to Little Jeezus, but he only shrugged and smirked:

"Okay. You've learned a valuable lesson every Marine must learn—cover yer ass."

Then, with a knowing wink, he suggested: "You don't get another GI issue. You can buy replacements at the canteen . . . or find some other way to cover yer ass."

The following week the newest class of recruits reported to their DI that items of their garments issue had disappeared overnight. I and my platoonmates enjoyed a rare snicker over that one. We'd shown Little Jeezus we could be resourceful. We'd covered our asses.

Came the day when the platoon was broken up into six squads of about ten each. To our surprise, Lewis, Gerrity, and I were selected by Little Jeezus to lead the three short-height squads. We felt good about it until we realized that the appointment was one of the ornery jokes Little Jeezus liked to play on us. The promotion turned out to be not an honor but a burden. The squad leader was also punished for any infraction by a member of his unit.

The sad fact is that we three unlikely-appearing prospects for the Marine Corps were even funnier looking as squad leaders.

At the head of our columns, we three earnestly marched and drilled abreast, but somehow couldn't keep in step or in time. Al couldn't hold the rifle on his shoulder at the proper angle, so that once when he left-faced, the low sweep of the rifle barrel conked the adjacent boot. Gerrity, suffering from extreme sunburn, bravely refused to fall out for medical treatment, and kept murmuring Ave Marias for support. And I was not only hurting from my bleeding blisters, but, worse, was fearful that I would replicate the booboo I had made during an ROTC drill in my Boston University days.

The incident occurred when I shifted my rifle from left shoulder to right shoulder arms. My rifle, instead of landing on my right shoulder, swung onto the jaw of the cadet on my right, knocking him out for the long count. I never was skillful with my hands.

We three tried earnestly, but our helmets just wouldn't stay on right and flopped over our ears. And every so often, when our taut nerves reached the snapping point, one of us would see how comical the other two looked and break into a fit of laughter, setting off hysterical hilarity throughout the platoon. Punish us as he might—and he did—Little Jeezus never did succeed in preventing those uncontrollable spells of silliness.

We drilled and drilled and drilled.

"A-whun-tuh-hee-fore . . . a-whun-tuh-hee-fore . . . Heft . . . rye . . . heft . . . rye . . . heft face . . . rye face . . . abow face . . . abow face . . . abow face . . . ho . . . march . . . halt . . . ho . . . march . . . halt . . . rip march . . . rip march . . . rip march . . . halt!"

Morning, noon, and night, ceaselessly, remorselessly, we drilled and marched . . . drilled and marched. To ourselves we cursed, griped, groaned—and we learned to drill and march in clockwork precision. All except Alfred, a nice kid but slow on the mental draw. He never did learn the rhythm of rip-march—to the rear march—and was the first to be cast out of the fold and sent home.

Some days, no matter how sweltering, there was no letup on the daily drilling. Six of the recruits collapsed one afternoon under the unrelenting glare of the scorching sun. Some of us were sure that Little Jeezus was trying to kill off all of us, but no, he remarked as he read our minds, he was only trying to toughen us up for battle in the tropics of Guadalcanal. Al and I got through the torturous exercise, but just barely; Jack, his sunburned face by then blistering, had to seek relief in sick bay.

We were ripped out of our sack at 4:30 A.M. the day we were scheduled for the first inspection by the battalion commander, and broken out for an extra drill on rip-march, but after breakfast, diarrhea swept through the platoon. Even so, we boots had to pull ourselves together because the inspection was too important to miss, Little Jeezus declared. However, the battalion CO failed to show up, and the word flew around the base that our highest-ranking officer had that morning learned that the running-willies was no respecter of rank.

My squad, No. 5, was barracked in Quonset hut A-6, and in deference to the DI's obsession for cleanliness, I made certain that our quarters were kept spotless, especially after failing in the first unscheduled scrutiny by Little Jeezus. For this transgression, Squad No. 5 had to clean up and wash down all latrines after our regular overload of drills and maneuvers. At other times, when our platoon leader became incensed over a miscue, we had to "ride the range"—scrub down and polish up the still-hot galley stoves.

One Saturday morning, while instructing us on extended order drill, Little Jeezus digressed into a tirade expounding his views on the state of the nation.

He denounced President Roosevelt as a "dictator" who would never give up the White House. He berated Secretary of the Navy Knox and the First Lady as "nigger lovers" who had compelled the Marines to accept blacks. He castigated the Army for accepting "rabble" under the draft. He hated the "Limeys" and wished the United States were fighting the British instead of the Prussians, whose military efficiency he openly admired. And he hated the Japs, too, not only for their sneak bombing of Pearl Harbor but also because they were "slanty-eyed, yellow-skinned heathens." He also made it clear to us that he was first of all a Marine who'd "fight for my country, right or wrong."

One of the few respites the boots received from the regimen of daily drill was an evening of movies. One night, the entire battalion was marched into the dining hall to see *To the Shores of Tripoli*, Hollywood's version of life in a Marine Corps training camp. And what a howl it was for us.

We jeered in derision when we saw the film's star, John Payne, given a neat haircut, complete with sideburns, when he arrived at boot camp. We knew better. We all got the standard three-minute bowl-style slash. We hooted when "Boot" Payne slugged the sergeant, a heinous offense in camp, second only to murder. Those who groaned the loudest were the patsies who had rushed to sign up with the leathernecks *after* having seen the film in their hometown cinemas, picturing themselves in the snappy blue dress uniforms of the U.S. Marine Corps, nonexistent for us boots.

It slowly dawned on me that Little Jeezus detested his assignment. The DI had to be up before the 5:45 A.M. bugle reveille and had to make sure the platoon was sacked in by 9:10 P.M. taps. His rank was only private first class, and he himself had not yet seen front-line action.

The DI well knew that if he was to be switched out of his unwanted task, he had to drive his platoon to the highest levels of performance demanded by his sergeants, and by their superiors all the way up to the battalion commander. The DI was an essential cog in the wheels of the Marine training system, and didn't dare permit himself, or his platoon, to ease up. The system demanded utmost effort from bottom to top.

Although deified by their boots, the DIs were treated with condescension by the sergeants, who had served in Haiti, Nicaragua, or China, and who trained the boots in rifle, bayonet, and pistol tactics, scouting and patrolling techniques, response to enemy fire, map reading, and jungle survival.

Little Jeezus was always there watching his company at the other training sessions, and I could hear him hollering, "Cover yer ass, stupid," even as the boots were crawling on their bellies under barbed-wire obstacles through a fusillade of "enemy" shot and shell. He would force us to practice our new skills until they met his idea of perfection.

Scorned from above and hated from below, Little Jeezus compensated by swilling suds when he could get away to the beer slops outside camp, and by pushing his boots relentlessly. The weak fell, were weeded out, and discharged. Only the strong in body and in will endured. Incredibly, Al, Jack, and I endured.

Those who survived boot camp would be prepared for the physical hardships of front-line combat. That was the theory. It worked, as we later learned in the Pacific.

Little Jeezus was a skinny guy, but wiry and tough, a cocky bully with clenched fists, humorless thin lips, an oversized Nicaraguan campaign hat wedged down on his head. He once boasted that his greatest satisfaction came from pushing his platoon to the limit.

Little Jeezus drove his charges beyond the brink one moonless night. He yanked the platoon out of the sack at 3 A.M. for a forced four-mile march to Elliott Beach, with light pack. We reached the beach without difficulty. On return, however, Little Jeezus decided to make faster time back through a shortcut in the marshy boondocks infested with myriads of slimy fiddler crabs. We trudged through ankle-high mud for a mile, came upon a deep, fast-flowing river, and came to a halt. What now?

"We'll cross it!" shouted Little Jeezus. He ordered the taller men to wade in first and form a human chain, so that the shorter boots, like me, could have help in wading through the stream while holding rifles high and dry. Maybe our DI saw the maneuver work in a movie, but it didn't work for us. The strong current repeatedly broke the chain every time it was re-formed, until several of the stalwarts in the support line, themselves overextended, began calling for help.

Furious, Little Jeezus threw himself into the pandemonium, belaboring the floundering boots with sneers, snarls, and oaths. To his credit, he quickly recognized the peril of the situation, coolly ordered into the stream all men who could swim to aid those who were faltering, and plunged into the whirlpooling waters to take direct charge. Little Jeezus used his "haid," demonstrating resourcefulness. He had covered his ass.

Gerrity hopped in with the rescuers. He wasn't much of a swimmer, but he splashed around like a walrus, barking orders like a seal, and carrying on heroically until he had to be pulled out.

One member of the platoon, himself struggling in the water but holding his own, hollered for help when he saw a comrade go under. A rescuer, thinking it was the yeller who was in trouble, grabbed him and started for the bank. When the Good Samaritan tried to protest, the rescuer knocked him cold with a jab to the jaw. Fortunately, the overlooked boot who was drowning was pulled out by other strong swimmers.

I was already making it across the river, rifle held high,

when the chain collapsed. I made it back on tiptoes. I clung to my rifle, keeping it high and dry, but ruined my watch.

Little Jeezus finally counted heads and found two helmets and three rifles were missing, lost in the stream. The DI would never be able to explain away so serious a loss, and he ordered a half dozen volunteer divers back into the surging waters to search the bottom. Little Jeezus gave the retrievers no words of thanks when they brought up the lost accoutrements, but showed his gratitude by marching us back to barracks at an easy pace.

(Six boots were drowned in a similar maneuver across that creek in February 1956.)

All the DIs were martinets, but Little Jeezus demanded that his company be faster, snappier, smarter. He was a tyrant in enforcing discipline, but he became the devil incarnate for rifle inspection. Scores of times each day I and my fellow trainees were ordered to break rifles apart and slap them together again in split seconds. A speck spotted inside the bore by the DI brought swift implacable retribution. When I, naturally clumsy in handling any mechanical device, dropped my rifle at drill one morning, I not only was punished with extra marches but had to sleep for a week with the rifle tightly tucked in my sack.

No matter how beaten down after a long day's workout, my first act on returning to quarters was to break, clean, oil, and polish my Springfield '03 to a shiny glow. The rigid routine inculcated me with the ethos of the Corps: A Marine is a rifleman, first and foremost. He is trained to handle the weapon and fire it accurately under all circumstances.

Over the torturous weeks, I gradually became aware that my rifle was transforming from a symbol of dread for me into a symbol of pride. One day, too, I came to the understanding that the Marine and his rifle are one.

From the day Little Jeezus formed his platoon, the DI perceived that Al, Jack, and I were different from other recruits. Most were in their teens, high school grads or dropouts; inexperienced, but resilient and crackling with energy. We three were obviously in the upper twenties. As ex-reporters, we were articulate and at first avoided the f-words, the lingua franca of the camp. The DI took an immediate dislike to us, for we were the odd ones.

One morning, I was pulled aside by Little Jeezus and sharply questioned:

"I found out you went to college. Why did you join as a private when you rated a commission?"

I replied truthfully: "I wanted to serve as an enlisted man."

"Don't believe it," snapped Little Jeezus. "I think you're a fucking spy checking on me. Only a fucking fool would pass up a commission."

He said no more after that incident, but poured it on me at every opportunity. I was determined not to flinch under the pressure. Once, I stared at Little Jeezus, who promptly announced that any silent sign of defiance against a DI could be considered a serious offense under the regulations. I stopped staring. I just took it.

Lewis took the buffets with a grin.

"Wipe that grin off your face," the DI ordered, but Al would soon be unconsciously displaying his unsquelchable broad smile. Gerrity not only took it but gave some back. He possessed a quick Irish wit and Blarney stone rhetoric that bamboozled Little Jeezus and forced the DI to yell "Attention!" whenever he found himself entrapped in a lengthy explanation by Jack.

The strict camp discipline incited hostility among the overstretched recruits. Fights broke out. The DIs generally turned their eyes away from the fisticuffs unless an officer happened by. Sometimes boxing matches were arranged between antagonists; other times, the challengers went at it with bare knuckles.

I studiously avoided any argument that might lead to blows, and accepted with feigned good humor the wisecracks about my peepers. I was, after all, the only boot in camp who wore glasses.

However, from the very beginning of my Marine enlistment, I had geared myself to strike the first blow at any joe who jabbed an anti-Semitic insult at me.

I had experienced my first encounter with mindless ethnic

animosity at the age of six, when my family moved into a predominantly shanty Irish neighborhood. The next evening, when I sauntered into the playground across the street, I was beset by a hooligan gang of tykes who wildly denounced me for killing Jesus. They hit me, scratched me, tore at my clothes. I was overwhelmed, not comprehending what the assault was about, but instinctively I clutched onto one of the smaller assailants and bit fiercely into his ear. The screams of my chance victim halted the attack long enough to let me escape and dash home.

As I rushed through the front door into the entry hall, I ran into my indignant father, who was standing there, glaring down at me, and scolding:

"Why do you come home so late, looking like a dirty little ruffian, my son, when you should be dressed and ready to go with me to the evening Sabbath service?" he demanded.

It was all too much for me to explain. All I could do was splutter:

"Papa, they beat me for killing Jesus."

Whack!

Papa slapped me across the mouth, not hard, but hard enough to smart.

"You are forbidden to utter that name in this house," Papa declared. "Now go get cleaned up and dressed by Mama so we won't be late for maarib" (evening prayers).

I was shocked speechless. First attacked, then whacked, for some terrible thing I had done but didn't understand. I didn't know who Jesus was. What made it all worse, it was the first time my gentle father had ever slapped me. I cried, but only inwardly to myself, because I was ashamed of having offended Papa.

There had been other such unpleasant incidents in my growing up, and even in my adult years. Along the way, I learned to respond to offensive racial remarks with verbal counterthrusts.

Boot camp, however, was a different testing field. There, I was aware, action was more effective than words, and my response to an anti-Semitic insult would have to be made with my fists.

The critical moment came one evening as I was walking down the steps from the camp canteen. A pace or two behind me an unfamiliar voice suddenly sang out: "Oh, Sam, you made the pants too long! Oh, Sam, you made the pants . . . !"

"This is it," I resolved.

I flung my glasses into the grass, and simultaneously swung around with a left haymaker intended for the offender's face. Instead, my southpaw sock landed on the massive chest of the hugest hunky on The Rock.

Surprised but hardly hurt by the blow, the "big Polack" did not strike back, but instead stopped short, rubbed his chest, and cried out:

"What's the fucking matter with you, guy?"

My left wrist in pain, head reeling, helpless without my peepers, I nonetheless squinted up at the perplexed giant and yelled accusingly into his face:

"I'm Sam. You were making fun of me."

"Hell, no," protested the puzzled gargantuan. "I never even saw you before. I just felt like belting out a song I learned last night."

Myself confused now, I slowly retrieved my spectacles and profusely apologized to the man mountain standing there quietly, still scratching his broad chest.

"That song drives me nuts," I tried to explain my crazy reaction.

I offered my right hand in a gesture of friendship. To my relief, the hand was accepted at once, and so vigorously that I wound up with both hands in pain, but it was a small price to pay for my reckless reaction. Big Polack could have smacked me into the infirmary for a couple of weeks.

I ran into no other physical to-do at camp, perhaps because the word got around that the little guy with the goggles had thrown a punch at Goliath and had come out of the imbroglio alive. Or maybe it was because Big Polack announced he was my friend, and if need be, my protector. I really liked the big lug.

We underwent intense firing drills. I had no trouble with the .22 pistol, scoring 81 percent in fifty rounds, just points below the qualifying score for expert. But with the rifle and without the specs, I was coming up with too many "Maggie's drawers."

As the boots entered the final phase of training, our time and effort were focused on snapping in with the rifle and practicing the firing positions: standing offhand, sitting, kneeling, prone in slow and rapid fire. Some of the boots, especially those from farm regions who had been brought up shooting squirrels and game birds, took to the Springfield tests with alacrity. But I, who had been a prominent member of the ROTC awkward squad back at BU, had trouble getting the hang of the operation.

When it came to the actual firing of the '03s, I was gunshy. That timidity was aggravated by having to wear my spectacles to see the test target clearly, and by the camp talk about rifle bolts flying out into eyes of maladroit shooters. I'd seen enough black eyes around the base to give credence to the tales.

The gunnery sergeant, expressing amazement that the Marines let me in wearing cheaters, gave me extra time and convinced me that it was shoulder jerking that created the shiners, not runaway bolts. All one had to do to be a topnotch rifleman was to hold on firmly to the rifle, take careful aim, and s-q-u-e-e-z-e it off.

Strangely, I found the offhand position easiest to handle, although it was difficult for most of my platoonmates. On the other hand, what was the easiest and highest scoring position for most boots—rapid-fire prone—gave me trouble. Worse, I could neither sit nor kneel exactly as the range instructor showed me. I could not keep my elbow from slipping from under the rifle after each shot, so my aim was thrown off for rapid-fire shooting.

The gunny tried every trick he knew, from encouraging words to holding down my shoulders, but it was no use, and he gave me up for a loss. So did the other noncoms on the butts.

Rifle Record Day was approaching, when tragedy hit. A savage squall lashed the island one night, and when the watch was relieved, one of the boot sentries was found dead, struck by lightning. The death, unexpected, shook up the boots. It was the first fatality of our war.

On Prelim Day, that is, the day before Rifle Record Day, I tried out all the suggestions of my coach, but I failed to qualify in the tests because the firing positions he insisted on were too uncomfortable for my joints. Thoroughly disgusted with myself, I decided the next day to shoot as I pleased. It was the score that would count, not the classic posture.

Amazingly, I somehow passed the tests and qualified as Marksman, lowest acceptable level, and only three points short of Sharpshooter. The rifle coach, enraged when I informed him that I was firing as I pleased—permitted on Record Day—had dressed me down and predicted I would fail. But when the target tests were over, he rushed up to me to declare, with pointed finger: "See, if you had followed my instructions, you would have made Sharpshooter!"

Bayonet practice—grim and realistic—was saved for last. I passed that test, too.

Two members of Platoon 388 with the lowest scores were immediately shipped off to purgatory—cooks and bakers' school. That was the system, and explains the well-earned reputation of Corps cuisine as the worst of the three services. I never could figure out why two members of our platoon were picked to be trained as DIs.

My chum Al Lewis got a bad break. Before he could finish his rifle tests, he was called back to Washington to testify in the trial of a serial sniper whose killings he had covered for the *Post*.

By the "lucky draw" among the boot platoons, my #388 won the booby prize—an additional week of mess duty. My galley-slave unit of twelve had to serve twenty-two platoons—1,300 men—three meals a day, and swab tables, benches, floors after each chow. We were up at 3:30 A.M. and crawled into the sack at 10 P.M. On my third day of dining hall duty, I slipped on a wet patch of the floor, two pitchers of iced tea tumbling down with me. I was given an uproarious razzing by the titillated trenchermen, and demoted from waiting on tables to scouring pots and pans.

Eyes inflamed from lack of shut-eye, feet swollen, skin singed by the hot plates, I staggered through the week. I had joined the Marines to fight, not to feed a mob of chow-hounds, and I was determined not to fall out in the final week of boot camp.

The happiest day in boot camp for me arrived on schedule a few days later, July 27. Platoon 388 was up at 2 A.M., breakfasted at 3, fell out for the last roll call at 4, and lined up for the ultimate dress review at 5.

The men—no longer boots—stood tall, confident, sinews flexed, spirits soaring, proudly aware they had earned their Marine Corps uniforms. They faced Little Jeezus for the last time with assurance instead of apprehension. They had attained the right to fight in combat, and already knew that their tormentor was doomed to more oppressive weeks of drilling the next incoming batch of raw recruits.

Little Jeezus, neck craned, chest out, chin in, defiantly delivered his farewell address:

"I know you guys hate my guts. Well, I don't give a shit about that. My orders was to whip a bunch of fucking slobs into Marines ready for combat."

He paused and glared into the faces of the Marines he had molded.

"And I did that!"

Little Jeezus spun around and strode off.

Not a one of the platoon cheered; not a one clapped. After an awkward lapse of silence, the freshly anointed Marine privates instinctively broke into "From the Halls of Montezuma." I joined in the chorus.

So went the bittersweet parting with Little Jeezus. I was happy to be rid of him.

But I was wrong; Little Jeezus, exemplar of Marine Corps training and discipline, would stay with me, indelibly instilled in my innermost conscience.

CHAPTER 3

Treasure Island

The ebullient covey of correspondents who had come through the rugged trials of boot camp was transferred back to Washington for indoctrination and to prepare the men for their assignments overseas.

General Denig, beaming with avuncular pride that his first brood of CCs had surmounted the hurdles of Parris Island, gave his protégés a warm welcome. He was chummy and chatty, and assured us that he was pushing the buttons that would speed us into the battle zones.

I was delighted with the prospect. I had given blood to get into the war, and craved quick action. So did my fellow keyboard commandos.

The objective of the CCs, our cheery commander said, would be to write a story about every one of the members of our squad, platoon, company, battallion, regiment, etc. These Joe Blow pieces, forwarded through official channels to HQ, would immediately be distributed to the regional press and radio embracing the hometowns of the leathernecks named in our dispatches. The media were hungry for front-line news about their local heroes.

General Denig wisely refrained from haranguing his fourth-estate volunteers with a litany of instructions. Concentrate on the enlisted man, he urged. It doesn't have to be about combat. Write about human-interest events, too. Sure, report the hero stuff, but don't forget the guy who wins his battalion boxing championship.

We CCs marveled that the general was talking like the managing editor of one of our newspapers. He had made a faster conversion to journalese than we had made to military jargon. We were amused, but we liked him for that.

The general's outline of the field operations was accepted with enthusiasm. Yes, I would turn out streams of local stuff, but I was already dreaming of finding myself in the middle of the Big Story that would make the national headlines. I suspected, with good reason, that my cohorts were secretly scheming a like scenario.

General Denig himself presented each one of his combat-ready CCs with the three-stripe armband that would from that moment on identify us as sergeants, and handed out to each a Swiss Hermes typewriter. The compact machine weighed eight pounds, and was to be borne on the backs of the CCs along with their regular field backpacks.

The indoctrination turned out to be a series of desultory lectures dealing with the Marine Corps code, regulations, traditions, and censorship rules.

The CCs were then given a brief furlough. I raced home to Massachusetts for a quick visit with my family, then dashed up to Vermont to spend a glorious day with Bernice, that summer a counselor in a camp for underprivileged children.

I returned to find that I had been posted to the Fifth Marines along with Al Lewis, who had finished up his boot camp course. We were tickled with the appointment. The Fifth was a famed regiment that had earned the fourragère for extraordinary bravery in France in World War I. Gerrity was designated for the Sixth Division.

Two days later, on August 7, the exhilarating news flashed over the nation, like a showering flare lighting up the sky, that the Marines, led by the Fifth, had landed on Guadalcanal and seized a foothold in the Solomons archipelago.

I was dismayed by the news. All through boot camp, I had sustained a vivid fantasy that I would be the CC in the initial Marine advance in the Pacific. My disappointment was exacerbated some ten days later with the nation-thrilling news that the 2nd Marine Raiders had annihilated the Japanese garrison on Makin Atoll in the Gilbert Islands, Central

Pacific. What in the hell was I doing in Washington listening to listless lectures?

General Denig, upset and irate, furiously phoned, button-holed, and harassed every one of his buddies holding top Marine positions, pleading and demanding that his CCs be dispatched to the field at once. He somehow cut the upper-echelon red tape and extracted the high-priority orders needed to send a batch of us to the West Coast for transshipment to our assigned outfits in the Pacific theater and to garrisons scattered around the world such as the Cocos Islands, Sitka, St. Lucia, and Balboa.

Al and I were overjoyed to have been chosen together to join the Fifth Marines on Guadalcanal. It was a prize posting the other CCs envied. General Denig assured us that he had arranged speedy travel orders for us, so that on reaching San Francisco, we would be flown posthaste to the Guadalcanal battle zone.

"I'll expect your first stories back in about two weeks," the general suggested. "I know you won't disappoint me."

Arriving in San Francisco, we CCs were quickly bused to Treasure Island, site of the Golden Gate International Exposition, since converted into a Navy-Marine base. Al and I were exhilarated with anticipation, like teens looking forward to their first major league baseball game. We waited, nervously alert for the flight call that would summon us at any moment. We kept on our toes—gear packed, Hermes and Springfields at hand—for the next forty-eight hours, and then, somewhat dispirited but still believing, stood by in futile suspense for several more days.

After a week of ants-in-the-pants anticipation and a series of frenetic, futile phone calls, Al and I came to the painful conclusion that the high-priority transport orders issued in Washington carried little weight with the Joint Military Port Command in San Francisco.

To the Port Command the CCs were an odd breed of Marine classified as low-priority personnel for the limited space available on Pacific-bound planes and ships.

The transient transfer to Treasure Island stretched into weeks. A few of the CCs managed to get away to offbeat destinations, far away from the battle zone, but Al and I, slated for Guadalcanal, were stuck. The Japs had sunk the U.S. cruiser shield off Guadalcanal three days after the Marine landing, and only a scattering of planes could get through the enemy blockade of the island. The beleaguered Marines there were in dire need of food, medicine, and arms—not CCs.

In the meantime, the old-time officers and NCOs (noncommissioned officers) running the Treasure Island base formed an instant antipathy to the marooned CCs, whose duties did not show up on the USMC Table of Organization and who, without any action experience, were already sporting three stripes, which normally could take ten years to acquire. Despite their protests, the CCs were shanghaied into loading gangs, standing night sentry duty, protecting ammunition dumps, guarding prisoner work shifts, even digging ditches.

I was randomly fingered to be a "chaser." I tensely cradled a loaded shotgun in my arms while standing guard over a pack of prisoners on a work project. The brig rats were plain fuckoffs, and had no intention of putting in a hard day's labor or trying to escape. Nonetheless, I was edgy. I had heard on the grapevine that the chaser would have to serve out the prison term of any escapee. Lips pursed, heart beating rapidly, I kept close watch over my wards. The work gang, however, was not intimidated by their bespectacled guard, and at times even heckled me, sneering at me, daring me to shoot. They had quickly recognized that their overseer was a stripling Marine, notwithstanding his sergeant's insignia.

The long transportation delay, like a heavy fog overhanging Treasure Island, cast a pall of gloom over the base for all of us CCs. The frustrating days mushroomed into discouraging weeks. Little by little, some of the dejected typewriter troops gave up their rifle drill and physical exercises. I, irrationally, hung in.

I drilled every day. I deftly tore my rifle apart and deftly put it back together again and again. I marched around with full pack, Springfield, and Hermes. I was determined to keep in shape. Some of my fellow CCs thought I was nutty, and said so.

At first, the languishing CCs took advantage of their off-duty spare time to explore the cultural charms and bounteous bistros of San Francisco, simply biding time as pleasantly as possible. My intent to get to Guadalcanal undiminished, I researched the libraries for background on that battle-field and learned little more than a sketchy outline of its topography of volcanic mountains and virgin jungles. Then, as ennui took over, some of us made a run to the offbeat bars on the north shore. We savored the sting of dry tequilas and other exotic concoctions for pleasant, conversational evenings.

One night when I showed up at a favorite saloon, my usual quaffers failed to turn up as promised. However, a couple of freewheeling sailors joined me for a round of mar-garitas and repartee. I was buying the second libation when Little Jeezus popped into my "haid" and hissed: "Cover yer ass, stupid!"

Too late!

I was already passing out from the furtive Mickey Finn. I came to in the misty early dawn propped up against a tele-phone pole on the sidewalk, my head throbbing from a knife-stabbing hangover.

When I mustered the strength to get on my feet, I discov-ered that I had been picked clean of cash. "So maybe they weren't sailors," I muttered to myself.

I made it back to the barracks by thumbing a ride from a passing Marine, who sympathized with my plight and had little good to say about the bluejackets, genuine or phony. Seems he had been cleaned out, too, that night, at dice with sea dogs.

I found an outlet for my suppressed energy by moonlight-ing for several weeks on the night copy desk of the *San Francisco Chronicle*, where I derived some little satisfaction writing rousing headlines about the war. I struck up a friend-ship with a *Chronicle* photographer, Joe Rosenthal, who wore glasses thicker than mine and who bemoaned his own rejection by all the armed forces.

(Months later, Joe got into the action as an Associated Press photographer. He took the acclaimed photo of the Marines raising the flag at Iwo Jima.)

The monotonous routine of Treasure Island was shattered one day by the arrival of Marine survivors of the carrier *Yorktown*, sunk in the Battle of Midway, June 4–6.

We stranded CCs, unable to get into the action, were so ravenous for eyewitness combat stories that we swooped down on the recovering Marines who had manned a section of the antiaircraft guns on the *Yorktown*. Pieced together, the accounts of the men unfolded an epic episode in the brilliant career of the flattop.

Launched five years before, the *Yorktown* was assigned to the Pacific, but early in 1941 was shifted to the Atlantic to help fend off the U-boats wreaking havoc on the U.S. lend-lease convoys to Great Britain.

The *Yorktown* was recalled to the Pacific after the Pearl Harbor debacle and the bloody Japanese conquest of Wake. The *York* joined a task force in U.S. naval harassment of Jap-seized strongholds, her planes raiding the Marshall Islands, and Salamaua and Lae in Papua, New Guinea.

Then, on April 18, 1942, America was electrified by the daring exploit of Army Air Force Col. James A. Doolittle, who led a formation of sixteen Mitchells from the deck of the carrier *Hornet* to bomb a surprised, unprepared Tokyo, 600 miles away. Doolittle's B-25s, unable to make a return landing on the accompanying *Hornet*, flew a thousand miles more to land on friendly Chinese airfields.

A couple of weeks later, the *Yorktown* teamed up with the carrier *Lexington* to provide the aerial clout for Admiral Jack Fletcher's Task Force 17 steaming out to confront the much more powerful Japanese sea might, then intent on making an amphibious landing on Port Moresby, New Guinea, off the Australian coast.

In the ensuing Battle of the Coral Sea, early May, in calm sea and clear sky, the opposing fleets, never in visible contact with each other, engaged in the first carrier-to-carrier conflict of the war. Dauntless dive-bombers from the *York* and the *Lex* sank a Jap flattop and the Navy's carriers were

themselves struck from the air. Critically damaged and listing, the *Lexington* was finished off by our own torpedoes after her crew was removed to destroyers standing by. Some of
the *Lexington*'s homeless SBDs (Douglas Dauntless dive-
bombers), finding no usable runway on the *Lex*, alit instead
on the return deck of the *Yorktown*, then refueled and flew
back into the raging battle.

The *York* was severely damaged by repeated attacks of
Vals, Aichi dive-bombers, and Kates, Nakajima torpedo
bombers, that broke through the Grumman fighter screen.
Three 500-pound missiles targeted the *Yorktown*, one crash-
ing through the flight deck and penetrating four levels down
before exploding. The Marine quarters were utterly destroyed, and a rash of fires broke out, accompanied by choking smoke. Through it all, with scores killed or wounded,
the Marine and Navy gunners stuck to their posts, firing
away without stop at the Japanese onslaught, shooting down
dozens of the enemy warplanes.

Disabled and slowed down, pumping water, the *Yorktown*,
commanded by Capt. Elliot Buckmaster, dragged herself
back 2,000 miles to Pearl Harbor and, after only a forty-
eight-hour layover for the most essential repairs, was ordered back to the Pacific to join the Allied fleet being
reassembled hurriedly in anticipation of a renewed and
mightier naval assault by Admiral Yamamoto's armada.

In terms of ship losses, the Battle of the Coral Sea was a
draw. But the United States rightly claimed victory on the
ground that the intended Jap invasion of Port Moresby, en-
dangering Australia, had been thwarted.

On June 4, off Midway—westernmost Pacific outpost
still held by the United States—our Navy took on the Jap
sea forces once more, again in placid waters and open
sky. Our planes went on the offensive—every squadron
from the carriers *Enterprise*, *Hornet*, and *Yorktown*, supplemented by obsolescent Brewsters flying from Midway and
Flying Fortresses from Pearl Harbor 1,100 miles away—tore
into the enemy sea and air forces.

Two bombs disabled the *Yorktown*, even as her gunners
shot down the planes that dropped the eggs on her, and later

that day two torpedoes slammed into the carrier's belly. Despite the resulting carnage, the AA guns of the *York* kept up a withering fire to blast the Jap torpedo planes. The *Yorktown* began to list and the order was given to abandon ship. The wounded were removed to destroyers and the dead were buried at sea. Surviving planes of *Yorktown*'s eighty kept on flying and fighting from the flight deck of the *Enterprise*.

The next day, the listing *York* was combed by a search party for a second time, and two wounded men, overlooked earlier, were found and rescued. Then a salvage crew of some 150 sailors and Marines came aboard in a risky attempt to lighten the carrier and hopefully save her. However, a Jap sub sneaked through the protective ring of our destroyers, sank one, the *Hamman*, and fired two more "fish" into the *Yorktown*. The gallant "Waltzing Matilda"—as her crew affectionately called her—slid down into Davy Jones's locker with her flags flying.

(The Battle of Midway proved to be a decisive triumph for the U.S. Navy in the Pacific. Four Nipponese carriers and scores of planes were eradicated. Americans at home did not learn until after the war that although our fleet was outclassed and outnumbered in ships, planes, and firepower in that crucial battle, our military intelligence had broken the Japanese code and our Navy command was aware of the enemy's plan of action.)

I and my fellow CCs interviewed the willing, wounded Marines, wrote a number of hometown-hero stories, and filed our reports directly off to Washington. All of our accounts that went beyond the bare details of bravery were penciled out by the censors, because—we were reprimanded—we were giving away critical information to the enemy. We CCs then realized that we would be contending from then on with two adversaries: the Japs and the censors.

One of my Joe Blow stories, about a Baltimore boy on the *Yorktown*, containing meager details of the carrier's valiant end, somehow slipped through the censors and was published in the Baltimore newspapers. The local item, which had been sent from San Francisco, 3,000 miles away, became a national story when it was picked up by the Associated

Press and relayed back to San Francisco, where it was given page-one play by the *Call-Bulletin*.

If Marine Corps public relations had dispatched the item directly to the West Coast daily, more likely than not it would have been thrown into the wastebasket for lack of the local angle. But the AP logo gave the hometown item national stature. The transformation of Hometown Hero into All-American Hero was often made during the war by the news wire services.

In the course of my naval hospital interviews, I came across a group of convalescing Devil Dogs who had participated in the daring, celebrated foray of Carlson's 2nd Raiders on Makin August 17, ten days after the Guadalcanal invasion by the First Marine Division.

The Raider mission, it was later disclosed, had been contrived by high command to throw the Japs, who were rampaging through the Pacific, off balance, and to divert some pressure away from our main thrust at Guadalcanal.

The nation's newspapers had trumpeted the sub-borne sortie as a resounding victory, cheering up our people at home at a time when the leathernecks were barely holding their own against the fierce Jap resistance on Guadalcanal, and after our Navy had lost four cruisers—a big chunk of its available fleet—to the enemy August 10, three days following the landing.

My immediate effort to interview the convalescing 2nd Raiders was blocked by the hospital OD (officer of the day), who maintained the Marines were off-limits. The ban on my talking with them aroused my reportorial curiosity.

I patiently proceeded up the ladder for permission—the three successively higher Marine public relations officers of the Western Recruiting Division; three successively higher Navy publicity officers; the executive officer and commanding officer of the base—to convince each that my story would surely add to the glory of the two services and to the morale of our citizenry. Besides, I argued—this was the clincher—whatever I wrote would have to clear their censorship.

I interviewed half a dozen of the wounded, and elicited the following account:

The 2nd Raiders' assault on Makin Atoll, in the Gilbert Islands, was led by Col. Evans F. Carlson, a famed China hand, and Maj. Jimmy Roosevelt, son of the president, his executive officer. Carlson had commanded the Marine unit stationed at Warm Springs, Georgia, to protect President Roosevelt, who was taking the waters there for his crippled legs. The two had become close, I later learned, and it was Carlson who persuaded the commander in chief to inject the Raider concept into the Marine Corps over the protests of the old-boy cadre who believed standard Marine training and tactics already made their leathernecks as tough and capable as the British commandos.

The Raiders, nonetheless, had undergone special training for commando tactics, and half of them had participated in the Battle of Midway after reinforcing the atoll's defense battalion against the Jap aerial onslaught and intended seizure of that outpost.

Two companies—some 200 Raiders—camouflaged in blackened fatigues and trained for rubber-boat landings from destroyers, undertook their first strike—against Makin August 17—from two big submarines, *Nautilus* and *Argonaut*. It was the maiden operation for the Raiders from S-boats.

The *Nautilus* had already gained glory by torpedoing and sinking the Japanese carrier *Soryu* in the Battle of the Coral Sea. The *Argonaut*, also a 2,700-ton old-timer, had undertaken yeoman assignments in mine-laying and troop transport.

The two pigboats required more than a week to churn the 2,000 miles from Pearl Harbor to Wake, and the Marines were miserably cramped for nine dank days, stuffed into the scarce spaces available to them, sardined among the stockpiled "fish."

Off the reefs ringing Makin Atoll, in the predawn darkness, the liberated Raiders set out on their motor-driven rafts for Butaritari Island in the atoll. High swells and wet weather snafued the landing plans, and one squad wound up on the opposite side of the lagoon, behind the defenders. Then someone accidentally fired a weapon, blowing open the covert operation.

The 2nd Raiders battled it out all day against the resisting

Japs, who had captured Makin only some weeks before. The Nip snipers played havoc with the Marines, until the Raiders turned their firepower on the trees instead of trying to spot the hidden individal sharpshooters. The Marines stopped cold several banzai-screaming charges of the enemy, and even shot down two Jap seaplanes aimlessly dropping bombs.

By daylight's end, the 2nd was rounded up to reembark to the two submersibles, but the breakers and tide were running too rough and fast for the rubber boats, which had to be paddled by hand because their engines had fizzled out. A few of the rubber boats made it back to the subs, but most, swamped, had to turn back to the landing beach, their weapons and gear swept into the sea.

As was his custom—unique in the Marine Corps—Colonel Carlson called his officers and men together for a confab, a policy called "gung ho" from the Chinese "working together"—a term that contrarily was later transposed into a Marine war cry meaning "Let's go!"

The council of war decided that, with a significant number of men wounded or missing and weapons lost in the vain struggle to rejoin the subs—and in the belief that the two S-boats had taken off without them—an offer to surrender should be made. Two Raiders were sent out that night to find and negotiate surrender terms with the enemy, but the enemy was not to be found.

Early next morning, after Major Roosevelt managed to paddle back to his sub with some of the Raiders, Carlson was informed by island natives that the Jap defense force, less than a hundred soldiers and "termites"—Korean laborers—had virtually been wiped out by the Marines in the first day of battle. The happily surprised 2nd Raiders were now free to move out at will and destroy the island's military installations, including a radio station. The Raiders then unhurriedly paddled out beyond the reefs to the subs and returned to an American base safely, to be hailed as heroes. Some thirty Marines were killed in the Makin raid, one of whom was awarded the first Medal of Honor in the Pacific War.

That vaunted Raider action was hailed by the Armed Forces as a brilliant victory, and was so proclaimed by the media, so that America reveled in the good news at a time when the Pacific war prospects—ten days after the landing on Guadalcanal, two days after four U.S. cruisers were sunk off Guadalcanal—were gloomy.

I had seen the headlines in San Francisco and had read the stirring story of the commando raid by the 2nd. I was dumbfounded, then, by the startling, differing version told by the men I interviewed. I talked to six, and each individually swore he was there in the council of war that decided on surrender. The Raiders, elite of the Corps, willing to surrender rather than fight to the death! Unbelievable!

Nonetheless, I had to accept the unpleasant truth, confirmed by the half dozen participants. I also, thinking it over, had to accept the unpleasant fact that none of the armed services' censors would, or could, let this disturbing account leak out into public knowledge. I didn't give the censors a chance to kill this incredible story. I killed the story myself. Why get another reprimand?

Little Jeezus danced around in my mind approvingly. "Covered yer ass!" he said. My ass, certainly, but not my conscience.

(After Makin, the 2nd Raiders later proved themselves to be a crack fighting force on Guadalcanal. The *Nautilus* lined up in its periscope and sank three Japanese *marus*, merchant marine vessels, off Japan, escaping depth bombs time and again. The *Argonaut* was not so fortunate. The sub attacked a Japanese convoy, pierced an enemy destroyer, and in the furious reaction was demolished by a barrage of shells and torpedoes. All one hundred crewmen were lost with her.)

Years after the war, the Marine Corps confirmed the version of the wounded Raiders I had interviewed. It was also belatedly disclosed that nine Marines missing after the Makin foray had been left behind, captured by the Japanese, and beheaded.

The morale of the CCs had been lifted when we threw our efforts into banging out hot copy about the *Yorktown* survivors on Treasure Island. Our original ambition to get into the action at the battlefront was revived. After all, we cried to one another, that's why we joined the Marines. In desperation, and in flagrant disregard of regulations that prohibited bypassing the chain of command, we bombarded General Denig with phone calls and letters, pleading with him to free us from our imprisonment on Treasure Island.

The CC creator, unable to break the blockade from Washington, flew into San Francisco and, unannounced, presented himself in formal blues at the Marine base.

"What in the hell are you doing here?" Denig demanded of his astonished Demons. We were momentarily made mute by the surprise visitation. Then we responded with a resounding babel of indignation.

"I get the picture," the general cried out above the din. "So you want to get out of here. Then why didn't you let me know?"

The general's sly remarks outraged us. We chorused in anger, but our chief turned a deaf ear to the uproar for a brief moment; then without any answers to the clamor of questions, he roared:

"Attention!"

We CCs froze instantly. It was the first time we had ever heard that rigid order barked by our general.

"I came here to get you out to your battlefield posts," General Denig declared. "Stay alert. Be ready to go." Without giving "At ease," without another word, he made a quick but dignified exit. Near the door, I thought I saw the perky general wink as he strutted by.

General Denig broke the bureaucratic shackles in three days. I never did discover how a one-star had blitzed the higher-ranking brass and braid bigwigs of the Port Military Command. But I loved him for it.

On November 21, some fifteen weeks after the "temporary" transit stop on the West Coast, I and five fellow CCs boarded the freighter *Juan Cabrillo*, destination unknown but somewhere in the Pacific. I felt certain the vessel was heading for Guadalcanal, and I was in a happy frame of mind again.

CHAPTER 4

Juan Cabrillo

Two days later, November 23, 1942, at 4 P.M., the 10,000-ton *Juan Cabrillo* lifted anchor. The Liberty ship was crammed with urgent cargo. Meager space was grudgingly doled out to 180 passengers—Navy personnel and a Marine contingent of six CCs and ten cooks and bakers.

The freighter, one of the fleet of 700 Liberty ships mass-produced by Henry Kaiser at record speed, was given a thrilling sendoff. A Navy blimp, like a frolicking kitten, circled overhead; a Navy plane dipped in a sendoff salute; Coast Guard cutters bobbed alongside and blew their foghorns in a show of respect. Marines, sailors, and crew cheered the surprising fuss made over our departure.

About an hour later, the *Juan Cabrillo* sailed under the glistening Golden Gate Bridge to behold the sun slowly sliding into the pot of gold that lay at the end of the rainbow overhead. A light mist purpled the elegant span, and the flickering hues of the clouds mingled with the swirling blues of the bay and the russet browns of the surrounding hills.

The six CCs aboard were among the original dozen Denig's Demons who were chosen by the general and assigned to Pacific war zone posts. The six were:

Joe Alli, Buffalo sportswriter, raconteur, hardly bigger than the fat cigars he habitually puffed, our leader by virtue of his surname beginning with the first letter of the alphabet. To First Marine Regiment.
Paul Long, of the *Chattanooga Times*, a gentle, professorish, but witty onetime schoolteacher. To Second Marines.

Art Mielke, of the *Washington Times*, athletic, acerbic, sharp of mind. To Marine HQ, South Pacific.

John Black, of the *Philadelphia Bulletin*, lean, eager, edgy. To First Marines.

Al Lewis, of the *Washington Post*, his smile ever ready to flash. To Fifth Marines.

And I, eager, impatient to go. To Fifth Marines.

All of us were relieved and glad to be advancing—even at eight knots—to the battlefront, after so miserably long a delay. However, the good feeling didn't last very long for me. I suddenly became aware that the vessel was rolling and pitching as it plowed through the choppy bay into the open sea. I abruptly lost interest in the exquisite view and, gasping violently, rushed to the latrine. I eventually recovered from the acute attack of malaise, but throughout the voyage the queasiness remained.

Before I could regain my composure, I suffered another setback—more fittingly, a sitback.

One night I had to make a hurried dash for the head. It was dark in the crapper, and I failed to notice that the primitive johns had been freshly doused with carbolic acid or some other antiseptic. As a result, I not only sat down in a hurry but rebounded even faster. I was truly painfully and visibly—from the rear—wounded before I ever saw the enemy, and could show, if asked, the unlucky horseshoe emblazoned on my sore butt.

So where was Little Jeezus when I needed to cover ass this time? Little Jeezus merely chortled.

Several days later, I informed the ship's surgeon that the seasickness pills given out to the passengers had not helped me much. Doc suggested that I give up smoking. It was no big deal for me to abstain, since I puffed a cigarette perhaps three times in any day. I quit cold, gave up the habit for good, but got no relief for my nausea.

There was more unexpected largesse that accrued to me during the ocean crossing. I sharpened up my poker and gin rummy skills and won enough pots to accumulate $600. I learned to play pinochle at a loss of $36. I improved my modest chess game.

I also made a start at Tolstoy's *War and Peace*. I had bought the bulky paperback edition of the novel so that I could roll it up and stuff it into my seabag, intending to wade through the classic tome by the end of my war service.

Several of the CCs, discouraged by the prolonged stay on Treasure Island, had long given up the daily routine of stripping down and reassembling their rifles. Not I. All thumbs in any mechanical operation, I had worked too hard at boot camp mastering the tricky feat to neglect it aboard ship.

First thing after morning chow, I diligently tended to my Springfield. Then I went through my physical exercises and followed up by walking at a fast clip on a circuitous route along the deck. I made an addition to my daily discipline. I began to carry out a series of eye exercises immediately after putting rifle and body through their paces.

Before boarding ship, I had taken along two extra sets of specs, especially reinforced to keep the lenses firmly glued to the frames, and had cached them into my backpack as replacements in the event of loss or breakage of my everyday pair.

Nonetheless, I seized upon the suggestion of the ship's first mate that I try "Better Eyesight Without Glasses," a system of eye conditioning aimed at raising visual acuity developed by Dr. William Horatio Bates. His regimen was based on the theory that six muscles control eyesight, and like all other muscles must be exercised to maintain healthy tone. His exercises were concentrated on blinking, central fixation, and shifting of the eyes. The Bates system, practiced daily, would end the need for spectacles. So it was claimed.

Every morning and afternoon, I sought out a quiet spot on the open deck where I would practice rolling my eyes up and down, left and right, and every which way. I ignored the stares and wisecracks attracted by this strange routine. The word soon got around the ship that I was a devotee of a special yoga. That rumor served to strengthen the widespread belief aboard that I was a kook who was planning to enter the battlefront wearing goggles taped to my ears. Another rumor had it that I was planning to carry a sign in large letters on my back, proclaiming I AM A MARINE!, so as to alert other leathernecks, especially those to my rear. Many of Tojo's soldiers wore spectacles, but a U.S. Marine?

Several of my shipmates pointed out to me that the peepers, reflecting sunlight, would make me a fat target for Jap snipers. The warnings convinced me that I could not afford to let up on eye drill even for a day. Each day, too, I tested my sight on an eye chart, and was encouraged by the seeming improvement of my vision. As a result, I later discarded my glasses in active combat areas and depended on my own eyes. During childhood I had won a lead medal for swimming fifty feet, barely, in the Y pool, but never improved that distance, so I wore my life jacket day and night. However, even those Marine comrades who were strong swimmers followed my example. They took it for granted that the cargo of the *Juan Cabrillo* was made up of munitions—stuff like explosives and high-octane gasoline—and so they clung on to their Mae Wests.

The ship's carpenter, two days out of port, had commented to me that the life preservers were useless, and ought to be scrapped as an unnecessary burden.

"One bomb from an enemy plane, one torpedo from an enemy sub, one lit match carelessly thrown, and we'll be blown to kingdom come with or without the jacket," the crewman confided. I and all the other CCs recognized the logic of the advice, but wrapped ourselves in the security blankets nonetheless. Just in case.

The passengers on the *Juan Cabrillo* were cut off from all news of the world during the entire voyage and forbidden to contact the ship's radio operator. As a result, wild rumors flourished. A mysterious light seen on the horizon, the third night at sea, aroused tense anticipation of an attack by an enemy destroyer or submarine. Jap subs—faster, more powerful, and longer ranged than ours—were ravaging Allied shipping in the Pacific, so that we had reason to be worried about them.

I and my fellow CCs were particularly edgy about the possibility of a "fish" attack since we all had interviewed the

Marines surviving the torpedoed carrier *Yorktown*. After a period of anxiety, the mysterious light vanished, and soon after so did our fears.

Two nights later, a flare lit up the storm-raging, foggy darkness ahead, and a sentry shouted he had heard a call for help. "Man overboard!" he cried.

The ship's captain turned the freighter around into the eerily whistling wind to search for the victim. All hands were broken out for a tally of noses, and when the body count proved to be identical to the ship's roster, the furious captain ordered his vessel back on course at top, sickening, speed.

The eleventh day out, we CCs were confronted by a new menace. We could see for ourselves unidentified planes hovering over the evening horizon, and so tensed for an enemy bombing or strafing run. The looming threat turned out to be scurrying cloud formations transfigured by the setting sun.

The *Juan Cabrillo* crossed the equator on the twelfth day and observed the ancient rites of initiation in which the first-timers aboard are transformed from pollywogs into shellbacks. My baptism included a dozen hard smacks on the fanny with a wooden paddle, a handful of vile-smelling grease slapped across my face, a large glob of garlic shoved into my mouth, and a ducking into a pool of filthy bilge water. I and the other CCs took our hazing good-naturedly.

December 6 was my birthday, and December 7 was the Day of Infamy, but neither date was celebrated aboard ship.

We CCs had been well fed on Treasure Island, and had heard that our vessel was similarly well stocked with food supplies. The *Juan Cabrillo* did carry an ample larder, according to its crew, but the meals served to the enlisted passengers, Marine and Navy alike, were poorly prepared and increasingly skimpy as the days sailed by.

We Marines grumbled, and feisty Joe Alli, our spokesman, formally complained to the ship's captain. "We all have to make sacrifices in the war," he lectured Joe.

"Crap," retorted Joe, noting that the regular crew and Navy officers were eating well, some visibly putting on weight. Joe's arguments fell like lead sinkers into deep waters. The Marines got no relief, and had to resort to buying extra food from the crew.

The Marines were worse off for drinking water. Only one cold-water tap was made available to the 196 enlisted men, and it was located in the gangway just outside the officers' mess. Apparently, the presence of the long line of enlisted passengers was a nuisance to the commissioned castes strolling in and out of their dining quarters. The lower ranks were barred from their lone source of drinking water from half an hour before to half an hour after each meal—that is, for six hours a day.

One by one, each of us CCs protested to the captain against the mistreatment, and also got nowhere. The CCs together then prepared and presented a joint letter, demanding free access to the water. We got neither response nor water. This rank-pulling practice left the CCs with a sour impression of the Navy and a low regard for its officers.

I take credit—with an assist from Little Jeezus—for improving the lot of the CCs in sleeping accommodations. We were assigned a musty recess in the hold for our night quarters. The pitch hole was stacked with huge gunnysacks of foul-smelling powder, and we had to scrape up whatever we could find as a substitute for bedding.

The ship's purser had run out of typing paper and went to Joe to see if he could "borrow" spare sheets from the CCs. Joe knew that I, squirrel-like, had tucked an extra ream into the bottom of my bottomless seabag, and referred the ship's officer to me. Typing paper was harder to come by than good scotch, but nonetheless I felt duty bound to make the sacrifice for the war effort.

That's when Little Jeezus rang the alarm bell in my head and sharply cautioned: "Cover yer ass, stupid!"

Thus alerted, I stopped being Mr. Nice Guy and demanded of the purser six folding cots for the CCs in return for fifty sheets of paper. The purser argued with a passion, but finally acceded. The six cots gave us combat correspondents leeway to sleep on the deck under the soft Pacific breeze, weather permitting, instead of in the black hole of Calcutta.

On the twenty-third day out of San Francisco an Aussie plane swept over the masts of the *Juan Cabrillo*, and soon a friendly destroyer scampered up to take a close peek. By evening, we sighted land. The next day, a harbor pilot came aboard and guided the freighter through the treacherous coral reefs that girdled New Caledonia, dropping anchor in the outer harbor of Noumea.

The *Juan Cabrillo* moved into the inner harbor the twenty-sixth day at sea and dropped anchor for unloading part of its cargo.

Although my nausea persisted, I was not entirely pleased with reaching firm land. Noumea was still some 1,200 miles from my coveted goal. Would the stop at Noumea turn out to be a frustrating repetition of Treasure Island? I wondered if I would ever get to Guadalcanal. I had to admit to myself that I was discouraged.

CHAPTER 5

Noumea

First seen in the rising sun from the inner harbor, Noumea, capital and principal port of New Caledonia, gives the appearance of a Camelot magical scene, with gay-colored, brightly shining roofs scattered pleasantly among the fertile hills and slopes that skirt the dozens of inlets and coves of the big bay.

Such was my first impression of Noumea, self-styled "Paree of the Pacific," seen from six miles out in the harbor.

Once I was ashore, however, that first reaction was quickly dispelled. For that pothole Paris turned out to be a frowzy city distressingly in need of a fresh coat of paint. The brilliant glare of the sun had played tricks on my eyes.

The sixteen of us Marines were sent ashore from the *Juan Cabrillo* the morning of December 17, with nary a tear shed for the unfriendly tub that had been our home for nearly a month. It was a six-mile bumpy ride through the chopping surf, and we were drenched by tall sheets of salty spray.

The huge, deep harbor was logjammed with cargo ships—freighters and tankers of various origin—and a goodly part of Admiral "Bull" Halsey's fleet, for at the time Noumea was our largest naval base in the South Pacific. The cause of the massive tie-up became obvious when we reached the wharf. There was only one pier to unload all the tightly packed vessels choking the harbor.

Seabees and Army engineers and service troops were frantically engaged in day and night operations, throwing up new docking facilities and constructing motor-driven rafts in a desperate effort to break up the congestion. Weeks went by, I learned later, before the *Juan Cabrillo* was unloaded.

Noumea was the headquarters for the Commander in Chief, Pacific Fleet (CINCPAC) and also HQ for the First Marine Amphibious Corps (IMAC), which oversaw the widely speading Marine operations in the Pacific.

We were greeted on the beach by a cotillion of gaudily costumed Javanese vendors dancing in and around us, shoving undersized bananas, heavy coconuts, and greasy cream puffs into our faces. Numbed, and outnumbered by the jabbering hucksters, we were liberated by a no-nonsense noncom who led us into a truck and drove to Camp "Gitchey," named after Lt. Col. Frank Goettge, a fearless Marine officer killed on a dangerous Guadalcanal reconnaissance mission.

The camp was laid out in a truly beautiful setting, along the palm-fringed beach in the bowl of a wide, natural amphitheater. The backdrop, a horseshoe-shaped hill, served as a grandstand for open-air movies, so that the spectators looking off beyond the screen could enjoy the shimmering sea as well. Beautiful, yes, in dry weather, but when it rained, the entire base was transformed into one vast slough.

Upon arrival at the island, the ten Marine bakers and cooks—the lowest scorers in their rifle tests at boot camp—were hauled off to the camp kitchen. We CCs were given scant time to find six billets, and without further ceremony or explanation were pressed into a supply-dump detail, despite our protests that as CCs we held rank of sergeant. The supply sarge, a six-striper, simply shook his head and snarled:

"Never heard of combat correspondents. I need hands, not typewriters. Get moving! And that's an order!"

Our work party pitched in at 2 P.M. and lifted cases of food and ammo until 4 A.M. The old sarge gave us no letup, and we were near collapse from the unaccustomed ordeal at hard labor. I made one consoling discovery. I had easy access to canned fruit juice, not seen or sipped by me since departing Treasure Island.

I had some qualms at first in taking advantage of the opportunity, but Little Jeezus darted into my ambivalent mind and whispered: "Cover yer ass, stupid!" The advice overcame my scruples. I also felt better about it when I became aware that the service-company men—and officers—were casually slipping a few choice cans into their deep fatigue pockets.

The following morning a youngish second lieutenant who identified himself as coming from C-2 (Intelligence) IMAC showed up at the CCs' tent and one by one interviewed the six of us. He asked questions about our backgrounds before joining the Marine Corps, but turned away all of our queries as to the purpose of his visit.

The next day official notification reached our tent that five of the CCs were to embark that night on another transport for Australia, but that I was to remain at the Noumea base pending further orders.

I was dismayed. After all, I had joined up to fight, not to wither away on a godforsaken island! Why was I being left behind? The other CCs, who were also in the dark, tried to comfort me with wild guesses, none of which assuaged my anger. The five destined for Australia were delighted with their own prospects, since it was an open secret that Marine forces were being organized and trained Down Under for coming operations against the enemy.

The six of us Denig's Demons celebrated with a few cans of beer that evening. I didn't even try to hide my disappointment; it showed on my face. Still, I toasted a fond farewell to my buddies of so many long weeks since departing from Washington, and I gave each a warm abrazo. To Al Lewis I promised, "I'll be joining you with the Fifth Marines. You can bet on it." The bravado didn't fool Al, but I meant it.

(I never met up with Al again during our Pacific war careers. Al caught on with Carlson's Second Raiders. He hit the national headlines: once, in a page-one photo showing him astride a jeep alongside the famous Carlson; a second time posing with the First Lady, Eleanor Roosevelt.)

The next day, before I could be whisked away to supply-dump duty, the same second looey intervened with orders for me to appear before the Chief of First Corps Intelligence (C-2). I was baffled. "Why the summons? What's it all about?"

But the officer shook his head solemnly and refused to respond. "You'll learn soon enough," he finally remarked.

The solemn face of the courier worried me. I imagined I had seen an ominous sneer flicker across his lips, and my curiosity gave way to trepidation. I cursed Little Jeezus, and berated myself: I've been turned in for swiping a couple cans of juice. And I'm going to go to the brig for it! I'm going to be cashiered!

Demoralized, I could not think of a single valid excuse for the orange juice heist. I pulled myself into rigid attention when I approached the colonel's desk, and waited fearfully for the guillotine to drop. Col. George E. Monson, a weathered warhorse of robust physique and stern demeanor, projected an intimidating presence. He slowly scrutinized me and locked his dominating eyes on mine. I could feel trembling in my legs, beads of perspiration rolling slowly down my back, and I fought to maintain an impassive stance. His visual inspection of me took an excruciatingly long time, before he rose . . . and smiled, and waving his hand, broke the tension with a friendly "At ease!"

Then he gestured and said, "Sit down, Sergeant. I want to pick your brains about the snafu we're having with the combat correspondents out here."

I could hardly restrain an outcry of relief. I trapped it in my throat. My eyes lit up and quivers of deliverance tingled down my spine. I fumbled around, pulling up a chair to the colonel's desk so I could slow down my reeling mind and pull myself together.

The colonel explained, "I sent my aide out to talk to all the Marine correspondents aboard your vessel in order to select one for a personal interview. I chose you because of your professional credentials and because, when I was stationed in Washington, I liked the *Post*.

"I've been flooded with queries from the field, but I've received no word from Washington about what to do with the combat correspondents. Unit commanders, lacking official instructions, are putting their CCs to work as company clerks, librarians, police, even stenographers. I want you to tell me all you know."

Relieved, I recomposed myself and quickly described General Denig's idea for raising the morale of the fighting men and simultaneously raising the country's appreciation of the Corps through CCs trained and tested to meet Marine combat standards.

"A great idea," the colonel opined. "Now tell me why a man of your age and qualifications would join the Corps as an enlisted man rather than as an officer."

I poured out in detail the history of my brief military career, my futile attempt to join up immediately after war was declared, my unusual entry into the Marine Corps, my frustrated determination to get into action as an enlisted man, my disappointment in failing to get to Guadalcanal.

The colonel listened without interruption, then said: "I think the combat correspondents will be good for the Marine Corps. I'll try to get you to Guadalcanal. Meanwhile, write me a detailed report on General Denig's plan as you know it, then poke around the Marine encampments on the island, and outline for me the news-story possibilities here."

Colonel Monson had me temporarily assigned to C-2, thereby snatching me beyond the clutches of the supply sergeant.

When I left the colonel's HQ, I was walking on air. I had come to face my executioner. Instead, I was being sent to Guadalcanal. Nobody will believe it, I murmured to myself. I scarcely dared believe it myself.

"You're on your own until called," the colonel's aide said. "Keep in touch with me every morning and make sure I can reach you any time of day or night."

The shavetail then offered me a piece of his own advice:

"Stay away from the Fun House. Every so often a drunken swab jockey or dogface will start a brawl, and the MPs will swarm in and drag all the cathouse customers to the brig. If you get into any jam with the security patrols, your hopes for getting to Guadalcanal are dead."

"Appreciate the warning," I responded, annoyed by the suggestion that I would consider joining the horny, serpentine queue lined up at the body mart.

The Fun House was the unofficial base clap-trap of Paree in the Pacific. According to scuttlebutt, the joint was a cohabitation of many colors. *Les femmes* included black, big-boobed Melanesians; white, small-breasted French *filles de joie*; tiny, tawny Javanese and Tongan *cocottes*; and a variety of mixed breeds and hues.

The clientele was given no choice of partners. The Yanks—Marines, sailors, and soldiers—had to share *la maison d' amusement* with French *matelots*, newly landed from long sea duty; Gaullist home-guard *soldats*; short-trousered Aussie diggers, and Limeys. Inside, you took what you got. First come, first serviced!

A military prophylactic station stood athwart the bustling sex emporium. When his allotted few minutes were finished, the departing joe—whether or not he had made it—was pounced upon by the MPs. A squad of medics gave each customer a short-arm injection; at times, in their haste, they gave the nasty treatment twice to the same victim.

The Fun House was off-limits to the officers. Instead they were granted exclusive social contact with the servicewomen, nurses, and Red Cross ladies on the base. In addition, they were given open season to hunt for female company—cuddling or coupling—all over the island paradise. Jeeps, recons, station wagons were at their disposal, and for the higher echelons, chauffeurs were available.

The brass and braid also had access to inexpensive liquor at the officers' mess, and, by pooling their funds, could order cases of the good stuff from the States, shipments that somehow found "urgent only" space on the restricted Pacific-bound transports. The enlisted personnel had to pay exorbitant prices for black-market rotgut.

The preponderance of perks for the officer created much resentment among the enlistees and draftees, and some wrote home to discourage their wives, sisters, and girlfriends from volunteering for the WACs, WAVEs, Nurse Corps, and even the Red Cross.

On leaving the lieutenant, I returned to my tent, pulled my Hermes out of its canvas covering, and by the end of the day had turned out a lengthy report on the Denig CC concept and forwarded it to the colonel.

I then set out with a light heart to fulfill the colonel's request for an outline of potential Marine stories on the base.

It was a soft assignment. I circulated around the camps for several days, chatting with Marines wounded on Guadalcanal and the close-by islands of Tulagi and Gavutu, culling potential stories for my second report. Every Marine I met had a story to tell.

After several days of nosing around, I had amassed scores of newsworthy episodes and experiences—so much good material, in fact, that I was tempted to bang out a dozen of the accounts to show the colonel what could be written from Noumea. As I was about to type my first example, the scornful face of Little Jeezus popped into my head. "Cover yer ass, stupid!"

I released my fumbling fingers from the keyboard to reflect. The wily DI was on the ball. If the colonel was impressed by my professionally written stories, he just might be persuaded to order me to write up the entire list of potentials, indefinitely delaying my passage to Guadalcanal.

Even so, my reportorial instincts overcame my caution, and I quickly tapped out a half dozen stories of their experiences from the Marines recuperating on Noumea. Little Jeezus all the while kept fluttering around in my head, moaning. I compromised and decided to submit several accounts to the colonel, and take a chance.

In my roundup of news-story possibilities, I visited the naval mobile base hospital—hastily thrown together, but nonetheless a pleasant place on a wooded slope overlooking the beach. I talked with Pvt. James G. Hall, who'd been severely wounded by a mortar shell. He was resting in his bunk, running his fingers through a lush beard.

The twenty-one-year-old veteran of the Solomons had plunged into Tulagi, across from Guadalcanal, on D day, with Edson's First Raiders, who met strong resistance by the defenders of the Jap seaplane base. The Jackson Heights, Long Island, scout saw his platoon leader cut down, and even though Hall himself had been nicked by a bullet, he crawled through a hailstorm of fire to drag the fallen officer back to safety, only to discover then that the lieutenant was dead.

Hall rejoined his undermanned unit in the continuing clash the very next day, and kept on fighting every day, even after Red Mike's Raiders were boated over to Guadalcanal to help beat back the crack Jap Special Landing Forces (Marines). Then, in the head-to-head battle of Bloody Ridge, with the elite enemy troops lunging toward Henderson Field, Private Hall was wounded by a shell fragment while scouting enemy terrain.

For two days he lay on the ground where he was hit, unable to move, surrounded by Japs who passed him by at arm's length. He feared through the day that he would be discovered by the enemy, but the nights were worse, he said, because of the frightful sounds made by the jungle's invisible inhabitants.

Somehow, during the second night Hall got the strength to drag himself about halfway back to the American line, only to be trapped again, by a hidden machine gunner. Again the Raider lay desperate, unmoving, until about 4:30 the following afternoon, when he was tripped over by two Marines, who carried the stricken scout back to friendly barbed wire. Evacuated to Noumea, Private Hall was on the mend, and he wanted to get back with his Raider outfit as soon as the medics permitted it. Platoonmates recovering at the hospital corroborated Hall's account.

The second story I gave C-2 described the remarkable experience of Jesse H. Youngdeer, of Doylestown, Pennsylvania. The parachutist, a twenty-five-year-old Cherokee, participated in the seizure of Gavutu, another isle off Guadalcanal, on D day. He was then thrown into the Bloody Ridge engagement in mid-September. A Jap sneaked up from behind in the dense brush and bayoneted Youngdeer through his right thigh. The surprised Indian dropped his machine gun, grabbed the bayonet from the Jap, and ran it through his assailant, killing him.

Fellow Marines in the hospital, who confirmed the episode, tried to make me believe that Youngdeer had also scalped his attacker, but the Cherokee just grinned and said, "When I got through with him, there was nothing left to scalp."

"Going home?" I asked Youngdeer.

"I'm going back to my outfit as soon as they let me," he responded.

The third account dealt with Cpl. Tom Meade, from Kingston, Pennsylvania. The twenty-two-year-old was a sniper on Tulagi, but had to start heaving hand grenades when the enemy closed in. He, too, served later at Bloody Ridge—renamed Edson's Ridge after the costly victory— and was trapped with his buddies on a recon mission behind enemy lines. The little band of Raiders fought their way out of the hole without loss, but right after that, Meade was maimed by a machine-gun bullet. He, too, was eager to get back on the line.

The following morning I delivered my second report to the colonel, who skimmed through it, then read to himself several of my example stories. He was impressed, and he said so.

"Sergeant, you've done such a great job that I'm tempted to keep you here for a few weeks so that you can write up more stories for the hometown newspapers."

My heart sank. Little Jeezus snickered.

Colonel Monson paused, as if to underscore his temptation. Then he added:

"But that would be a cruel reward for your work. I'll have to snag some other combat correspondent coming through this sector to follow up on your suggestions. You did your part well, and I'll get you to Guadalcanal."

I thanked the colonel profusely. Then I jeered at Little Jeezus, who shrugged.

In my conversations with the rest-and-recreation Marines, I came up with the elements of a human-interest yarn about Graddick, an old-hand NCO who had served in Cuba and China, in Haiti and Nicaragua, in Guadalcanal, who was always there when his commanding officers needed help in an emergency situation. All Marines are expected to be resourceful—"Cover yer ass, stupid!"—but Graddick was special.

A problem popped up and the top sergeant yelled, "Where's Graddick?"

A map was missing and the captain called, "Get me Graddick!"

The red tape was snafued and the colonel bellowed, "Find Graddick!"

At Tenaru River, when a battalion commander needed a truck and there was none around, it was Graddick who "borrowed" the vehicle from the only available source—the Japs.

When the company commander said he could spare only one man from the thin line to set up tents in the rear, it was Graddick who rounded up a gang of natives and did the job. There was even some talk that Graddick, who had charmed the Melanesians, had been offered the vacant office of village chief.

Most of the Marines I interviewed knew about Graddick and his exploits, but when I pressed them, none had ever met Graddick or even seen him. Graddick, it appeared, was always attached to another unit. But he was there—and every one of the men swore to it.

Back at IMAC headquarters I asked several of the old-timers about Graddick. Sure enough, they knew of Graddick. They had heard of him in Shanghai, in Cuba, in the banana-country expeditions, but no one had laid eyes on Graddick.

I made a mental note to track down Graddick. His story was bigger than I'd first thought.

Now confident that the colonel would make good his promise to get me to Guadalcanal, I relaxed and strolled around the neglected streets of the grungy port, the paint on its houses weathered and peeling. I enjoyed chatting with the storekeepers and sidewalk hawkers in broken English and a smattering of Franglish, and from them I collected bits and pieces of island lore.

I was told that the island had been discovered by Captain Cook and had been named New Caledonia because its coastline reminded him of Scotland. The French snapped up the Melanesian island in the mid-1850s, after a French survey ship had anchored unhappily in time for dinner with the cannibalistic aborigines.

The island was renamed Port-de-France and converted into a penal colony for criminals and political dissidents.

Descendants of the involuntary settlers—*naioulis*—in due course became the ruling class, and as patricians shunned manual labor.

The French had subdued the tall, powerfully built, dark-skinned "broussards," but the indigenous inhabitants preferred hunting and fishing to working. The master class then had to import as indentured servants Javanese and Tongans, who by thrift and diligence bought their freedom. The Japanese arrived on their own, and through their steady enterprise took over the industry of the island: the retail trade and the chromium and copper mines.

When World War II broke out, the French overlords were only too happy to arrest all the Japanese citizens as spies and saboteurs and clap them into a concentration camp, simultaneously confiscating their property.

A popular, bloodless revolt overthrew the governor-general, who was loyal to the pro-German Vichy government of France, and the island swore allegiance to General de Gaulle. Shortly the American forces, on March 29, 1942, landed and secured the twenty-five-by-thirty-mile alligator-shaped island, even as the Japanese forces were advancing on it from their conquests in the Solomons. New Caledonia, some 750 miles east of Australia, was essential to protecting the Allies' southern supply line to their ally Down Under.

I found some good things about Noumea to write home about. In dry weather, the island is a pleasant place, in the seventies for the most part, with the evenings delightfully cool. The country is subtropical, and though it gets nippy at times, it never snows, not even on its mile-high peaks. Live volcanoes tower over some of its surrounding isles. The animals were mainly rats and wild pigs, and the birds were of many colors, including the crested kagu.

I also learned that New Caledonia was free of malaria despite its infestation of mosquitoes. I was told that the bark of the native tree—*niaouli*—exudes a greenish oil that in some way blunted the ability of the local mosquitoes to transfer the malaria bug to humans. I personally discovered, however, that the *niaouli* had no softening affect on the fierce bite of the local fleas, which were much more savage than their cousins in the San Francisco cinemas.

The residents also claimed there were no snakes in their paradise, but even when sober, a number of Marines inisted they had seen snakes in the water.

At first I enjoyed browsing through the quaint stores and shops in the center of town, but my interest quickly waned when I realized that there was little to buy, the prices for what was available were outrageously high, most of the merchandise had been manufactured in Japan or the United States, and none was of native craftsmanship. The black market for booze, beef, and gasoline flourished. Every storekeeper and street vendor demanded payment in American "doh-lars."

Noumea, I quickly saw, was also a thriving rumor factory. Every time a destroyer pulled anchor for firing practice, the whispers were that the Jap fleet was approaching. If a cruiser failed to return from maneuvers in three or four days, the smart scuttlebutt was sure it had been sunk.

Most popular and frequent were the tidbits of inside info on sabotage. When an overworked air transport taking a party of fighter pilots on furlough to Australia crashed at the Noumea airport, the poop was that saboteurs had watered the fuel. When an Army ammunition dump accidentally blew up one night, scaring the hell out of everyone and scattering all hands to their fleet stations, Noumeans "knew" that Japs had set it off. (New Caledonia is today an overseas territory of France.)

Christmas Eve on Noumea was a gasser. Beer flowed the whole night through at Camp Goettge. It was the first 3.2 brew to reach the island. Every tent had a case or two, and the tent flaps were open to all comers. I quaffed at every tent pole, or thought I did. How could I remember?

That celebration was an especially happy one for the Marines, because rumor had it that the leathernecks had pulled a fast one on the Army, which was in overall command of New Caledonia.

The Army, it seems, insisted on commandeering convalescing Marines, who had been wounded on Guadalcanal, for ship-unloading parties. The recovering combat veterans resented the enforced work detail, and retaliated with mischief. They often expressed their anger and defiance by yelling: "Get off your hatch, Patch!" whenever their trucks dashed by the headquarters of Maj. Gen. Alexander Patch, the Army commander.

The Marines' heaviest avenging blow fell the early morning of the day before Christmas, when the Guadalcanal veterans were ordered by the Army command to unload the beer destined for Yuletide cheer of the GIs. The normally reluctant convalescents responded quickly, by loading the cases of brew onto dozens of Marine vehicles, which had inexplicably rolled up from all over the island, and speedily carried off their booty into eager friendly hands.

Camp Goettge celebrated Christmas with a mass hangover.

That afternoon, the imminent call came through. I responded instantly, despite a throbbing headache, rushing to C-2. The colonel said, "Sergeant, to get you to Guadalcanal, I've had to issue oral orders for you to fly there and carry out a special mission for me. No one will question orders from C-2. Your job will be to find out how the combat correspondent operation is working in Guadalcanal and how it can be improved. Get back to me within four weeks."

Then he added, "And while you are there, report and write as many stories as you find, and bring them back to me."

Colonel Monson stepped forward from his desk and gave me a warm handshake. I left aglow.

Early the next day, December 26, I was driven thirty-five miles to Tontouta airport, which had been built by our forces, and boarded an Army C-47 transport heading for Espiritu Santo, New Hebrides, en route to Guadalcanal.

I marveled at the sudden change in my fortune. Unlike the other CCs, who were to be attached to specific Marine units, I had been given a roving assignment. I would be free to venture anywhere I had the guts to go in the battle areas to write the story of Guadalcanal. My fortune was up again!

CHAPTER 6

Espiritu Santo

It's approximately 500 air miles from Noumea to Espiritu Santo, New Hebrides, a northwesterly four-hour flight on the Army's C-47. The transport was loaded down with high-priority materials, including two cases of whiskey and a shortlist of passengers—all brass including a couple of two-star generals—and me, the lone enlisted man.

I didn't rate a bucket seat, so I selected a vacant space on the floorboard and stretched out to sleep, my head still jangling from the revelry of the night before.

From the sky, Espiritu Santo looks like so many other Pacific islands—a big blob of lustrous green in a sea of lustrous blue, a swirl of coconut trees fringed by a coral beach. From the ground, Espiritu Santo looks like so many other Pacific islands—a big blotch of mud in a swirl of coconut trees fringed by a coral beach. Espiritu was a mass of mud, shouldered by a rain forest, and soaked by a forest of rain.

On landing, I was summarily informed that I had been bumped off the continuation flight to Guadalcanal. I never did learn whether I was pulled off to make way for one high-ranking field officer or for two cases of whiskey. I attached myself to a convalescing echelon of Marines that only a few days before had been evacuated from Guadalcanal after five grueling months of combat.

I was eager to meet these men—there are no boys remaining in a unit that has seen combat—who had smashed the Japanese foothold on Guadalcanal. I relished the prospect of mining a rich lode of incidents from them.

When I entered the regimental bivouac, I was appalled by

59

the poor physical condition of the men and the poor living conditions of the camp.

The Marines, many wounded, were dead tired from their strenuous weeks of action; the sightless thousand-mile stare was visible in their reddened eyes. Many were emaciated, and all were sick—sick of malaria and dysentery, sick of the jungle and swamp, sick of the rotting corpses. . . . Their faces were drawn, hollowed, and jaundiced from malaria and from the Atabrine swallowed to alleviate the high fever and nausea.

In contrast to the simple but comfortable R & R facilities in Noumea, where the wounded and afflicted battle survivors had tents to hunker down in and bedding to lie down on, in Espiritu only the fortunate evacuees had cots or ticks, and many had to sleep on the soggy soil huddled in their thin ponchos. I was furious about the pitiful situation, and made a mental note to report it to C-2 when I got back to Noumea.

I, too, had to sleep that night on the slimy ground, wrapping myself up in my own flimsy poncho—which would serve me more or less adequately as raincover, stretcher, windbreaker, sunshade, water catch, pack, and shelter-half. The tent flaps offered slight protection from the relentless rain that night, and the downpour drenched the earth. Puddles of water oozed around me.

That first night could have been worse, I learned from the more experienced evacuees. The groundwater that kept me from sleeping also kept away the ferocious ants whose bite was like fire.

First thing next morning, I foraged for slats of wood and two-by-fours in order to build a bunk about eighteen inches above the dark earth. As ever manually inept, it took me all day to construct the crude crib. I could scrounge up neither a make-do mattress nor a blanket, so I slept on the boards. I hoped that would safeguard me from the marauding insects, and from snakes too. I had an innate fear of snakes and refused to accept assurances there were none of the slithery reptiles on the island.

I was proud of my crude carpentry and cockily boasted of it to Little Jeezus.

"Covered my ass."

Little Jeezus looked over my klutzy handiwork and made a face in disdain.

Just before dawn of the following day, I was awakened by a sudden, acute attack of the "screaming willies." The runs dominated my daily routine for the remainder of my six-day stopover on Espiritu and, together with the oppressive wet heat, sapped my vitality and enthusiasm. In a couple of days, I was looking as sallow and feeling as debilitated as the recuperating Marines who had undergone the punishment of battle. I had to give up my rifle drill and eye exercises. I had neither the will nor the energy to continue with the daily routine.

The paregoric and bismuth doled out by the medics brought little relief. Only after dosing myself with sulfa guanidine could I find respite. American medicine at the time knew little about the tropical diseases, and the military was testing new compounds like the sulfa drugs.

The trots were endemic and everywhere, and often struck when least expected. When that happened, the victim had to race for the nearest head. One evening, I got caught in such an emergency situation, and I tore off for an enlisted men's latrine I sighted nearby. Only after I was safely perched on the john did I notice the eagle insignia of the grunter squatting next to me.

Why in the hell was the brass in the enlisted men's can? I asked myself, but politely said nothing, and averted my eyes from the "chicken" emblem. The colonel must have read my mind. "The runs respect no rank, son," he said. I thought that was a reasonable excuse for breaking the rules.

There was no permanent relief possible on Espiritu then, because the dysentery was spread by hordes of coconut flies, winged tormentors that overran the Hebrides. At times, like a beekeeper, I had to wear a head net to shield my face from the buzzing beasties. And at night, I rolled netting over the bunk I had built to stave off the bloodthirsty anopheles mosquitoes, whose females sting and inject into the bloodstream the parasites that produce malaria.

During my seizures, I couldn't even drag myself to the galley, some distance away, to refill my canteen with scarce potable water. Little Jeezus came to my rescue. "Cover yer ass!" he advised.

"Makes no sense," I responded to myself. But after a minute or two trying to comprehend, a shaft of light penetrated my feverish "haid."

I fished up my helmet, removed the liner, and, with some fumbling, managed to kindle a small fire and boil a quart of water in the hard hat. I had found a source of potable water.

Oh, sure, I did thank Little Jeezus for reminding me of the emergency measure, and he took a bow with a sweep of his Nicaraguan campaign hat.

Before the Yanks came in to convert the seventy-five-by-forty-five-mile island into an air and sea base in mid-'42, Espiritu Santo was only another of the indistinguishable islands clustered on the map of the Pacific Ocean, inhabited by the indigenous Melanesians and governed by an Anglo-French condominium. Espiritu was a mass of jungle, poked through by peaks running to more than a mile high, with plantations of coconut relieved only by colorful spreads of orchids.

Another of the New Hebrides, until taken over by American forces as a bulwark against the Japs battering their way down the Solomons, the archipelago had had few occupants or visitors.

When I arrived, a part of the Pacific fleet—the carrier *Enterprise*, the cruiser *Minneapolis*, the repair ship *Rigel*—found anchorage in Espiritu's bosomy harbor.

The esteemed *Enterprise*, which had paired up with the *Hornet* in the fabulous Doolittle bombing of Tokyo, had been hit in the Solomons in battle, and was wounded again by warheads off Santa Cruz in October. She was in port for substantial repairs.

The *Minneapolis*, which had been in the thick of the clashes around Guadalcanal, was gouged and knocked out in November. The cruiser also had to be rebuilt. The *Rigel*, which had served as the headquarters for Vice Admiral

Robert L. Ghormley in New Zealand early on when he had few vessels under his command, was there to help get the two fighting ships back into condition for more action.

All three ships made cold beverages available to recovering Marines who could climb aboard. In that port, unlike on the *Juan Cabrillo*, the Navy made friends of the leathernecks.

Before the bouts of diarrhea laid me low completely, I interviewed and chatted with a score of the Marines. I was surprised to discover that many of the men were in no mood to talk about their experience at the front. Unlike the spirited men eager to fight again whom I'd found in hospital on Noumea, most of the leathernecks on Espiritu Santo I found to be lethargic, listless, with no inclination to get back to the front. What they talked about was fresh milk, fresh eggs, big juicy steaks, and a reunion with their girls back home. There were a slew of stories to be had, but I was too ill to write them. I concentrated on recovering my strength so that I would be in condition to take on Guadalcanal.

I did, however, keep asking the evacuees if they had run into Graddick. Several said they had. No, they had not met him personally, but they had heard all about him and his quick-fix feats from friends in other units. One grunt did come up with a clue. He had served for a short stretch with a salty topkick who was a whiz at troubleshooting, but didn't know if his last name was Graddick because everyone called him Vic.

My curiosity overcame my malady long enough for me to search around the base and catch up with Vic. I was disappointed to learn that Vic was not Graddick but Sergeant Major Troutman, a career leatherneck, from Troutman, New York. He had been the key man who kept things humming, smoothly if possible, but running no matter what, at the battalion command post, control center of the front-line operation.

Vic's team was made up of three clerks. Each of the trio was a fully trained Marine, capable of using all the Marine weapons when called upon, but their principal duty was keeping Vic happy. Vic became very unhappy when some unexpected blip screwed up his daily flow of intelligence reports, operations reports, personnel reports, medical reports, and all those other documents, orders, messages—the red tape that holds a military organization together.

The topkick's staff was envied by the grunts on the front line for their cushy jobs crunching papers at clean desks while they were scrunching in filthy foxholes; the all-too-common image of the headquarter document stampers, I found, did not fit the image of the Troutman team.

The leathery-faced sarge and his clerks—Staff Sgt. Allen J. Lynn, a Detroiter; Cpl. Edward J. Catallo, from Waterford, New York; and Cpl. Douglas S. Reid, of Syracuse—pushed off from their landing craft onto Guadalcanal D day on the heels of the assault troops. They proceeded forward, as scheduled, following a given azimuth (angle of direction) to set up the command post, as directed, about a hundred yards behind the front line, which was to be formed by the leading echelon of Marines.

The four order-cutters first cut their way through the jungle for a couple of hours without coming up to the front. Eventually, the steaming, stinking heat of the jungle forced them to take a break and to take stock of the situation. They concluded they were lost.

The four sat quietly deliberating their next move, when rustling sounds to their rear tensed them to alert. They hid behind broad-trunk trees, rifles cocked and ready to shoot. It was not the ocher-green faces of the enemy that broke through the jungle shadows but the point patrol of the lead Marine echelon. For the past two hours, it turned out, the clerks had been preceding rather than following the assault troops.

The front line now found, the sarge and his squad set about creating the command post. They dug out a large foxhole, covered it with leafy branches and canvas, and presto, they had created an office equipped with running water—from the rain.

However, the troublesome absence of office equipment remained a problem to be solved, since all their supplies had gone down with the USS *Elliott*, the first American transport sunk by Jap bombers in the Guadalcanal landing.

Sergeant Major Troutman, with fifteen years of service in

the Corps, was unfazed by the dilemma. He pointed out to his men that according to the sketchy map drawn by a former coconut planter, the Japs had thrown up a headquarters of sorts in a native village some distance away.

The office staff, following their leader—after all, he had learned a few things about jungles in the Central American campaigns—descended on the abandoned Jap HQ and helped themselves to the spoils—paper and carbons, pens, pencils, and even typewriter ribbons. They could figure out no useful application for the Japanese typewriter they dug up, nor for the Nipponese rubber stamps.

So where obtain an English-script typewriter? Troutman disappeared and came back with a beat-up Underwood and never did explain to his mystified men how he had "just come across" the aged machine. At first the cranky machine refused to respond to the tinkering of the men. But after much puttering, muttering, coaxing, and cursing, they got the keys to cooperate. And Sergeant Major Troutman was happy again.

Since the clerks were first and foremost riflemen, like all Marines, they were rushed up to the line during skirmishes when every man and every rifle was needed. They all responded to trouble calls. One night, when the observation-post telephone line went down in a storm and no signalmen were available, clerks Lynn and Reid were sent out to find and repair the line break.

They groped through the creepy dark without stirring up Jap snipers, and came to the bank of a river. It appeared to the pair that the gap in the line was on the other side.

"We pushed a log into the river, and with our hands, paddled across," Lynn recalled. "Bodies of dead Japs floating downstream bounced off our log—gave us the shudders. We were scared stiff." But they repaired the line.

Later, Corporal Catallo had a close call. He had just rushed up to the command post with a message when "One Lung Charlie" dropped a bomb plumb on his jeep. Only Catallo wasn't in it at that moment. Corporal Reid wasn't so lucky. An aerial bomb splattered shrapnel into his knee while he was on night sentry watch. Sergeant Major Troutman's left foot swelled up double in size from a fungus infection, but he stuck to his post. After all, he still had a lot of Japanese stationery around and reports to write.

As I was about to leave, I asked the sergeant major whether he knew of Graddick. "Sure," the veteran six-striper responded. "Graddick was down there in Nicaragua with us."

"Did you meet him?" I persisted.

Troutman scratched his balding, sun-burnished pate and took a few seconds to think about it. "No, I never did meet him," the old sarge confessed. "But he was there, I can tell you. Stick around, and I'll tell you about Graddick."

My stomach signaled that it was time for me to go. "Thanks. I'll be back, but I have to go now." I ran, and made it. I never did get back to Troutman.

I filed one story out of Espiritu. The incident took place on Guadalcanal, which I had yet to reach, but the account was vouched for by several officers and enlisted who had taken part in a mission of vengeance.

The episode began with a routine but always dangerous reconnaissance patrol deep into enemy territory, ten volunteers led by 2nd Lt. James L. Jordan Jr., of Mansfield, Louisiana. They ran into an ambush, but barely managed to hole up, hold off their assailants, and radio back word of their predicament.

Immediately, 2nd Lt. Gordon Maples, of Middlesboro, Kentucky, a Washington & Lee alumnus, was dispatched with a relief party. It took twenty-four hours for Maples and his men to make contact with the trapped Marines. Then, joining up, the leathernecks fought their way to friendly terrain through a superior Jap force without losing a hand.

No sooner were they back than Lieutenant Maples was ordered to assemble a company of Guadalcanal veterans and go after the ambushing Japs. The lieutenant, commissioned from the ranks only a few weeks before, took off with fifty-six leathernecks eager for revenge. Ten, headed by Sgt. Merle F. Roy, of Edwight, West Virginia, and guided by Pfc. Charles V. "Red" Carman, of Weehawken, New Jersey, former catcher for the St. Louis Cardinals—who had been a member of the ambushed scout patrol—advanced ahead of the main force as decoy.

It was believed that the Japs they were looking for were encamped on a knoll one day's slog inside the enemy's line. The bait was to approach the foe frontside; the larger posse would steal up from the rear through the jungle.

The early morning of the second day, Lieutenant Maples's men closed in. Just before the larger party reached the top of the hill from the rear, two Jap soldiers were spotted, and Maples riddled them. The Marines then closed in rear and front and caught seventy-five or so enemy soldiers lined up for morning chow. The Marines opened up with rifles and tommy guns, and mowed down the bewildered Japs.

From the flanks, four enemy machine guns began spraying the Marines. The leathernecks quickly shot down the gunners, but as soon as one was killed, another took his place. The lieutenant and several of his men then crept up on the machine guns and silenced them—permanently—with hand grenades.

A Nip officer attempted to outflank the Marines from the left, but he crossed into the sights of a tommy gunner named Tracy, who with a single burst felled the officer and four of his men.

But the Japs were still fighting on. About forty of them, who had been busy trying to ambush the decoy squad, tried to charge the main combat patrol, and in so doing had to dash through a clearing. Fired on from both front and rear, the Japs were annihilated. A handful escaped into the jungle.

Lieutenant Maples counted heads. Two of his command were wounded, but not seriously, and a third was missing. A Navy corpsman attached to the patrol, Pharmacist's Mate (21c) Kenneth Gorton, of Andes, New York, was found, smoking rifle in hand, poking around for Japs. He had accounted for three.

"Hey," shouted the lieutenant to the corpsman. "Don't you want to come back with us?"

The dazed medic looked around. "I thought the fight had

just begun," he replied. The skirmish had lasted no more than thirty minutes.

Back to the American line, Lieutenant Maples reported the successful raid to his commanding officer. The CO listened to the recounting of the foray and chuckled.

"I wonder," he mused, "what the Japs were having for breakfast?"

"Hot lead and hand grenades," the lieutenant said.

(Lieutenant Maples, who had celebrated his twenty-eighth birthday on December 7, the first anniversary of the attack on Pearl Harbor, was recommended for the Navy Cross.)

The ambush, a daily period for reconnoitering patrols in the jungle, worked both ways. The Marines at times suffered painful losses too. Lieut. Col. Frank B. Goettge, a powerhouse of a leader in the Marine invasion of Guadalcanal, and all but three of his twenty-five scouts died with him on a patrol caught in a Jap trap, and there was some talk that the outstanding officer had been set up by a prisoner who gave false information. The Marine base on Noumea was named after him.

On New Year's Eve I joined the ambulatory sick and wounded to attend a vaudeville show performed at a nearby Seabee camp. The show gave us all a lift. We sang ourselves hoarse with nostalgic ballads like "Home, Sweet Home."

One of our bombers crashed in the boondocks New Year's Day. With scores of other gyrenes, I forced myself to trudge to the wreckage to pay personal homage to the dead pilot and crew.

Two days later, I said good-bye, without regret, to New Hebrides.

(New Hebrides gained its independence in 1980, then renamed its V-form aggregate of thirteen islands Vanuatu, meaning "Our land forever" in Bislama, the Pidgin English lingua franca—and official language—of their South Pacific region.)

At dawn of January 4, 1943, I was shaken out of my makeshift sack and unceremoniously jeeped down to the airfield, where I piled into a SCAT supply plane bound for

Cactus, the code name for Guadalcanal, 500 miles away at the bottom of the Solomons.

SCAT stood for South Pacific Combat Air Transport. It also stood for a courageous, committed pioneer outfit that was able to provide the Marines on Guadalcanal with the bare essentials during the dark weeks that followed the August 10 destruction of the Allied fleet of covering cruisers, only three days after the Marines' amphibious landing.

The old crates, Douglas Skytrains—C-47s to the Army, DC-3s to the Marines—were slow and unarmed. The pilots had to depend on their skill—and prayers—to get through the Jap fighter squadrons patrolling Guadalcanal.

Only a few days after the leathernecks had landed, the first SCAT flew into the newly captured Henderson strip, and the transports—boxcars with wings—never halted their daily visits, even when the field was under enemy shelling. No sooner did the DC-3 roll to a halt than its load of ammunition and provisions was carried off to the lines where fighting was in progress. Some days the SCAT pilots landed in the midst of skirmishes rattling around the landing strip. I paid tribute to SCAT with a news feature. Later Admiral Halsey paid tribute to SCAT with a special order of the day.

But my SCAT touchdown on Guadalcanal, January 4, 1943, was uneventful and routine for the pilot. For me it was a momentous occasion. I had at long last reached my tantalizing goal!

I ran down the ramp of the transport and, without thinking about it, kneeled down and kissed the runway tarmac. I quickly looked up to see if anyone was laughing at my odd behavior, but no one paid any attention to me. They probably didn't even see me do it, but I felt—I strangely sensed—that Zedel saw me do it and approved.

CHAPTER 7

Guadalcanal

My SCAT transport alit on Henderson Field, Guadalcanal, January 4, 1943, five months after the Marine landing, nine months after my taking the oath in the Marine Corps, thirteen months after trying to enlist the day after the Japs bombed Pearl Harbor, fifteen weeks after being assigned to the First Division in Guadalcanal and making a transit stop in San Francisco.

Late, but nonetheless I was elated to reach my fervently desired destination.

I was already vaguely familiar with Guadalcanal from visiting the library in my more-than-ample spare time on Treasure Island. I had learned that Guadalcanal was part of the Solomon Islands discovered in 1567—not by Captain Cook, but by an obscure Spaniard, one Álvaro de Mendaña. This voyager was, like so many ocean adventurers of his era, seeking the fabled Solomon's gold mines, but all he found was coconuts. Nonetheless, unable to come up with the bullion, he bullied his avaricious patrons by titling the long string of primitive, worthless chains the Solomon Islands. He named the biggest, southernmost island Guadalcanal in honor of his home town in Valencia.

I also was somewhat acquainted with the battle zone from the accounts of the wounded Marines I had interviewed on Treasure Island, Noumea, and Espiritu Santo. So I was not surprised by the thunderous, pummeling rains, the humid, sweltering heat that drenched clothing and skin. I already knew that omnipresent mosquitoes were lusting for my blood, that scrub typhus lurked under every bush leaf, and that crud (fungus) had a predilection for the toes but also thrived in the inner ear.

Indeed, I had been warned that the jungle was thick, tangled, tough to penetrate, beset by snakes, scorpions, spiders as big as my hand, and other repellent denizens. One of the sick-bay patients had even claimed to have had a hand-to-mouth encounter with a charging open-jawed crocodile.

Curiously, I was more apprehensive of the possibility of a heavy, ripe coconut falling on my head and paralyzing me. The coconuts, their perches having been weakened by bombing and shelling, would drop unexpectedly. Once I had verified that peril with several seasoned grunts, I kept my steel helmet virtually glued to my skull in the presence of the noble-looking palm trees.

I had also learned that the 250-mile-long volcanic island, only ten degrees or so below the equator, was split by a double chain of high mountains, a peak or two stretching upward for more than a mile, and pitted by ravines and caves, ominous terrain in which the enemy could lie in ambush or conceal snipers in trees.

When I checked in at administrative HQ, I asked to be attached to Fifth Marines, First Division, the prize posting I had been awarded by General Denig. To my dismay, I was told that the First Division had been relieved and most of its elements sent Down Under to rest and recover after five months of incessant face-to-face combat.

I then reported to the Second Marine Division, which with the Army's Americal Division had taken over the final stage of the Guadalcanal campaign. The Second included the 2nd, 6th, and 8th Regiments, plus defense (artillery) battalion units. Hurriedly, I found a billet with a headquarters unit, where I arranged to have my Hermes safely stowed away during my story-seeking spurts, and in return I would write a hometown piece about each member of the section. Those quickly accepted arrangements opened my eyes to the potential bargaining power of my Hermes when I should run out of typing paper, carbons, or even beer.

Exhausted by the hectic running around of my first day on

Guadalcanal, I scraped up a cot, covered it with netting, and prepared to sack in for the night.

"Expecting a Jap bombing run over the camp tonight?" I asked the senior noncom in the tent, a tall, rangy fellow, who spoke with a longhorn drawl.

"He might," offered the Texan. "Washing Machine Charlie paid a call last night, and it's possible he won't be back tonight."

Worn out, I grabbed for the straw. "Then I can dig my foxhole tomorrow, right?"

The sarge was noncommittal. "Suit yourself, chum," he said. "It's your butt."

Instantly Little Jeezus whizzed into my cranium and cried out, "Cover yer ass, stupid!"

"You heard the man," I muttered to my stalker. "Tonight I sack in, tomorrow I dig in."

"Were you talking to me?" inquired the lanky NCO.

"No," I tried to explain. "I was talking to Little Jeezus."

"That's good," responded Tex. "I pray and talk with Jesus every night. It makes me feel safer."

About 2 A.M. that night I was jolted awake by the drone of oncoming planes. I ripped the netting apart in my haste to hit the sod below my cot, my face shoved down into the reeking muck as the bombs exploded violently at a distance, but close enough to shake the ground under my tightened belly. My tentmates, used to wake-up calls by the Bettys—Mitsubishi bombers—had swiftly dropped into their adjacent foxholes. I, exposed on the surface, lay there trembling and sweating until the Klaxons sounded all clear. I could see Little Jeezus shaking his head at me.

As soon as the sun broke through, I started hacking a foxhole out of the stubborn coral. It was palm-blistering, backbreaking work, and it took me half a day to chop out and spade up a dugout deep enough and wide enough to cram myself into it so that my derriere was a few inches below the surface. When I completed my herculean labor, I plopped into my sack and slept uneasily, glimpsing in my fitful sleep the simpering told-you-so smirk of my phantom DI. By then I was too fatigued to eat the powdered eggs or drink the powdered milk available—or consume the other canned, condensed, concentrated, and dehydrated delicacies available at chow.

My third day on Cactus I got the answer to a question that had been gnawing at me ever since I had departed Parris Island. Boot camp survival and graduation had officially declared me to be physically and mentally ready for combat, but how would I react under real enemy fire? Notwithstanding the intensive discipline and training I had endured, I was not so sure.

That very day, I ran into Bob Davis, like myself a former Washington newsman and CC attached to the 8th Marines, a Second Division regiment. Davis had been a hard-nosed, hard-drinking reporter at the rival *Times-Herald*. At Parris Island a hear-tell had been flying around that Bob had had a plastic flask of bourbon mailed to him concealed in a cake, and that he had gotten away with the scam. To be fair, another rumor credited Andy Knight, a *Times-Herald* compatriot, with pulling off the deception. Whoever did it, there was sufficient appreciation among the thirsty CCs in boot camp to invest each with a halo of admiration.

We abrazoed and exchanged brief rundowns of our experiences for a few minutes. Bob, his baggy civilian tummy trimmed to Marine firmness, was in a hurry, due to show up for his turn at the observation post overlooking the battlefront about a mile and a half away. He offered to take me along, and I jumped at the invitation.

We slogged through the gluey mire and jungle underbrush for more than an hour and came up to a line of barbed-wire rolls running from a ridge to the shore.

"We're at the front," Bob suddenly announced, pointing to the concertina barrier.

I was taken aback. All I could see was a long, wide field of low growth running into a dense forest. I could see no enemy out there, nor could I hear any shooting.

"It's the front, all right," Bob assured me in response to my skeptical look. "It's been quiet for the past week, so we can take a shortcut to the OP."

Before I could ask Bob what he meant by a shortcut, he

had hurdled a segment of the barbed boundary and stretched his arm out to help me over. I hesitated. I could see in my mind's eye Little Jeezus yammering, "Cover yer ass, stupid!", but it was too late. I simply couldn't show fear to a fellow CC who was so casual about being at the front lines, could I? After all, Bob knew the ropes, didn't he?

We started across the open swath toward the ridge where the OP was situated when a strange staccato stuttering broke out around us.

"Down!" yelled Bob, throwing himself down. "It's a Jap machine gun!"

I panicked.

I lunged for a tree some yards away as the bullets clattered noisily about my feet.

"Cover yer ass, stupid!" Little Jeezus screamed, virtually tumbling me into the brush. I lay there prostrate, breathing heavily, heart pounding so loud that I was sure the sniper could hear it too.

After a long pause, Bob whistled softly and slowly crept up to me, whispering, "Sorry, Sam, but that's the way things go out here. Don't move until I give the signal. Then we'll creep out slowly to the trees and find cover. I'll get you to the OP and back to safe ground later."

That was hardly reassuring, but I had no alternative. I didn't even know where I was, let alone where to go.

The observer on duty was glad to be relieved, and remarked that it had been boring and uneventful on his watch except for a machine-gun burst or two from the other side about a half hour earlier.

"I couldn't see what the shooting was all about. Wasn't much," he commented.

No, it wasn't much, I said to myself ruefully. Just my ass.

During Bob's two-hour vigil, I peered from time to time through the field binoculars and spotted a beached Jap transport, but failed to locate the machine-gun sniper. After I cooled down, I questioned Bob and he briefed me on the CCs still stationed on the island. When his watch was over, we carefully—very carefully—crept back to our side of no-man's-land.

Only after I clumped back to my tent later did I come to realize, guiltily, that my first encounter with the enemy might have been my last. Little Jeezus said nothing, but he was clearly disgusted with my performance. So was I. I vowed to myself I'd never let my guard down again.

That night when the blackout blanketed the bivouac, I joined the headquarters staffers around the radio savoring the hit tunes of the week, singing along with Dinah Shore and chuckling at the antics of Charley McCarthy, the deft-tongued dummy, and listening amused to the rantings of Tokyo Rose.

Newscast time swelled the gathering of listeners. Over-head, our shells were swishing, outbound, their nightly lul-laby, and a few thousand yards up the rifles and machine guns were chattering in deadly debate with the other side, but the little crowd around the low-pitched radio was wrapped up in an update of Russia's winter offensive.

I concentrated for several days on collecting information for my report to C-2. The CCs were unhappy, I found, be-cause for the most part their reportorial functions had been limited or stymied by puzzled, angry field-command offi-cers who had received no instructions from the top on what in the hell to do with the hybrid Marines.

I later recommended in my report that a high-level policy directive spelling out the double duties of the CCs and more reasonable censorship of their copy was urgently needed. Both suggestions were later put into effect, though I doubt that my report had any bearing on belated organization or-ders. The military red tape runs inexorably on its own cir-cuitous course at its own tortoiselike pace.

I also discovered from the eight CCs I tracked down how they had beaten me to Guadalcanal while I was chafing rest-lessly on Treasure Island. They had circumvented the West Coast transport blockade by crossing the Pacific with the Marine units they had joined and trained with in Cuba, Samoa, Australia, and New Zealand.

Even as I traipsed about "The Island" interviewing my fellow CCs, I gathered up the experiences and exploits of the grunts. Just about every one of the Devil Dogs had been involved in at least one of the fierce daily skirmishes in the critical pitched battles at Bloody Ridge, Tenaru, and Matanikau.

Armed with single-shot Springfield 1903 rifles, the leatherneck infantrymen were at a disadvantage against the automatic firing power of their entrenched, battle-tested foe. Nonetheless, the leatherneck loved the Springfield on which he had been weaned, because it was part of him, and because it was deadly accurate. The leathernecks overcame their lesser firing power and seasoning—and numbers— through sheer tenacity and courage.

The Marine fighting units also had suffered an acute lack of supplies. The Imperial fleet had early on sunk the Allies' four-cruiser squadron that was screening the landing, so that the leathernecks had been cut off from their transport ships and the flow of food, medical supplies, guns, and ammo. Tojo's Zero fighter planes and Betty bombers dominated the daylight skies, at times restricting the Marine SCATs to furtive night drops, which sometimes fell into enemy territory.

Five days after hitting the beach on Guadalcanal, the already underfed Marines were so low on provisions that they were reduced to two skimpy meals a day, at times no more than brown rice salvaged from the foe. Four weeks of savage fighting was carried on with the meager diet before the normal, unappetizing but more belly-filling three chow calls a day could be restored.

During that cruel month, a crescendo of calls went up for Graddick.

When the Marines' guns or machines or tanks ran down or became disabled, the call went out for Graddick. Somehow, he showed up and came up with the essential bolt or cog or other gizmo that was missing. He was quick about it, too. Graddick scooped up the needed part by cannibalizing cracked-up weapons, broken-down vehicles, wrecked warplanes. When fuel ran out, Graddick scavenged the rear areas for scattered gasoline cans and drained the leavings of the fuel tanks in abandoned trucks and tracs.

No matter the trouble—and there was trouble every day—Graddick found a way to fix it.

By then I had come to the conclusion that my search for Graddick, begun in Noumea and continued in Espiritu Santo, was on a false scent. Graddick, it began to dawn upon me, was not a specific troubleshooter, but the paradigm of the Marines' resourcefulness when confronted by unanticipated problems.

Graddick was the ingenious individual Marine who knew when and how to cover his ass and use his "haid" when faced by an unforeseen problem. Graddick was always there when needed.

I looked inward, and there was Little Jeezus beaming in agreement with my slow but inevitable deduction.

Meanwhile, there was no letup for the undernourished, overspent, sickened men. Our losses ran into the hundreds, dead and wounded or stricken by malaria and forced out of action. Even two months after the landing, in October, the Marine perimeter was so thin, strung out like an overstretched ribbon, that the field commanders were at times compelled to round up clerks and bandsmen, bakers and cooks—they were after all trained riflemen!—and throw them into the bitter fighting.

Despite their desperate straits, the First Marine Division troops, inch by inch, foot by foot, overcame each of the strongly prepared, camouflaged defenses thrown up by the enemy, and before being relieved in December had, with the support of fresh, green National Guardsmen called up by the Army, driven the Japs' fanatical Special Landing Forces into their final toehold at Cape Esperance, on the northwest corner of the island.

I reveled in the trove of tales I collected on Cactus. I wrote fast and furiously, trying to make up for the time squandered in San Francisco. I wrote about the actions I witnessed, the actions I took part in, and the actions and reactions of the men whose experiences I could reasonably verify.

Heroism in the face of death, sacrificing a life to save teammates, killing and being killed by fire, shell, bayonet, and knife, all provided scores of reports for the local newspapers and radio. But there were also many stories of human interest that reflected the indomitable spirit of the fighting men and created new legends for the stirring lore of the Marine Corps.

There were a few instances, too, when our artillery shells fell short and killed our own troops; when our bombs from the air dropped onto the wrong target and killed our own grunts. On January 10, for instance, our guns blew up our own ammo dump. That's a "normal" happening in war; but, of course, I didn't write about the "bad" incidents. I knew such fatal mishaps would never clear censorship.

I was story hunting in the Kokumbona sector, the last front on the island, when a Japanese knee-mortar shell burst close by and I threw myself into a water-filled gully. When I felt it was safe again, I pulled myself out of the mush and peered around. The canister fragments had showered a jeep nearby, but the baby-faced driver had escaped untouched. The kid was furious, and swore a firecracker string of curses.

"Hurt, Mac?" I inquired.

"Hell, no," the driver responded.

"Then why in the hell are you beating your gums, chum? You were lucky not to get blown apart."

"Lucky, my ass," the kid howled. "How would you like to change a flat tire in this shit?" Without further ado, he kneeled into the mud to replace the flat.

I looked at the youngster with admiration. The driver had no concern for his personal danger; his only concern was for his beloved jeep.

The kid said he was eighteen, but I suspected Pvt. Roy McKenzie had added a year or two to his birth-certificate age, like so many other impatient enlistees, when he had signed up in May back in his native Oklahoma City. Roy was already a combat veteran of five months. He and his jeep were carrying a message to a unit lost somewhere out there in the amorphous battlefield, lost because its field radio or phone communications had been broken off.

I asked to go along.

"Hop in." He beckoned.

Private McKenzie was proud of his funny-looking, squat, ducklike vehicle with its six-shift creeper gears. He boasted, from experience, that his jeep delivered ammo and supplies where no truck could get through, brought down the wounded from heights no ambulance could reach, delivered vital messages to front-line units when other contact failed.

Roy claimed his low-slung conveyance could traverse the worst terrain. He proved it to me in a wild four-hour drive through a caterwauling downpour that transformed the wooded ridge trails into a treacherous labyrinth of slime. Up steep hills and down slithery slopes, the jeep bucked and sideslipped, wobbled and twisted, jerked and spun, jolted and churned, tilted to the left and tilted to the right—but it never turned over. It was a hairy ride. I was shaken up and had to pull myself together, but the kid only patted the driver's wheel, pressed on, and found the missing platoon.

The first story I filed from Guadalcanal was not about guts and gore. My first dispatch was about grit and esprit, about a kid from Oklahoma who drove a funny-looking jeep named Lindy Lou.

Sometimes, waiting tensely at the line for the Japs to attack, the Marines would try to goad the enemy into action. At Bloody Ridge—as related to me by the grunts—a weary company was manning a tense line against an expected assault, but the attack failed to materialize. An antsy squad leader came up with a ploy to provoke the foe into attacking, and got the okay from his commanding officer to try it.

At dawn the next morning, the squad leader jumped up and, at the top of his voice, yelled: "Tojo is a bum! Tojo is a bum!" The Jap ranks reacted to the insult thrown at their Imperial Commander by firing a series of fusillades.

When the uneasy quiet resumed, the squad leader leaped up again and hollered even louder: "The Mikado is a bum! The Mikado is a bum!"

The Japs, outraged by the contemptuous disparagement of their revered God-descended emperor, charged out of their dugouts, screaming, and were cut down by the sweeping enfilade fire from the expectant Marines.

The next morning, as the sun crept up, the Japs tried the same trick, and yelled out in resounding chorus: "Loosevelt is a bum! Loosevelt is a bum!"

There was no reaction from the Marines.

The Japs, after a long pause, hurled the insult again, this time repeatedly and louder: "Plesident Loosevelt is a bum! Plesident Loosevelt is a bum!"

"Who cares?" the Marines cried out.

(A year later, on New Britain, Japs charged the Marine line, screaming, "To hell with Babe Ruth!" under the delusion they were desecrating an American idol. Even the Sultan of Swat was unruffled when he heard about the incident. "To hell with the Japs!" the home-run king retorted.)

Killing the enemy did not always give a sense of satisfaction, I found. On January 16, concealed in foliage, I kept vigil from the top of a deep ravine during a "routine" mop-up operation, as weary, dogged Marines spread out slowly, warily weaving down a growth-shrouded gorge to flush out a scattering of holdout Jap soldiers who though cornered refused to surrender.

The Marines had to go down into that hellhole and eliminate the diehards one by one. The worn-out leathernecks were neither enthusiastic nor eager to finish off the suicide-bent resisters; they were acutely aware that they or some of their buddies in the execution squad would have to pay with their own lives, but all followed the killing order without complaint.

I watched uneasily through the afternoon, detecting only shadows or blurs of the exterminators, but also hearing bursts of gunfire and the violent sounds of close combat . . . tommy guns, rifles, hand grenades . . . flashes of fire from the flamethrowers.

Late in the afternoon, the shooting and blasting abruptly ceased. Then the American wounded and dead were carried up, and the survivors of the grim death-squad emerged.

"Killed all the yellow slant-eyed bastards," one returning Marine announced aloud to no one in particular.

He didn't look happy, nor did any of the others who made it back. They were too beat, too tired, too drained to feel any glow of victory. Four skinny, starved, wounded, and unconcious Japs were dragged out. The rest were dead: shot, bayoneted, blasted by grenades. Rooted out. Grubbed out. Rubbed out.

Nobody seemed to know—or care—how many of the Japs were slain, nor could I learn the extent of our own losses in dead and wounded.

"It's over, guys," the grim lieutenant told his grim men. "That does it. Tonight we'll be relieved." Not one of the taut faces broke into a smile. Not one uttered a prayer of thanks. Some cursed, hot, bitter curses. They were past relief; they were spent.

This gory scenario was played out again and again over the weeks as the leathernecks slowly, tenaciously overcame soldiers who refused to give up, accepting death rather than surrender and shame, as they had been indoctrinated by their military credo. Japanese officers at times committed hara-kiri with their swords rather than accept defeat. It was their code to live by . . . to die by.

I fell in with a Marine howitzer battery whose crack crews on this very day had established a new record for speed and accuracy, loading and firing a dozen sixteen-pound high-trajectory shells in two minutes flat. The 75mm pack howitzer, a favorite Marine weapon for island incursions, was capable of flinging its missiles some five miles distant. Its odd-sounding name is a variation of the Czech word for slingshot.

The artillerymen were not participating in playful rivalry with another Marine gun crew. They were shooting for keeps, at an invisible target several miles out in the jungle, where a concentration of Japs was making a last-ditch stand.

The crews of that battery had for days been experimenting with a variety of operational steps in order to shave the number of seconds required to load and fire the workhorse cannon. Three to four rounds a minute, I was told, was generally accepted as good shooting.

With the enthusiastic encouragement of their commanding officer, Capt. Guido F. Yerbeck, a Syracusan, the five-man gun teams tried out hairsplitting timesaving motions.

The opportunity for testing their refinements came on January 21, when the entire battery was ordered to lay down a barrage at a specific objective. One of the barrages was to last two minutes, and the Marine gunners immediately accepted that time limit as the measure of their firing skill and speed.

At the sharp command "Cannoneers! Posts!" the crews sprang to their places. "Fire!". . . and they fired at will. At the end of the two-minute interval, the crew of No. 4 gun had rammed home and fired an even dozen of the howitzer projectiles.

The prize teams also demonstrated that not only could they dish it out, but they could take it as well.

Camouflaged in a deep draw a mile or so behind the lines, the big cannons, which did devastating damage to Jap ammo dumps and supply depots, were prime quarry for the Millimeter Mikes (Jap artillery) and Washing Machine Charleys (Jap night bombers). And the batterymen were constantly harried by snipers who filtered in through the bush.

This howitzer outfit arrived on the island in November and set up its position at the very same hour that a Jap task force was shelling their sector from the sea. Their heavy cannon had to be broken down into six loads and lugged on the backs of their crews through terrain impassable for vehicles or wheels. Since that first day, the howitzer gang had been pounding the Japanese entrenchments day and night.

In the ordnance tradition, the Marine crews wrote messages on each shell, like "A Red Hot Mamma for Yokohama," "Kiss the Japs Good-bye," and "From Mike to the Mikado."

On December 7—the first anniversary of the treacherous attack on Pearl Harbor—all American guns on the island observed the occasion by battering the enemy lines and rear without halt. The Marine howitzers joined in the island-shaking chorus and later referred to that occasion as "Special Hate Shoot No. 1."

Brig. Gen. William H. Rupertus, assistant commander of the First Division, and Pedro A. del Valle, commander of artillery, dropped in on the battery and lent a personal hand. With General del Valle barking the firing order and with General Rupertus taking over the gunner's position, they boomed out an anniversary greeting inscribed: "To Tojo— Dec. 7."

The eyes of that outfit was Capt. Robert E. Collier, a twenty-six-year-old Texan from Aspermont, who took to the air in an observation plane over Jap lines, tree-hopping to elude enemy antiaircraft fire while picking out the targets for the howitzers.

As of 7 December, the battery was officially credited with neutralizing twenty Jap field pieces, and with direct hits on three more guns; with demolishing six ammunition and gasoline dumps; and with destroying or damaging a number of bridges and roads in Jap territory.

The cannoneers emphasized that I should not overlook another claim to fame of sorts. They pointed with pardonable pride to Corporal Franz Geiger, of Melbourne, Florida, who in civilian life had been a human cannonball with Kaus Carnivals.

The prize battery included Sgt. Ray Moore, Roanoke, Virginia; Cpl. Frank Sexton, Memphis, Tennessee; Cpl. Mike Fidali, Newark, New Jersey; Cpl. Matthew Jackson, Wyoming, Pennsylvania; Pfc. Andy Conrad, Scranton, Pennsylvania; Pfc. Andy Sopriak, Ambridge, Pennsylvania; Pfc. John Morrison, Brooklyn, New York; Pfc. Guy Steele, Harlan, Kentucky; Pfc. Joseph J. O'Connell, Hyde Park, Massachusetts; Pfc. Gordon Furney, Fulton, New York; Pvt. James Spurlin, Spartanburg, South Carolina; Pvt. Donald Simpson, New York City; Pfc. Alex Bolevich, Youngstown, Ohio; Pfc. John Keyser, Columbus, Ohio; and Pfc. Peter Saltonstall, twenty-one-year-old son of the governor of Massachusetts, who had quit his senior term at Harvard to enlist.

By January 1943, the Japanese land offensive had been beaten back, but they were still formidable in the air. When Secretary of the Navy Frank Knox, Admiral of the Fleet Chester W. Nimitz, and Vice Admiral John S. McCain undertook an inspection tour of Guadalcanal, they were put up at the headquarters of Maj. Gen. Francis P. Mulcahy, commanding the Second Marine Air Wing.

That night, when Condition Red was sounded, the brass and braid had to race into the foxholes in their pajamas and helmets like every other Yank. Came the dawn, Washing Machine Charley had left, and Secretary Knox—General Mulcahy vouched for this tidbit—called on his admirals to join him in morning calisthenics. It was an inspirational sight, and comical.

Another day I unexpectedly observed the Marine tanks in action.

The fourteen-ton General Stuart tank appeared to be an impregnable mobile fortress. More than fourteen feet long, seven feet wide, and seven feet tall, it should have been more than enough to scare the pants off any soldier confronted by its weapons. In the hands of the trained, toughened four-member crew, it proved to be crushingly effective on the beaches and in the tall, knife-edge kunai grass.

The Stuart mounted four guns, one firing two-pound projectiles, and was capable of crossing a ditch six feet wide, fording a 3.5 foot stream, and climbing a 50 percent incline.

Considered a light tank, the Stuart was not impenetrable. Its armor was thin, 1.5 inches of steel or less. An unlucky shell could decapitate it. A hand grenade thrust into its treads could stop it. Jungle brush or mangrove roots could snare it. The sheer slopes could balk it. And it was the best—perhaps only—tank available to the Marines on Guadalcanal.

That day five tanks had been directed to take out three enemy nests holding up the infantry advance. It turned out that there were a helluva lot more pillboxes out there, and the Stuarts trampled a dozen or smashed them to smithereens with cannon shot.

It was then that one of the tanks, commanded by Sergeant William T. Unger, a twenty-two-year-old from Wichita, Kansas, was knocked out of commission 300 yards inside the enemy sector. Unger and his three mates—Pvt. Merle McVey, nineteen, Pine Valley, California, Cpl. Maurice Mensch, twenty-three, Leavenworth, Kansas, and Cpl. Jean Baker, Burbank, California—hopped out of their stricken

Stuart and set up a ground machine-gun defense under heavy fire from the surrounding foe.

Noting their predicament, Lt. Cal Hansen, twenty-four, of Kansas City, Missouri, who was leading the operation, radioed for another tank to join him. The two tanks, both hit but still mobile, formed a V with the disabled machine so that their wedge faced the Jap fire with their backs protected by the sea.

For more than an hour, the enraged enemy pummeled the tankmen with bullet and mortar shell, but the Marines fought on, and fought back, shouting encouragement to one another.

Then Sgt. Gene Roush, twenty-two, of Pampa, Texas, sneaked up on one of the enemy gun emplacements and tossed in two grenades with explosive impact. Sgt. Irvin Neely, from Peniel, Texas, seized two light machine guns and fired them simultaneously from the third tank. Another Texan, Pfc. Henry McPherson, of Corpus Christi, celebrating his twenty-first birthday, exultantly cried out, "Today I am a man!" as he squeezed the trigger of his tommy gun. Cpl. Duane Branaka, from Wisconsin, joined the hullabaloo with "This sure ain't like Beloit!" as he fired repeatedly.

After an hour's battle, Lieutenant Hansen radioed for help, and under the cover of Alligator (amphibian tractor) guns, led nine of the tankmen through waist-high water back to their own line. Three of the men—Roush, Branaka, and McPherson—volunteered to stay behind to keep the Japs from capturing their battered tanks. Aided by friendly artillery support, the trio held out for another sixty minutes until the advancing Marine infantrymen could relieve them. Two of the three tanks were then successfully withdrawn and all crews got back safely.

The day's action was a rousing homecoming for their battalion commander, Maj. Robert L. Denig Jr., of Richmond, Virginia, returning that day from a hospital siege. The thirty-three-year-old son of the CC chief, General Denig, the major was a graduate of the U.S. Naval Academy and Army tank school and had served with the Marines in China.

I asked to be assigned to a tank mission as a member of the crew, but Major Denig adamantly refused. Perhaps the major heard Little Jeezus moaning.

Untrained for the tank's urgent demands on its skilled crew, Denig declared, I would endanger the mission and his men.

Major Denig instead suggested that I take part, inside the tank, in a practice maneuver. That shakedown—which shook me up—forever stifled my yen for the treads. I suffered a severe attack of claustrophobia inside, and I was very glad to pop out of the opened turret when the demonstration was over. I had a crazy impulse to blurt out, "Tanks for the memory!" but I swallowed it. The tankmen deserved better of me, and I shook hands all around, promising to send their story to their papers back home. I did.

I next tried to track down a tank-destroyer platoon that I had heard had blasted apart eight Tojo tanks in a critical stage of the fighting around Henderson Field. I never did find it, but I did catch up with another tank-destroyer outfit engaged, as artillery, in smashing the enemy's defenses west of the Matanikau River, where the fighting was in progress.

The tank-destroyer, officially LVT—Landing Vehicle Tracked—is half truck, half tractor. The front part of the vehicle has regular truck wheels; the rear runs on tractor treads. Mounted with a 75mm gun, the destroyer and its seven-member crew are effective against enemy tanks, and its .50-caliber machine gun is likewise effective against enemy aircraft and personnel.

The half-tracs, led by Lt. Stephen K. Pawlawski, from Brooklyn, Connecticut, twenty-eight, and up from the ranks, had rushed up to the front line to fire a preparatory barrage of shells for the infantry push, and the following day blasted out three unyielding pockets and six machine-gun nests. The third day, the enemy line cracked when the half-tracs cleared the way with a series of salvos that took out two more machine-gun emplacements and a 40mm gun. When Jap snipers tried to pick off the tank-destroyer crew, the Marines fired high-explosive projectiles into the camouflaged hideouts, blowing down trees and snipers alike.

Lieutenant Pawlawski and his seven-member team had

first seen action in the August landing on Tulagi, and were transferred to the Guadalcanal front line in December. The platoon leader and two scouts slipped into enemy territory to reconnoiter. All three were hit and pinned down by an enemy machine gunner, one hurt so badly he could not move. The bleeding officer lifted the wounded boy onto his back and catwalked him to safety, while the other wounded Marine covered their escape.

Pawlawski's platoon was cited—as I watched—for "courage, resourcefulness, and skill" by the regimental commander, and as a "big factor" in success of the infantry operation.

The little guys in the "big factor" were Marine Gunner Ernest E. Smith, twenty-five, of Cochrane, Georgia, second in command; Sgt. Joseph Casignao, thirty, Benton Harbor, Michigan, section chief; Cpl. James Monay, twenty-six, Westwood, California, gunner; Cpl. John Metz, twenty-nine, Pueblo, California, radioman; Pfc. Robert Mitchell, twenty-three, Harvey, Illinois, driver; Pfc. LeRoy Dedrick, twenty-eight, El Paso, Texas, firer; Pfc. John S. McLaughlin, twenty-two, Ponca City, Oklahoma, loader; Pfc. Juest J. Domamngue, New Orleans, machine gunner; and three ammo runners: Pvt. John E. Meyers, twenty, Waukegan, Illinois; Pfc. Louis Mendel, eighteen, New Orleans; and Pvt. Elmer Judd, eighteen, Bliss, Idaho.

I witnessed many selfless acts on different fronts in different sectors, and I wrote a hometown-hero story about the participants in every instance. I didn't make the heroes; I simply gave them recognition.

One day on the island, I had an unexpected Boston University reunion. During my undergraduate years at BU, I had covered several college football games for the *Boston American* as a stringer at twenty-five cents per inch of published copy. I got to know some of the gridiron players. So, when I bumped into Pat Hanley, the Terriers' coach until his recall to active duty as a lieutenant colonel, we were both happy to meet a familiar face from the campus.

We were joined by strapping George Morris, a Scarlet and White tackle, and trim Al Amirault, a tight end. The varsity gridders had both hit the Guadalcanal beach in the first wave with an amphibian tractor outfit and had been in action for five months.

Lt. Col. LeRoy "Pat" Hanley had fought in World War I and was a line officer with the "Butcher Battalion," so called for its bloody engagements over two months. Hanley's closest call had been a stray bullet that whistled by his thinning hair.

Pat's more famous older brother, Dick, coach of the top ten Northwestern University eleven, was also in active service as a Marine major; his younger brother, Lee, was a Marine flier.

The two BU gridmates were privates first class, Bay Staters, and twenty-two, Amirault from North Weymouth, Morris from Hyde Park. After Parris Island boot camp, they had been assigned to an Alligator unit, and had been under fire for 131 days.

What did we talk about? Football, of course.

Major Hanley, a veteran pro on both the battle and football fields, compared the two arenas this way: "This war is like a football game. The breaks count, sure. But what matters most is the training, the organization, the leadership, the strategy. That's why we're licking the Japs."

There was another reason why our grunts were licking the Japs. Our guys never lost their sense of humor. In their worst hours, they would joke about their lot. One example:

"Why do we eat evening chow so early in the afternoon?"

"If we eat in the dark, the Japs will grab all our places in line!"

The phenomenal feats of the outnumbered Marine airmen on Guadalcanal fascinated me. Each squadron, virtually each pilot, gunner, and crewman, provided hot copy for a thrilling news dispatch.

In the early days of the Guadalcanal incursion, the Marine fliers were few in number. Their Grumman Wildcat fighters were less maneuverable and climbed more slowly than the lighter Zeroes, which were piloted by the more experienced Jap aviators. Our Douglas dive-bombers and torpedo bombers were not as fast as the Vals (Aichi dive-bombers). The commissioned pilots were so few that enlisted men who could fly were encouraged to take over the cockpits. Volunteers also were needed and accepted as rear gunners on the Dauntless dive-bombers.

The Marine fighter pilots, however, discovered they also had three advantages. Their stumpy-looking Grummans were better armored and more powerfully armed than the Zeros; and the Marine airmen, though dogfight fledglings, were daring and fearless. They clobbered the enemy, but also suffered severe losses in planes and pilots.

Of course, the CCs were not permitted by the censors to send home the bad news. But there was plenty of good news to write about the fliers—for instance, Dive Bomber Squadron 142.

Maj. Robert H. Richard, who was a twenty-eight-year-old Diamond Bar rancher at Cody, Wyoming, before giving up his broncos for bombers, flew his Dauntless Scout-Bomber Squadron 142 into Cactus on November 12, and within twenty-four hours led half his fliers against a Japanese armada off Savo Island, in that battle at sea that ran four days and nights.

First strike was made by one of the squadron's two enlisted pilots, Master Technical Sergeant Donald S. Thornbury, a twenty-five-year-old Iowan, in a screaming dive on a battleship of the Kongo class, he made a direct hit with a 1,000-pound bomb. Marine and Navy torpedo planes finished off the battle wagon. Next day the Waterloo recruit followed up his spectacular debut by finishing off two transports.

In the two succeeding months of daily action, Squadron 142 also sank seven enemy cruisers and destroyers, eight transports and freighters, and fourteen motor barges; damaged one more battleship, four cruisers and destroyers, four transports and freighters; and downed twenty Zero interceptors. With few exceptions, the pilots and gunners alike had been called up from civilian life.

On December 3, the full squadron, flying through thick weather, attacked a Jap fleet of five cruisers and seven destroyers 240 miles away from their base. Led by the squadron's executive officer, Capt. Lionel W. Pool, a school-teacher from Hiawatha, Kansas, the Marine dive-bombers tore into the enemy warships fifteen minutes before sundown and ran into tremendous antiaircraft fire. They sank two and left three more in flames, before returning to their home field through the soupy dark. Captain Pool, twenty-three, alumnus of Hastings College, had to make a crash landing because his dive-bomber had been shot up by the antiaircraft fire.

The notable performance—all in a day's work—earned the praise of Admiral Halsey and of Brig. Gen. Louis Woods, who only a few days before had taken over command of the Cactus Air Force and who made a surprise visit to the wingmen.

Four days later, December 7, the SBDs remembered Pearl Harbor by striking out at eleven destroyers, 200 miles off, sinking one and damaging two more. En route, 1st Lt. William McL. Ellison, twenty-four, of Wassaic, New York, spotted a two-man submarine. The Harvard graduate promptly finished it off.

Eleven was a lucky number for Squadron 142. On December 11 the squadron ran down another formation of eleven destroyers, 175 miles out, and took out five of them with direct hits. This time it was Adm. Chester Nimitz, Commander in Chief of the Pacific, who radioed congratulations.

The Dauntless fliers savaged five more destroyers on January 15. First Lt. Austin Wiggins, out of Amherst, Texas, dove through antiaircraft salvos to drop one bomb on one tin can, and score a near miss on another, before bailing out with his gunner into the sea. They patiently floated around on their emergency rubber raft until lifted off by a Navy patrol plane.

Squadron 142 was dubbed the "Munda Maulers" for its damaging assaults on Jap fortifications defending Munda, a major Jap garrison blocking the route to Rabaul, Tojo's military hub in the Solomons, 1,000 miles north of Guadalcanal. Several of the dive-bombers were hit, and the pilots had to make crash landings; yet in their two months' activity, remarkably, not a man was lost. Twenty-three pilots and gunners were recommended for decoration. Six of the rear gunners, all enlisted men, were credited with shooting down at least one enemy Zero.

Pumped up by those episodes, I made a pitch to join a dive-bomber raid on Munda as volunteer rear gunner. I was so intent on getting into the air, I simply brushed off the frantic flappings of Little Jeezus.

The squadron leader looked me over and responded to my request with one word:

"Nuts!"

Later that day, two of the dive-bombers collided in the air; the pilots bailed out, but one gunner failed to clear. I experienced a strange reaction, a reaction I could not explain to myself. I was not scared off by the tragedy. Maybe because it was so easy to get killed anyplace in and around Guadalcanal.

I pestered the squadron leader. By then the Zeros had been driven off, and were busy defending Munda from our air attacks, I argued futilely. Then I said I'd settle for a routine "Pistol Pete" mission prowling after hidden enemy machine-gun nests and hidden pockets of holdouts. The squadron leader relented only when the rear gunner scheduled for the next flight came down with dysentery.

At 3:30 P.M. on January 20, the pilot, Staff Sgt. John L. Milby, a twenty-seven-year-old West Pointer—that is, West Point, King William County, Virginia—reported to the squadron operations pagoda. He'd joined up as a groundling mechanic at the Anacostia Air Base and earned his wings the hardest way. I reported too, and Milby accepted his unexpected substitute gunner without a qualm.

"Nothing much to worry about on this run," Navy Lt. Harold Payne, twenty-nine, of Washington, D.C., the intelligence officer, commented. "There hasn't been a daylight Zero attack here in a couple of weeks, and there's been hardly any antiaircraft fire from Millimeter Mike below." He laid out a panoramic photo map of the northwestern sector of the island, where the Japanese troops were making a stubborn last stand. The area was marked off in chalk with an inscribed invitation to American airmen: "Open season."

Lieutenant Payne's reassurance had a familiar ring and stirred up some misgivings, which I immediately suppressed, but Little Jeezus was not so easily mollified.

"I'm due back to Noumea in couple of days," I pleaded with my mental watchdog. "It's my one chance to get into the air on a dive-bomber."

"Cover yer ass, stupid," my jinni sputtered. Guiltily, I ignored him.

"Here," the intelligence officer pointed to a map, indicating Tassafaronga Point, three miles beyond the Marine lines, "you'll spot a rubbish heap in a clearing. We think it's a camouflaged Jap supply dump. Blow it up."

Sergeant Milby nodded. I nodded too, without any real idea where the target was located.

"Farther up, at Bunina Point, look around for enemy activity. Our last air patrol sighted movement in that sector." Again the pilot nodded. Again I nodded.

"Okay. Good luck, guys."

A truck shuttled us to "Dot," her nose painted white like an overpowdered saucy dame's. Dot had been around, as evidenced by the bullet holes on her frame and by the two Rising Suns emblazoned on her fuselage, one for a transport she had sunk, one for the Zero she had blown away. A quarter-tonner was strapped to the bomber's belly and a 100-pound bomb was fastened under each wing.

The incapacitated regular rear gunner, Cpl. Simon Cavage, at twenty-one a veteran, gave me fifteen minutes of instructions on operating the dual guns, and on handling the interphone, radio, life jacket, and parachute.

The corporal, from Wilkes-Barre, Pennsylvania, then added a couple more minutes explaining how to disengage the machine gun and throw it overboard in the event of a forced water landing. The gunner's parting advice: "If a Zero pounces on your tail, just keep firing."

I gulped, climbed briskly into the rear gunner's slot, shifted the swivel seat to face the rear, adjusted the aviation goggles, and raised my arm to indicate I was ready, shaky but ready.

"And don't forget," the grounded gunner shouted, "if you have to bail out, dive for the wing and you'll clear the tail."

With those comforting words, Dot took off like a breeze. One swoop around the airfield, and the Douglas flashed out to sea to begin the two-hour patrol.

Pilot Milby dipped his wings in greeting to a nine-plane formation returning from a bombing run. He dipped them to a Navy transport lolling in calm waters. He dipped to Navy torpedo boats skipping below like swift water bugs. Dot's shadow chased after her like a porpoise on a lark. Off Kokumbona, I saw a Navy destroyer skirting the shoreline, belching fiery salvos into the enemy redoubts.

Then Milby announced that he saw the guideposts of his mission: four enemy transports blasted and beached in the shallows, and several wrecked landing craft scattered around.

He glided Dot along the beach at about 500 feet along Tassafaronga Point and dropped a 100-pounder on the conspicuous rubbish pile, then returned and let go the other. The two explosions eliminated the trash heap and suspected supply dump. Dot then zoomed upward to 6,000 feet and dived at 280 miles an hour as Sergeant Milby celebrated his hits. The breakaway from the sharp dive left me giddy, like the first time I had drunk too much champagne.

Milby then warned me he was going to seek out the second target and that we might encounter antiaircraft fire. I crouched deeper into my seat and tightened my fingers on the gun grips. The pilot descended, zipped swiftly along the shoreline, and picked out a trail trickling into the jungle. Over the interphone, he yelled something unintelligible to me, immediately followed by a sharp outburst of firing.

"Hey!" I screamed into the phone. "The Japs are shooting at us!"

"That's me shooting, dumbo!" Pilot Milby screamed back.

Well, how was I to know? We'd been warned we might run into enemy fire, hadn't we?

"Mission's over," the pilot abruptly proclaimed. "Time to fly back."

Crestfallen, I argued for permission to fire my machine guns. After all, I went up as rear gunner, didn't I? I didn't go up just for the ride, did I?

Milby, a reasonable guy, accepted my logic and dove back over the second target. This time ready, I fired away at the trail where it ducked into the jungle. I didn't see any enemy, but I fantasized that I was getting back at the sniper who had nearly nailed me my first day on the front.

After a graceful landing on return, Pilot Milby climbed out and clapped me on the shoulders, announcing to all: "Today Sam earned his wings. He fired his guns, he hit the designated target, and . . . and . . . he didn't hit the tail."

Nonetheless, I was satisfied. I scrunched my nose at Little Jeezus as if to say "So there!"

Several days later I was typing out a sheaf of notes when a tentmate brought the news that a Marine fighter pilot name of Voss had shot down his twenty-sixth Jap warplane.

Voss? I had never heard of Voss. My C-2 mission to Guadalcanal was just about over, and I was due back Noumea by January 25, two days later. Voss, twenty-six kills? Didn't Capt. Eddie Rickenbacker achieve a record twenty-six kills in World War I? It was too good a story for me to pass up.

I quickly tucked away my notes and Hermes, thumbed a ride to Henderson Field, and chased down Voss, who turned out to be Capt. Joe Foss, leader of "Joe's Flying Circus," a division of Marine Fighter Squadron 121, "Cactus" Air Force. Foss had shot down three Zeros in nose-to-nose passes a few days before, on January 15, for an official total score of twenty-six kills, not counting "smokers," enemy planes hit and emitting smoke but not actually seen collapsing into the sea.

I found Foss at the operations center of his F4F Wildcat command, an unimposing-looking individual in dungarees and baseball cap, his sun- and windburned face and slow, deliberate manner of speech identifying him as a farmer—

which he was back in Sioux Falls, South Dakota, before relinquishing the haycock for the cockpit.

Joe's nose showed definite signs of multiple collisions, fractured—he confessed under questioning—by a pair of boxing gloves, a kicking horse, and quarterback's knee.

As a Golden Glover, Joe had been so-so, and as a college football player at South Dakota University he had been a benchwarmer, but as a Marine fighter pilot he was today the Ace of Aces.

Some of his fellow fliers broached the theory that it was Joe's frequently broken schnoz that provided him the uncanny ability to smell out—and snuff out—enemy planes. More seriously, members of the Circus said Foss was a natural. Not a flying fool, but an instinctive sky fighter who knew exactly what he was doing up there at 20,000–30,000 feet, where the pilots rarely got more than one guess.

It took Foss six years to earn his business administration degree, because he also had to earn the tuition. He took on odd jobs—packing plant worker, gas station attendant, hired farmhand, butcher's assistant, waiter, and dishwasher. He had fallen in love with planes as a youngster, the first time he saw an aerial barnstormer, and had vowed to become a flier.

In 1940, at the age of twenty-six, Joe joined the Marine Corps and earned his wings at Pensacola, staying on as an instructor after being turned down, because of age, for fighter pilot duty. But he persisted, went into combat training at Camp Kearney on the West Coast, and was primed to go when Squadron 121 was urgently called up to relieve the depleted fighter force defending Guadalcanal against the nonstop Jap counterattacks.

The Flying Circus flew into Henderson Field from a small escort carrier, *Copabee,* early in October, when the Marine fighter strength was at its nadir, and made an inauspicious initial sortie several days later. Then the aerial action exploded.

October 13: Captain Foss drew first blood when a Jap bomber fleet, escorted by a cover of Zeros, struck at Henderson. As Joe's Wildcat shot skyward, a Zero pounced on his tail and raked him with machine-gun fire, but then made the mistake of diving under the Wildcat's belly. Joe blasted his assailant down in flames. He had little time for elation, however, as three enemy fighters ganged up on him and riddled his Wildcat. Joe barely managed to slip away to a dead-stick landing.

October 14: Joe went up in another Grumman and down came another Zero.

October 17: The Japs roared in high, above 29,000 feet. Joe knocked off a Zero in a dogfight and headed for a bomber, but one of his Circus buddies got there first and eradicated the Betty. So Joe lashed out at another Mitsubishi and watched it streak away, smoking. Joe made a third try and that time perforated a Jap bomber, which plunged to an official death. Then, confronted by a challenging Zero, Joe made it three for the day. Five kills in three days—and Joe had become an Ace.

October 20: Two Zeros for Foss.

October 23: Four for four. All raiding Zeros. The Flying Circus had a field day. The division chalked up twenty-two sures. Joe had to make another dead-stick landing.

October 25: Five for five. All Zeros again, between breakfast and lunch. Six Zeros jumped the Circus and five would never jump again. More Zeros poured in, and Joe pulverized four more Zs and managed to land with a smoking tail after being hit. The division was credited with sixteen more enemy warcraft. For Joe, it added up to sixteen definite kills in twelve days of aerial combat.

November 7: Take three. The Circus escorted Marine dive and torpedo bombers in an attack on a Jap fleet of nine destroyers. The Circus knocked off six Zeros, one by Joe, who then fired fatal bursts at two Rufes, Jap seaplanes. Joe's motor, however, was crippled by bullets, so that he had to make a water landing. His Wildcat sank, but Joe managed to pull himself free, floating some five miles off the island of Malaita, on the other side of Sealark Channel. As night enveloped the sea, Joe made out canoes paddling toward him, but fearing them to be enemy, he made no outcry. This game of hide-and-seek kept on for two hours, when Foss heard someone shout:

" 'E's hover 'ere!"

There was no mistaking the accent of Tommy Mason, a sawmill operator and coastal watcher.

November 12: Two torpedo bombers and a Zero for Joe.

November 16: For Foss, one Zero, his twenty-third kill, and himself taken out by malaria. He was flown to a rear base for treatment and recovery.

Joe came back to Squadron 121 on December 31, face wan, eyes flushed, cheeks hollow, and weight down from 190 to 160. He nonetheless insisted he was in shape for action again.

January 15: Joe proved his contention, and picked off three Zeros. The Circus celebrated its leader's return by bagging three more.

Total to date: Foss, twenty-six; the "Circus," sixty-nine.

How did he achieve his remarkable record?

Joe was reluctant to talk about it.

"We fight as a team," Foss tried to explain. "We cover each other, and I keep getting the best breaks."

As a team the Flying Circus had accounted for sixty-nine enemy fighters, dive-bombers, torpedo bombers, and float-planes, and had suffered painful losses too. More than half of the original eight pilots of Joe's flight had gone down with their Wildcats.

Lt. Bill Marontate, a twenty-three-year-old University of Washington grad from Seattle, was credited with thirteen kills before being listed as "missing in action" on the day that Joe Foss scored his twenty-sixth.

Seven witnessed flamedowns were attributed each to Capt. Greg Loesch, twenty-four, of Montrose, Colorado, and Lt. Roger Haberman, twenty-six, of Ellsworth, Wisconsin. Loesch, out of Colorado College, had to be rescued twice after forced water landings. Haberman, out of Stout Institute, had flunked the civilian pilot test just before he joined the Marines.

Lt. Bill Freeman, twenty-four, of Bonham, Texas, and Texas A & M, connected with six Jap warplanes; and Lt.

Frank Presley, twenty-two, of Encinitas, California, and California Polytech, had five.

Lt. Oscar Bate, twenty-four, of Essex Falls, New Jersey, was forced to make a water landing and a parachute jump, but still accounted for three kills. He was a Yalie, studying law at Harvard, when he opted for flying. And Lt. Tom Furlow, twenty-three, University of Arkansas alumnus from Ogden, made the honor roll with two confirmed shoot-downs.

On February 17, Joe Foss was ordered to return to the States for the customary war bond tour and was awarded the Medal of Honor. A number of his Flying Circus comrades were awarded the Navy Cross and Distinguished Flying Cross.

I flew back to Noumea on January 24, the day following my interviews with the Flying Circus, my notes carefully stuffed into my backpack along with my report for C-2 and a stack of news stories.

First thing, I banged out the Foss story, happy in the thought I had come up with a Big One. First Amphibious Corps Intelligence cleared it quickly, and General Mulcahy, the wing commander, personally okayed it. Nonetheless, at some anonymous checkpoint my Big One was held up by censors for three months—I later was informed—on the grounds the story would reveal vital information to the enemy.

Could it be that Tojo was unaware he had lost sixty-nine warplanes?

Sixteen days after I left Guadalcanal, the Jap forces also pulled out, officially declared to be driven off the island on February 9.

The Marines had slain thousands of the foe, and had suffered losses of 1,250 dead, 2,700 wounded, and as many more stricken down by the jungle diseases.

I did not realize it then, and I doubt if our military leaders at the highest level realized it then, but the Japanese juggernaut, which had overrun the American and Allied ramparts all over the Pacific, had ground to a dead stop on Guadalcanal.

CHAPTER 8

Pavuvu

I flew back to Noumea via SCAT—this time on a bucket seat—and reported to Col. George Monson, C-2. He and his deputy, Col. John T. Selden, a campaign-toughened expeditionary officer who succeeded to the Intelligence command, liked my report on the CCs on "The Island"; they also liked the news stories I had turned out.

At Colonel Selden's suggestion, I went aboard the *Chicago* to interview the Marine survivors of the intrepid heavy cruiser that had blazed through a half dozen sea battles and had been mortally wounded a few days before, on January 29–30, in the battle off Rennell Island, the last major naval engagement around Guadalcanal.

The ship had been launched twelve years earlier, and was one of the oldest ships on Pacific duty.

The *Chicago* had fought ferociously in the Coral Sea and at Midway, surviving bombs and torpedoes launched by Admiral Yamamoto's naval forces and, once, mistakenly, by Army Marauders. Next, off Savo Island, August 10, our fleet protecting Guadalcanal was caught flat-fleeted, and was ravaged by bombs, torpedoes, and shells. The Allies lost four heavy cruisers that disastrous night: USS *Astoria*, *Quincy*, *Vincennes*, and the Australian *Canberra*.

The *Chicago* was severely chewed up in that shocker but survived the crushing defeat of our fleet and returned quickly to fight again.

The seagoing Marines, who had manned antiaircraft machine guns on the *Chicago*, related how three members of their detachment, although painfully wounded and under raking fire, stuck to their posts, blazing away, and even as their cruiser was lanced by several torpedoes, shot down every one of the eleven Nakajimas screaming down at them.

Pvt. Harold M. Dixon, nineteen, of Bisbee, Arizona, his leg smashed and in agony, was lifted by two buddies and carried eighty feet down the vertical ladders from his anti-aircraft post on the mainmast. His gunmates, Sgt. Willard B. Johnson, twenty-one, of Swanville, Minnesota, and Pfc. Jacob Baraban, twenty-three, of Kansas City, Missouri, then lowered Dixon by rope over the side, where Pvt. Cecil E. Stanley, twenty, of Eureka, Kansas, a powerful swimmer, freed the trussed Marine and lugged him, Red Cross method, fifty yards onto a bobbing raft.

From his adjacent gun post, Pvt. William L. Stander, nineteen, of Promontory, Utah, his back perforated by shrapnel, shot down two of the torpedo planes, then managed to squirm down from the high mast on his own. A third wounded AA crewman, Pvt. Vernon A. Brown, twenty-seven, of Kansas City, Missouri, called on his four years' experience as a civilian fireman to clamber down by himself as the *Chicago* listed.

At the Naval mobile base hospital, the Marines described the action at sea:

"The Japs had roared in on us for the second day," Private Dixon recalled, "and three of them came right at us in the mainmast. I was loading, and my gunner (Pfc. Alessio S. Di Paolo, twenty-three, Cleveland Heights, Ohio) knocked off one in a hurry.

"Stander got the second one, but the third came in strafing, and that was when Al and I got hurt. Stander, though, didn't budge from his gun. As cool as a cucumber, he picked off the third. That was some shooting, I tell you."

Private Stander, who had joined the Corps only seven months before, didn't have much to say. "I didn't even know I was hurt," he said. "But Dixon, his leg bone was cracked open, and he was suffering terrific pain, but you didn't hear as much as a whimper out of him."

Dixon, like Stander, refused to quit his gun when wounded "because there was no one to take my place."

Every member of the Marine contingent, two officers and

forty-one men, were rescued, some after more than an hour in the open sea, the interviewees said.

Last to leave the gun mounts were members of the crew of No. 1: Cpl. Harold Johnson, twenty, Tucson, Arizona; Pfc. Robert S. Ebert, eighteen, Memphis, Tennessee; Pfc. Jack E. Chuda, twenty-two, Omaha, Nebraska; and Pvt. James Baker, twenty, Cincinnati, Ohio. They were still firing away when ordered to quit station and ship.

The Marine leader, Capt. Walter F. Cornnell, twenty-five, of Alexandria, Virginia—a onetime *Washington Post* newsboy—confirmed the version recounted by his men. He also expressed admiration for the commander of the *Chicago*, Capt. Ralph C. Davis, "coolest man on the ship, and the last to abandon her."

Cornnell, a University of Virginia alumnus, and 1st Lt. Frank M. Granucci, twenty-four, his deputy from San Francisco, described the last battle of the *Chicago*:

"The *Chicago* was proceeding south of Guadalcanal with Task Force 18 about 7:30 P.M. Friday, January 30. Our air escort had just left us when a swarm of Nakajimas swooped down on us.

"The guns of the *Chicago* were first to open fire, and as if infuriated by the action, twenty of the torpedo planes dove at us, scoring two hits. We knocked them down, at least four of them, including the two that had scored.

"Our engines were out, the ship was listing and dead in the water. We had to be towed.

"At 4:15 P.M., the next day, Saturday, the torpedo planes lashed at us again. This time we had fighter protection and many of the enemy planes were destroyed or beaten off. Eleven, however, got through, and these were all blasted by our ack-ack and the fighter planes.

"But the paralyzed *Chicago* was doomed. Four more torpedoes tore into her starboard side. She had to be quickly abandoned, and Captain Davis cleared the ship, able and wounded, about a thousand men, in twenty minutes.

"To the very end the morale was high among both sailors and Marines. Over the sides they went shouting to the rescue boats: 'Hey, taxi! Going my way?' "

The *Chicago* was given the traditional honorable coup de grâce by sister ships and slid down 2,000 fathoms to its final port of call.

It was an upbeat story, and C-2 assured me it would be cleared by the censors. I was not so sure, but it did make it through, and made a big splash in the Stateside media.

After my initiation into combat on Guadalcanal, I was happy to be back to "Paree," shabby and scruffy as it was. I was happy to enjoy the simple comforts of Noumea after the physical punishment of Guadalcanal. I had lost weight and was drained of vigor and enthusiasm. I eased up by visiting our newest battleship, *Indiana,* and other vessels in the harbor, ostensibly to glean Marine action stories, which I wrote, but also to satiate my craving for hot, appetizing food.

I now found myself entangled in a struggle for survival as a freewheeling combat correspondent operating under the aegis of C-2 Intelligence.

Unannounced and unexpected, a Company X—as it was officially designated—presented itself in Noumea, dispatched by General Denig to carry out psychological warfare against Tojo's troops. The concept had merit, to be sure, but the CCs in Company X, all experienced newsmen like myself, had received no training in psyching the enemy. Nevertheless, they were supposed to undermine the morale and will of the Mikado's revering subjects with loud, vociferous mikes and clouds of leaflets.

C-2 reacted to the proposed psych offensive with derision, and turned thumbs down on the project. The commander of Company X, Capt. Brooks Peters, a onetime *New York Times* reporter of sorts, was then ordered to regroup his men into a standard public relations section. Captain Peters had to find make-work for his disheartened CCs, but nonetheless, as he was senior PR officer on the base, he officiously demanded that I be placed under his command and control.

Determined to retain my independence, I called for help among the friends in high places I had made in C-2 and these took the necessary steps to save me from the grasp of the pompous empire builder.

(Company X was soon dissolved and its CCs sent to the battlefront units, where they served with distinction.)

My confidence and well-being renewed, I enthusiastically accepted an invitation to join a deer hunt, my first. Out there, deep in the boondocks of New Caledonia, succulent deer were to be found, game worthy of the most avid sportsman and venison gastronome. The lithe animals were not indigenous to the island, but had been imported generations earlier from Sumatra.

The deer idea spread around the encampment because of the vivid reports of Tech. Sgt. Bill Noll, who'd been hunting in the forests of the Great Northwest since his Tom Sawyer days. "There's a lot of climbing to be done," he said, "but it's worth it. There are scores of deer out there—if you can find them."

Noll, a mailman and gun-and-rod enthusiast back in Salem, Oregon, had returned from a three-day chase and, with two fellow hunters, had sighted fourteen antlered beauties. He returned with a prize portion of his stag, providing a lucky gaggle of gluttons with venison steaks "less gamey in flavor than our American deer."

Our hunt was organized on a pragmatic basis, made up of the NCOs in charge of the motor pool, arms depot, kitchen, and PX (post-exchange) so as to ensure sufficient wheels and ammo, choice food, and, not least, the essential beer. Mott, a photographer, and I would be there to record the historic event for posterity.

We nimrods six departed at 2 A.M. from Camp Goettge on a jeep that bounced over the jagged east-west coastal road, reaching a native village eighty-two miles and many jarring hours later. The aborigines spoke no English, but understood two words: *deeer* and *doh-lar*. We chose as our guide a scrawny friendly fellow, untypically short among the tall, brawny Melanesian males, who called himself Charlie, pronounced "Sharlie."

The guide wore jungle-stained shorts, raggedly cut from a pair of khaki trousers, and a faded khaki overseas cap perched precariously on his pear-shaped head. He saluted snappily whenever any of the huntsmen spoke to him or looked at him. We felt honor bound to salute back each time.

"Sharlie" strode into the spiky kunai grass with the expectant adventurers plodding closely behind. Surprisingly, the skinny short-legged leadman took uncomfortably long steps by hopping through the bush, so that the stalkers behind him had to skip and jump forward every few paces to keep up with him. After overcoming several hills and dales, we protested we were being taken on a wild-goose chase, but the grinning guide kept pointing and pressing forward.

At last Sharlie stopped, and with hand over mouth to signify silence, raised his rifle pointing directly ahead. Several hundred yards away, I caught sight of a handsome five-pronged buck and a graceful sleek-bodied doe grazing on the rise of a hillock. The nibbling couple, sensing danger, hesitated an instant and bounded into the woodland. But we were mesmerized by the sheer magnificence of the idyllic scene and failed to pull our triggers.

Sharlie, anger showing in his eyes, started to turn back. He resumed the trek only after the reanimated marksmen waved two more "doh-lar" in his face. At that point three of the huntsmen gave up the chase to return to the village, the jeep, and—doubt you not—the beer.

One more weary hour later, Sharlie again signaled a halt, then aimed his rifle toward an open patch perhaps 600 yards away. This time the guide, I, and the other two sportsmen fired simultaneously. Each of us hunters claimed a bull's-eye. But when I reached the fallen quarry I noted that each of the animals had been felled by a single bullet, and, without saying so, I suspected that our guide, tired of tracking, had himself done the trick.

Still, who was there to deny our boast when we got back to base with two huge hind quarters for all to behold—and to feast on at a venison barbecue that evening? There was plenty of fresh meat for all comers, even though the bulk of the spoils had been left behind for the grateful villagers.

No sooner had I returned to Noumea than I ran into Capt. John C. "Tiger" Erskine, of Washington, D.C., who was raised in Japan by missionary parents, and had earned degrees at Bethany College and Clark University. Captain Erskine had left the relaxed pace of the Library of Congress for the quickened beat of the Marine Corps and had participated in the First Raiders' initial assaults on Tulagi, Gavutu, and Guadalcanal.

A little guy, Tiger would hop into Jap foxholes as the Raiders advanced, nabbing prisoners for interrogation, grabbing maps and documents for information.

The twenty-five-year-old soft-spoken interpreter insisted he didn't really know why he was called Tiger. His friends gave two differing explanations for the nickname. One: Despite his small physique, he had ferociously pounced on his unwilling prisoners during the Raider drive on Tulagi. The other: He possessed a voracious appetite, so that despite the uninviting fare, he pounced on the iron rations like a famished wildcat, even boosting his 105 pounds to a short-lived 120 on The Island.

On Tulagi, a mud-splattered hand-drawn map he dug up in a destroyed dugout revealed the enemy's positions. Later, at Kokumbona, on Guadalcanal, info he extracted from a rare Japanese NCO captive foiled a Jap trap for a Marine recon column. When we met in Noumea, Tiger was quizzing the few enemy taken alive, who were impounded in the military stockade.

With Captain Erskine by my side as interpreter, I sought to interview the captives. I was surprised to discover that the prisoners were "dead"—as dead to their families as their countrymen who had been killed on Bloody Ridge or at Kokumbona. According to samurai code of Bushido, the warrior could return home only as triumphant victor or as revered ashes. There was no return for the vanquished. Capture in battle disgraced both a soldier and his family.

That creed explained why the Japanese troops fought so fiercely; why they fought to the death even in hopeless situations; why many took their own lives by hara-kiri rather than submit; why they blew themselves up with hand grenades, taking along their captors; why they would raise the white flag of surrender, then shoot to kill, knowing they would be slain for their treachery. That belief explained why so few Japanese prisoners were taken in the Solomons, and perhaps it also explained why the Japs also took few prisoners and mistreated those they did.

The POWs in the stockade had, for the most part, not given up voluntarily. They had been taken unconscious or dazed, or wounded, overcome by hunger or disease. They could not comprehend why they were not killed off by the Americans and given an honorable end as a defeated enemy.

The "dead" prisoners had little to say in response to my questions. To a man, they insisted: "Shinda ho ga ii"—To have died would have been better.

Some sought to justify being taken alive, as much to themselves as to me. "I was out of my head from the loss of blood," explained a soldier. "I was numbed by my long immersion in the sea," protested a sailor. "I lost my wits in the crash," claimed the rescued pilot.

None would admit to surrendering voluntarily, although, I later learned, a few had done so.

In spite of the widely publicized word-of-mouth stories of Japanese mistreatment of the American troops overrun at Corregidor, and the fresh rumor of the day that a parachuting U.S. pilot had been machine-gunned by a Zero, the Japanese prisoners were decently treated. They were provided with the same simple rations and bedding that the leathernecks received.

The captives were model prisoners—disciplined, courteous, obedient. None would discuss his past life. They gave false names for fear word would get back to their homeland and bring shame on their families. Likewise, they scrupulously avoided being photographed.

And what of their future, what did they expect? I asked.

They shrugged. They were resigned to their fate—to be "dead."

"Shikata ga nai," they said. So let it be.

Within a fortnight I was off again, this time to Button (Espiritu Santo) to join the Third Raider Battalion. I was excited by the assignment.

The raid on Makin had been carried out in the Commando style, quick in and quick out. But the hit-and-run precept was soon found to be impractical in the jungles of the Solomons. After Makin, the Raider battalions were thrown into action as assault troops in the invasion of the islands, and as strong links in the front line. Instead of hit and run, it was strike and seize for the Raiders.

I reported to the Third Raiders, then bivouacked in a camp overlooking the Renee River, commanded by Col. Harry Liversedge, a big bear of a man, standing six feet four inches with his boondockers off.

The men of the Third had undergone four months of intensive jungle training on Samoa and were itching for a fight, eager to demonstrate that the outfit could whip the Japs as Edson's First Battalion had demonstrated on Guadalcanal.

Liversedge had personally picked his top officers: Lt. Col. Samuel S. Yeaton, a Missourian, second in command; and Maj. Michael S. Currin, a Californian, Operations.

The Third was to lead an amphibious operation into the Russell Islands, forty miles northwest of Guadalcanal, next target of the Marine offensive. Colonel Selden had given me oral orders to participate in the operation and report back.

The 800 men of the Third Raiders were tough, lightly equipped and weaponed, picked for their specialties, and put through extra, longer training for their assignment: seizing beachheads, launching spearheads, penetrating enemy flanks through swiftness and surprise. Four months of the most rigorous conditioning—beyond boot camp—and tactical training for jungle warfare, beach landings, thrusts over mountains, and through ravines and swamps, gave these Raiders a battle edge: confidence in hand-to-hand combat. The officers had to outmatch the men in the daily grind.

All Raiders were volunteers, and in addition to passing the other screening tests had to be capable of swimming 200 yards. They were hardened by long, forced marches over torturous terrain. They were thrown into hand-to-hand fighting in rough-and-tumble tilts, knife and bayonet jousts. They played games like diving over a double apron of barbed-wire. Or like blindman's bluff, in which a blindfolded Raider tried to break through a ring of blindfolded opponents armed with switches. These and similar play were aimed at developing hearing faculties and the art of stealth. Like every Marine, they were riflemen first, but also trained to kill with fists, knees, and feet, with knives and bayonets, with tommy guns and Browning automatics.

An official Navy release following the Marine raid on Makin proclaimed that the Raider learned to throw his knife "accurately and with force to kill or disable an enemy at close range." This was utter hype. I never met a Raider who could throw his knife into the bull's-eye. He did learn—the hard way—to jam the point of his dagger into a can of Spam without cutting off his thumb. However, he could when necessary thrust his blade with lethal impact in hand-to-hand combat.

In theory, I had to be capable of meeting the Raiders' requirements. As a preteener I had won a lead medallion for learning how to flounder across the narrow width of the YMCA pool, but the 200 yards swimming minimum of the Raiders was far beyond the capability of my thrashing crawl. But since I was operating under the aegis of C-2, nobody asked me if I could do it. Nor could I have met the superman skills demanded of the Raiders. On the other hand, I had been through front-line action and was battle-tested, an experience that, with few exceptions, the Third Raiders had yet to undergo.

On February 14, 1943, the first echelon of the Raiders, to which I was attached, boarded the minesweeper *Southard* in Espiritu harbor. The *Southard* had been in the thick of the sea battles off Savo Island and Cape Esperance and had sunk a submarine only a few weeks earlier. This time the minesweeper rendezvoused with eleven APDs, light destroyers of World War I vintage converted into personnel carriers for landing operations, and took the point position in the V-array proceeding warily through "Torpedo Junction," the sub-filled course to Guadalcanal.

Just before midnight, strong sonar contact was made with

a submarine. The *Southard* pulled out of formation and heaved four ashcans on the unseen foe. When they went off, the depth charges reverberated like heavy iron doors slamming shut, and a fan of flame belched from the surrounding sea.

Like most of the other passengers confronted by an imminent possibility of a torpedo attack, I dived for my life jacket before rushing to the rails to watch, anxiously, as a division of the destroyers churned around the contaminated area scanning for the underwater threat and dropping lethal charges.

Did our ashcans destroy a sub or a school of big fish? Opinions were many and loud, but no one in command gave us any definite answer, so each Raider had a story to tell later in proportion to his imagination.

Two days later, our convoy reached Koli Point, Guadalcanal, where the Marines and Army units were being organized for the invasion of the Russell Islands. I took advantage of the stopover to hitchhike fifteen miles over spine-damaging roads to Henderson Field to visit the new bomber strip under construction, looking for stories, and returned at dark bone-jarred and exhausted, without having pinned down a story that would clear the censors.

On February 20, the Raider complement took off on four APDs—I on the *Stringham*, an aged destroyer converted into a transport that had been active hustling troops, arms, and supplies in the long struggle for Guadalcanal. We made landing on Pavuvu a little after dawn, February 21, behind schedule due to the treacherous shallows. Simultaneously, Army's 169th Regiment surged over Mbanika, the other invasion point.

We charged ashore . . . only to meet no opposition.

The enemy had pulled out, unnoticed, some days earlier.

Instead, we were welcomed by English-speaking Melanesians who had worked on the Lever Brothers' coconut plantation before the island had been grabbed by the Japs.

The unfought "Battle of Pavuvu" was technically a victory, but it was a botched-up operation *despite* the lack of opposition. The Yanks had anticipated having to overcome a sizable force of dug-in defenders prepared to die for their emperor. The Marines and GIs had been geared up to expect fierce resistance. The opposition was nil. The American forces had failed to carry out sufficient reconnaissance of the objective.

Two of the destroyers messed up their screws in the shallows of Paddy Bay and two of the APDs unloaded their troops via rubber boats on the opposite sides of the bay, so that one was at the wrong beach.

Raider scouts had slipped into Pavuvu only two days before, but only on the morning of the landing could they report they had not scared up a single Jap on the island. The Raiders, who had trained four strenuous months for this shot, were keenly disappointed and frustrated.

The letdown spread out, like a miasma, over the island and through the ranks. Our admirals and generals kicking off the invasion of the Russell Islands had been led to believe that the some 12,000 Japanese soldiers who had been skillfully withdrawn from Guadalcanal, had been embedded on Pavuvu. It didn't happen.

During the following days the Raiders' shooting was confined to craps, go-for-broke encounters that sprang up like mushrooms throughout the bivouac. I amassed all of $20 American for my round-the-clock efforts.

I visited nearby Byce Island to see for myself that there, at least, the Japs had been prepared to give us a hot reception from solid entrenchments, but those too had been abandoned, along with munitions, before our arrival. I poked around for souvenirs, but all I could come up with were a couple of Japanese dime novels.

The next day, intent on bringing home a more worthy prize—a Japanese flag—I trekked out to West Bay, where two Zeros had crashed in the brush after an aerial dogfight and, having been sanitized by Intelligence, were available for pickings by all souvenir hunters. I was late in reaching the fighter planes, by then completely stripped, so that I had to be satisfied with a piece of the fuselage.

I hacked off a slab of aluminum siding with my Government Issue knife, used before only to tear open a can of Spam. My booty bore an inscription in Japanese characters that—as translated for me—proudly proclaimed participation in the Midway battle royal.

It was not until March 6, the fourteenth day of occupation of Pavuvu, that the Nips took official notice of the Marines by raking the island from the air, and then returning every day. Shockingly, not a single one of the Army's antiaircraft guns was prepared to fire back at that first enemy aerial assault. Many of them were still in their crates. The ack-acks were not mounted and ready for action until the following day.

I was pecking away on my portable that morning in an abandoned plantation folli (hut) when the Japanese bombers roared out of a low cloud bank and spotted a batch of Higgins boats busily bringing in supplies. Down streaked the Bettys, strafing the small-fry craft and scattering a wide arc of bullets along the beach. I scrambled out of my folli and, despite warnings from Little Jeezus, failed to make it to a nearby foxhole. I hit the ground on the beach between the boathouse and couple of lighters—both natural targets—and inexplicably turned face upward to gape at the immense silhouettes of two Mitsubishis, their Rising Sun meatballs staring me down, their guns spraying tracers and shells.

The awesome scene vanished after an eternity-long instant when three Grumman Wildcats plummeted out of the sky and drove off the bombers. The Bettys had already dropped their bombs over Mbanika, the Army's bailiwick, and were just making a neighborly hit-and-run call on Pavuvu on the way back to their Georgia Island base. Six GIs, caught in the open like myself, were cut up badly by shrapnel. I escaped unscathed. I raised my head and thanked my lucky stars. Little Jeezus snorted in disgust.

One morning my attention was drawn to the open water, where a group of swimmers was flailing toward the shore. I counted seven swimmers and wondered why the crash boats weren't scooting out to rescue them. It turned out that one Marine had thrown himself into the sea as the Bettys raced toward his Higgins boat. When he came up for air, the Higgins was churning off in the distance. The coxswain had been hit by a fragment and had lost control of the craft. The others, six Raiders, had also plunged off their targeted Higgins. All made it safely to the beach, more than 200 yards away. Two hundred yards! I wouldn't have made it.

After that incident I had little to do but dig up hometown stories and answer a few long-delayed letters that had reached me via "airmail." I wrote to my parents and sent a long, passionate letter to Bernice. I also sent her a native grass skirt, which I had purchased for one doh-lar, unaware that all such verdant handicraft was destroyed on arrival by the customs inspectors.

I also wrote to George Juskalian, my close friend and lockermate at Boston University, where we had majored in journalism. George had been named the outstanding ROTC student at the university and had decided on a military career. He had risen to captain when the first American troops had invaded North Africa, and had been taken prisoner by the Germans. I wrote George through the Red Cross to encourage him, and we kept up a long-delayed correspondence throughout the war notwithstanding strict censorship both ways.

Although the Third Raiders got into no action on Pavuvu as a battalion, several of the leathernecks got into plenty.

Two Texans, Sgt. Jack Boyd, from Houston, and Pfc. Leonard McKenzie, from San Benito, had been hospitalized and were moping around after being left behind on The Island when their Raider units had embarked for the Russells invasion. Boyd, a twenty-one-year-old three-striper, had developed blood poisoning from a scratch on his trigger finger; the single-striper, only eighteen, had been sickened from one of the jungle diseases. They were determined to catch up with their outfits.

First they hitched a ride on a supply ship to Mbanika; there they bummed another lift on a Higgins boat heading for Pavuvu on the other side of Sunlight Channel. They were halfway over when six Zeros plunged down on the light craft. The two Raiders grabbed the boat's two machine guns and blasted away. They caught one Zero with a solid burst that smashed it into the sea about a quarter of a mile away.

The coxswain, Seaman First Class George E. Wall, nineteen, from Lexington, North Carolina, had been running Higgins boats for the Marines since the landing on Guadalcanal six months earlier. He had been under air attack before and stuck by his throttle. He was proud of those Marines.

"Those two Marines were shooting like veterans. I saw them hit two other planes besides the one they shot down."

Well, it must be admitted that Sergeant Boyd, an intelligence platoon scout, had served with a machine-gun company and knew a little something about antiaircraft weaponry. But Private First Class McKenzie, a scout and expert rifleman-sniper, was a post–Pearl Harbor volunteer with little antiaircraft experience.

The episode was confirmed by Capt. Thomas R. Shepard, twenty-six, Cincinnati, and the other passengers aboard: 1st Sgt. Allan Carlson, thirty-four, Long Beach, California; two Chicagoans, Pvts. Raymond E. Marston, twenty-one, whose canteen was pierced by a bullet, and Thomas R. McNichols, twenty, whose helmet was nicked; two Detroiters, Pvts. Kenneth Wilds, twenty-one, and Glenn Hewitt, twenty; and Pvt. Irvin Herak, nineteen, Elk, Washington.

Several days earlier, I learned, six other Marines, caught in a rubber boat in the middle of Hooper Bay, were not so lucky. Two Zekes (as some now called the Zeros) pounced out of the clouds, strafed and sank the slow-moving craft, but all seven—one gob and six gyrenes—swam hundreds of yards ashore to safety. Not so lucky, perhaps, but lucky enough.

Then there was the incident of the missing Raider, nineteen-year-old Bill Greeley, who had been left aboard a destroyer-transport to watch over the spare landing boats when his battalion disembarked for the invasion of Pavuvu. Young Bill, from Milton, Massachusetts, was a distant kinsman of Horace "Go West, Young Man" Greeley, and had certainly gone farther west than any other relative. He had joined the Marines one year earlier after quitting his senior year at high school and marrying his sweetheart, Jean.

An unscheduled switch in the Pavuvu operation shifted the troopship out of the Russells to Tulagi, taking Greeley along.

That night in Tulagi harbor, Greeley was assigned to routine gun watch. Bill had never handled an antiaircraft gun before, but as a fledgling Marine, he dared not question orders.

"Suddenly, without warning, a Jap plane dropped three bombs within 300 yards of the ship," Bill related. "Then, before anybody could shoot at it, the bomber roared off.

"I guess they forgot about me in the rush of things. Or maybe they figured I was a gunner. Anyhow, I just had time to figure out how the piece was cocked when the bomber returned to drop six more.

"So I just started firing away, giving my shots a long lead. The plane blew up about a half mile out, and the rest of the gang said I was the guy who shot it down."

When normal order was restored, the captain of the destroyer assembled all hands and dressed down Greeley for violating regulations by shooting away before the command to fire.

Then, having adhered to the sacrosanct naval canon, the captain announced he would also have a few other things to say in his letter of recommendation for meritorious conduct to the Marine's battalion commander.

The Japs were gone from Pavuvu, but there were other vicious enemies visible and hidden there everywhere. The disease axis undertook its own powerful offensive against the Marines and GIs in the Russells.

Diarrhea, dengue, and dysentery, fungus and coral infections, malaria and mumu felled even the hardiest of the Raiders. Mumu—filariasis or elephantiasis—spread by mosquitoes in Samoa, where the battalion had trained, broke out in epidemic proportions. A terrifying symptom of mumu is the enormous swelling of the testicles and scrotum. The psychological impact on the men was worse than the pain.

Marine Corps training stressed personal hygiene to combat the tropical diseases. Each Raider carried a single change of dungarees, underwear, and socks for the Russells mission, one pair to be washed every night with boiling water and soap. "Soap," according to Navy Lt. Bruce W. Milligan, of Jacksonville, Illinois, senior medical officer attached to the Raiders, "is our best weapon against disease."

Soapy water did prove to be the most effective antidote against the outbreak of skin eruptions. There was ample soap, but water was in extremely short supply, especially for drinking, and then it was brackish, salty, or tasted of rust. At times, rainwater could be caught in a helmet or trapped in a poncho, but the latter left a rubbery taste. Chlorination made the water safe but nauseating. At that, the drinking water was limited to two canteens—two quarts a day. Hardly enough in that sweltering, enervating heat.

But it was impossible to keep the body dry in the torrential rains, even with the extra set of clothing.

The Raiders, inoculated against a list of diseases before their Pavuvu expedition, were given a series of booster shots, vitamin and salt pills, all as health precautions, and urged to turn into sick bay even for minor scratches and skin rashes. Even common athlete's foot could immobilize the grunt unless treated. A coral cut required immediate attention to prevent the rapid and painful spread of infection.

The food situation was tight, and the Raiders were limited to two meals a day—iron rations—a diet of corned willy, Spam, canned salmon, and powdered eggs for some thirty days. Sickness and the sheer tedium of the drab diet dulled the appetite, and the men lost weight. I lost fifteen pounds, skinnied down to 151.

As a result, on Pavuvu the main topic of conversation was food. During the long nights, the Marines gloried in reminiscing about the flavors of mother's cooking back home. Spam became the repugnant metaphor for all their monotonous meals.

For some lucky Raiders the chow crisis was eased by the exploits of Mott, of deer hunt fame. Allan A. Mott, thirty-two, of Brooklyn, New York, was a photographer with a Marine engineer unit. Mott, the next-to-shortest man in the battalion, was endowed with a huge head, a Charlie Chaplin mustache, and a quarter-moon mouth that spread from ear to ear when he grinned.

Mott was on a patrol that set out in motor-driven rubber

boats to reconnoiter the far-out islands. Expecting to return to base by evening, the scouts took along no rations. However, motor trouble developed so that the patrol had to seek refuge for the night on one of the islets far from camp, since movement after dark was forbidden.

At that critical juncture, Mott suggested to their leader:

"How about steak for dinner, sir?"

Steak! Did Mott say steak? Every eye fastened on his gargoyle noggin.

The lieutenant scrutinized Mott's beaming face. Was Mott kidding, or just cracking up?

"I'm serious, sir," Mott insisted. "I need a five-man detail."

The officer, for lack of an alternative, picked out you-you-you-you-you volunteers. Mott and his skeptical squad marched off into the dusky boondocks. Half an anxious hour later, a shot rang out. More long, tense minutes passed, and then a dumpy guy, wearing a smile like a crockery Buddha, rifle riding jauntily on his shoulder, strutted into the clearing . . . alone.

"What have you done with my men?" the officer demanded.

"Bringing up the rear, sir," Mott replied.

And so they were soon to be seen, staggering under the weight of a hindquarter of beef. Mott had earlier spotted cattle-gone-wild grazing in an open patch, surely fair game for hungry Marines. The half-starved recon men stuffed themselves with steak on the spit that night.

Sad to relate, the battalion medical officer later prohibited all further rustling on the grounds that the loose livestock might be unsafe for humans, even leathernecks.

Graddick—I mean Mott—scored again a few days later when it was discovered that the 169th Army Regiment had brought in enough provisions to feed its doughboys three times a day, along with a stock of luxury rations—peanuts, popcorn, dried apricots, cocoa, hard candy, and the like.

While his mates conspired aimlessly on how to get their hands on the pogey bait, Graddick—no, Mott—showed up at the Army camp on Mbanika Island shooting pictures here and there but assiduously avoiding the doggies watching over the supply depot. Word got around that Mott was taking photos for hometown newspapers, and the guardians of the goodies wanted in. Mott drove a hard deal: a case of delectables for a photo of the guards, plus two GIs to motorboat the goodies back to Pavuvu.

Only later did Mott realize, he confessed, that he had been snapping shots without film.

I confirmed the first of Mott's ploys by partaking of the beef; the second, by sharing in the tasty loot. Later, in another campaign—I heard through the grapevine—Mott raided an Army post exchange. Marines will tell you the Army always travels with a PX in tow, one stocked with cigarettes, shaving lotion, hair fudge, and other such indispensable items.

Four men dressed in Army fatigues marched up to the barbed-wire PX compound one day fifteen minutes before the customary relief detail was to show up, then disappeared with their plunder before the regular GI sentries showed up for duty.

When the Army officer in charge complained to the Marine officer in charge, the latter asserted that his men would never commit so nefarious a deed. It was strictly against the rules. To be fair to him, the Marine officer in charge had no way of knowing that the haul had been cached under his sack.

Mott had joined the Marines at age thirty-one, giving up his State News Service job in New York City to enlist. His brother, Jean, younger by ten years, had joined the Army. They had an unexpected brief reunion at the Red Cross hut in Noumea.

The Third Raiders, their military ambitions unfulfilled, riddled with jungle sicknesses, were glad to pull out of Pavuvu March 20, 1943. The Army, which had quickly built an airstrip on the Russells, stayed on to defend the field against counterattack.

I departed on the destroyer *Manley*, a workhorse which among other tasks had slipped "Red" Edson's First Raiders onto a beach, outmaneuvering the Jap defenses in the critical stage of Guadalcanal operations. I slept on a bench topside under a full moon. I found the bare bench comfortable compared to the high, shaky table in the plantation folli that I had claimed for my bed to discourage the ravenous rats that ran amok every night on Pavuvu.

On March 27, I got back to Noumea. I brought back two souvenirs from Pavuvu—the slab of the downed Zero and a fungus infection in my left ear.

CHAPTER 9

"Big Mamie"

It felt good to be back in Noumea. In the course of only three months, the dowdy Paree of the Pacific had been transformed, in my eyes, into the City of Lightheartedness.

In Pavuvu, the downpours had been cold and hostile, but in Noumea the rains felt warm and hospitable. In Pavuvu, my bed had been a miserable foxhole most nights; but in Noumea I now slept on a mattressed canvas cot, in a comfortable floorboarded tent, in a neat company row on the slope of a hill overlooking the luminescent bay. I slept the night through: no Charley cacophony, no blaring alerts, no bomb bursts.

In Pavuvu, the bugles had been silenced lest they give away battle position; there in Noumea the reveille calls were sweet to my ears.

Noumea had many little comforts, like flickering electric bulb lights until taps, old fluttering films, cold beer, pogey bait, freshwater showers, and neatly laundered clothing; and the chow was varied and plentiful. Oh, yes, the Fun House was still there, doing a bang-up business.

A couple of days of the good life, and I was already sorting out the latest scuttlebutt for clues to potential stories. My quest led me to the port and the transport *President Jackson*, a converted liner that had conveyed the Marines to Guadalcanal and surrounding islands.

Officers of the *Jackson* maintained that their Higgins boats hit the beach on Tulagi minutes before the main incursion force waded into Guadalcanal.

Attempting to pull into Tanambogo, six of the landing craft ran into a heavy fusillade, their situation aggravated by

119

the explosion of a Jap fuel dump, the flames silhouetting the Higginses like sitting ducks for the enemy gunners.

Five were driven back by the massed enemy fire, but the sixth, guided by Coxswain John S. Evans, twenty-five, of Columbus, Ohio, noticed a small band of Marines on the shore, fighting off the encircling foe. Evans rode into the firestorm and plucked the stranded 2nd Marines to safety. For his act of heroism, he was awarded the Navy Cross.

The gunnery officer also mentioned that when the *Jackson* was carrying a large contingent of leathernecks into the battle for Guadalcanal, the transport and her destroyer escort were attacked during the night by seven torpedo planes, which dropped flares that formed a ring of fire around the two ships. But the troopship shot five of the Kates down aflame into the sea. The other two warplanes flew away.

"We threw up a tremendous volume of ack-ack, and we didn't have to see them to shoot them down," recalled Navy Lt. Comdr. J. R. Daix of Philadelphia.

"We maneuvered the ships with such coordination, all but turning them inside out, that we made the Japs dizzy. We confused them, confounded them, and shot the hell out of them!"

A few days later, I became aware that a cluster of warships was amassing in Noumea harbor, and I suspected that Adm. William F. "Bull" Halsey, the Commander in Chief, Pacific (CINCPAC), might be planning a naval thrust that would lead to a sea battle in the manner of Coral Sea and Midway.

I immediately decided I wanted in. I had already interviewed and written a spate of stories about the leatherneck machine gunners of the doomed carrier *Yorktown* and the cruiser *Chicago*, but I had a yen to take part in a sea clash, so I wheedled a four-week hitch with the Marine contingent stationed aboard the USS *Massachusetts*.

The one-year-old battlewagon was a new breed of battleship: fast, big, and armed with the latest 16-inch guns, the Navy's most powerful, that could hurl their shots at targets twenty miles away. For the first time in the war, the Japanese 14-incher was at a disadvantage.

Laid down at Bethlehem's Quincy shipyard, the "Big Mamie" was commissioned in May 1942, and four days after its shakedown cruise, in October 1942, caught up with the Western Task Force to serve as the flagship of Adm. H. Kent Hewitt for the Allied invasion of North Africa.

Off Casablanca, when the untried "Mamie" underwent baptismal fire from the 15-inch guns of the Vichy French battleship *Jean Bart*, the *Massachusetts* responded with its 16-inch cannons and destroyed its opponent's main battery turret. "Mamie" then smashed two destroyers and pounded the shore batteries around Casablanca, blowing up an ammunition dump in the process. It was the first time that the 16-inchers had been turned on the Axis.

After the Vichy government surrendered a month later, "Big Mamie" was shifted to the Pacific theater to strengthen Admiral Halsey's scrappy but crippled fleet.

"Big Mamie" pulled into Noumea harbor March 4, 1943. The proud cannoneers of the *Massachusetts* had already fired 800 rounds from her big guns, more than the average battleship fires in a lifetime. A charmed ship, "Big Mamie" had been twice hit, and more than 200 enemy shells had fallen within 500 yards of her, but she had suffered no casualties.

I boarded the "Big Mamie" April 29 and reported to the Marine commander, Maj. Jackson B. Butterfield, who hailed from Lyndonville, Vermont. The twenty-nine-year-old Norwich University alumnus had served on the battleship *Wyoming*, and then six months on the carrier *Hornet*, and had already earned three campaign ribbons.

Major Butterfield and his two subalterns, Capt. Roy D. Miller, twenty-three, of Dresden, Ohio, and Ohio University, and Capt. Littleton K. Smith, twenty-six, of Bound Brook, New Jersey, and Rutgers University, were jumpovers from the Army. Each had been an honor student in the college Army ROTC (Reserve Officers' Training Corps) but had transferred to the Marine Corps after brief service with the Army.

Viewed from land, the 35,000-ton *Massachusetts* seemed to loom over us like Godzilla. The battleship seemed to have a limitless capacity for absorbing guns, planes, armament, machinery, and personnel. In fact, however, the living space aboard "Big Mamie" was cramped for its more than 2,000 sailors and ninety Marines.

Every modicum of space not devoted to other essential uses was utilized for the sailors' and Marines' hammocks and lockers. The spring-type hammocks were stacked like sandwiches five to a tier, with little headroom between. The guy sleeping below couldn't raise his knees without banging the butt of the fellow above him. I drew a middle bunk, not as airy as a tent sack, but free of inquisitive crabs and omnipresent mites.

Most of the berths faced an aisle or gangway busy with pedestrian traffic, so the hinged hammocks were swung up vertically against the bulkhead during the day. From reveille to tattoo there was little opportunity to catch a little extra sack time. Anyhow, as I quickly discovered on being integrated into my new company, the Marines' many duties left little time for a quick shut-eye, what with drills and schools, preparations for inspection, and inspection, musters and watches, and general quarters drills.

The mess was bounteous and varied, a delight to my palate. A weekly allotment of fresh khaki and underwear to permit a change of clothing every day was an unbelievable bonus to me, who on Guadalcanal and Pavuvu had been compelled to wear the same uniform and apparel, often wet, for days before obtaining fresh or dry replacements. And clean sheets and pillowcases! "Come on, guys," I said, and shook my head in envy.

The Navy had a clubhouse called Shangri-la on the docks for the sailors and sea Marines on liberty, every ninth day in port. But Shangri-la was not another Fun House; shenanigans were not permitted.

The sea Marines also carried on with traditional duties as orderlies to the ship's captain, for the task force admiral when he was aboard, and as color guards, guards of the day, bow sentries, and brig sentries. But the Marines quit their special duties and raced for their antiaircraft posts when the alarm was sounded.

The brig sentry role created friction between the bluejackets and the leathernecks, and ashore the resentment might lead to a name-calling bloody-nose row between the "swab jockeys" and the "seagoing bellhops." But the rivals had mutual respect for each other's performance in battle.

As a landlubber, I had to absorb, quickly, a new vocabulary of naval nomenclature, since my acquaintanceship with the sea—before boarding the *Juan Cabrillo* in San Francisco—had been limited to the swan boats in Boston Gardens when I was a youngster. In order to understand commands and conversations, I had to be aware that on the dreadnought, floors were decks; ladders were stairs; overheads were ceilings; screws were propellers; and a score of other seafarer terms.

I also picked up that battleships are named for the American states; cruisers for cities; carriers for presidents or famous Navy ships; destroyers for heroes of the sea; and frigates—smaller than destroyers—for respected admirals who didn't quite make the hero pantheon.

More important, it quickly became clear to me that on the "Big Mamie" the skipper was a zealot for cleanliness.

Aboard, in port or at sea, sailors and Marines alike were relentlessly run through a fervent daily ritual of cleansing. Clean, clean, clean . . . decks and bulkheads . . . overheads and metalwork . . . pipings and fittings . . . furniture and furnishings . . . long-range guns and antiaircraft guns . . . topside and bottom . . . Sweep down, wash down, clamp down!

The ninety Marines do it! The 2,000 sailors do it! Scrub it, wipe it, shine it!

This rhythmic routine exploded into a frenzy of activity on Friday field day, when all other activity was suspended for the Big Sweep to get set for the Captain's Inspection on Saturday. No ship's officer dared risk the commander's disapproving eye. Spit-and-polish perfection was demanded, and given.

The strict, strenuous shipboard discipline recalled my boot camp training days, and I mentally gave my ghostly DI a belated nod of appreciation.

"Jes' cover yer ass," Little Jeezus retorted.

At sea, the fetish of cleanliness was augmented by air

raid drills, gun testing, and more frequent calls to general quarters.

On reporting in, I requested a quiet nook where I could finger-skip on my Hermes in my spare time. The obliging officers scrounged up just enough space in a stuffy, window-less clothing closet for me to assemble an unused crate as a desk and an empty box as a seat. I was grateful for my tiny sanctum. There I could ease my aching feet, which were un-accustomed to the unyielding steel decks, and once in a while read a page or so of *War and Peace*.

In the privacy of my hole in the wall, I resumed my eye-ball calisthenics on a daily basis. I had been wearing specs only infrequently by then, and had been getting by without them. In "my office" I could also catch a few winks because, despite all the fresh linen, I found it difficult to get a good night's sleep in my bunk, what with the foot traffic, the ship's bells and noises, and the overhead lights.

From reveille at 5:45 A.M. to taps at 9:10 P.M., the bugle regulated the twenty-four-hour day of the battleship.

The two buglers with the Marine detachment had to memorize ninety-five calls covering every order and com-mand. They averaged fifty calls a day between reveille and taps. The bugle notes reached every part of the man-of-war via the electronic bullhorn, backed up by verbal orders over the ship's PA system from the bosun's mate.

In port and at sea, under normal conditions and in emer-gencies, all ship's activities were proclaimed by the bugle. The ships were fueled, hands mustered, hammocks lowered, doors made watertight, air alerts sounded, church services announced, the admiral's barge heralded by the bugle. Tat-too, sounded five minutes before taps, lasted fully sixty sec-onds, and was generally regarded as the most melodious call. The shortest was the single blast signaling cast off. Then there were the notes every bugler must learn but can utter only once, mournfully: "Abandon ship!"

The bugler also had to know his boats. There was a differ-ent call for the admiral's barge, for the captain's gig, for the officers' motorboat, for the launch, and for the whaleboat. There was even one for the garbage lighter.

There were no official lyrics for the bugle calls, but many had been celebrated by tradition. The lilting notes of liberty call, for example, aroused the following verse:

Who's goin' ashore?
Who's goin' ashore?
Who's got the price for a two-bit whore?

Officers' call inspired the following from the ranks:

It's a good ship,
It's a good ship,
For the officers;
But it's horseshit,
It's horseshit,
For the crew.

The buglers, despite their welcome notes to chow, pay, and liberty, were never quite forgiven by their compatriots for the 5:45 A.M. reveille wake-up call, followed by the jeering voice of the bosun: "Up, all idlers!"

Oh, how they hated the bugler!

"A cross we have to bear," the buglers sadly agreed. "But," they assured me, "there are specific regulations against punching the bugler in the mouth."

Each of "Mamie's" two Marine buglers took to battle stations during general quarters, air raids, or torpedo attacks. Field Music First Class Walter H. Hausman, twenty-three, of Bellevue, Kentucky, a conservatory grad, became an antiaircraft machine-gun loader. Field Music First Class James D. Bell, of Miami, Florida, younger-looking than his official eighteen, stood by the Marine commanding officer to toot his battle orders.

Bell had failed to pass the height standard required by the Marines, but, determined to enlist, he drew a waiver offered to buglers. At the time, Bell didn't know a bugle from a bagel, but he learned from scratch how to blare out the ninety-five bugle blasts.

I was assigned to the time-honored Marine gun station

high on the housetop—fifth level—of the battlewagon's superstructure. Ever since the first Marines helped John Paul Jones attain respect for the U.S. Navy with their accurate musketry in the Revolutionary War, sharpshooting leathernecks have manned the shrouded masts and fighting tops of our warships.

As on the *Bonhomme Richard*, where the topmast Marine gunners were the last line of defense against boarding by the enemy, so on the *Massachusetts*. But in World War II the storming aboard was carried out by Aichi dive-bombers, Nakajima torpedo planes, Mitsubishi bombers, and Zeros.

My toploft post—between antiaircraft gun crews 8 and 9—made me giddy at first. I was given intensive training, so as to be capable of stepping into either team as needed by the white-haired gunnery sergeant, Ernest F. Gore, who had retired to Southport, North Carolina, after sixteen years of service, had married, raised two children, and even built a hunting lodge only to be recalled for war duty. The gunny was a taskmaster who quickly brought me up to par with his antiaircraft crews. There were moments when I could hear the unmistakable voice of Little Jeezus as the sarge demanded more and better from me, but Little Jeezus simply sat back with a smile of satisfaction.

The gunners were as doting on their guns as on their girlfriends, after whom they named their guns: Lillian, Edith, Dukie, Muriel, Mary, Frances, Helen, Viola.

From my high vantage point I could easily overlook starboard or port, and even observe below the movements of ship's captain Robert A. Glover and task force commander Rear Admiral G. B. Davis.

It was hard for me to climb up to my battle post during the daylight, but at night, when the vessel was blacked out, I had even more difficulty getting up there in the stampede that ensued after the call to general quarters. I had to clamber my way topside through a maze of passageways and compartments, deliberately misaligned, with their steel doors set a foot or so above the deck—an arrangement of watertight precautions. Rare was the night call to quarters that I failed to crack a shin or bang my head when racing through the darkened gangways. Then I had to find and pull myself up the broken series of ladders from the main deck to the housetop.

On a wet night, the footing was also treacherous. Cpl. Ralph S. Butcher, of Meadville, Pennsylvania, fell four decks down—about fifty feet—through an open hatch, landing backfirst on the steel flooring. The husky twenty-two-year-old former Golden Glover rose dazed but otherwise unhurt.

A crewman was seriously injured when he slipped off a ladder one moonless night; another was critically hurt when he fell into the path of a swinging 16-inch gun. It was not the slippery surface that worried me, it was the towering swinging guns.

Early in the morning of May 14, the "Mamie," screened by three destroyers, took off for target practice at sea but had to chafe around in circles when enemy subs were sonar-sounded in the outer harbor, while the destroyers snapped around to "decontaminate" the waters. Then for three days the "Big Mamie" sailed out some twenty miles and tested all her guns, even at night under the showering light of star shells.

Planes launched from the deck flew overhead at various heights and angles, dragging behind a long white sleeve for the antiaircraft gunners to shoot. I enjoyed my practice whacks at the moving targets.

The gigantic guns—which I one day observed from the crow's nest atop the mainmast—hurled 2,600-pound missiles at invisible targets with a volcanic blast of flame and white and black smoke from their muzzles, sending tremors through the mountainous framework of steel.

It was Tuesday, May 18, when my antiaircraft section was at midday mess, that the bugle abruptly, shrilly, jarringly blew: *"Air Attack!"* A couple of the Marines grabbed their pieces of pie and gobbled them down as we scrambled topside, without confusion, to our stations. By the time I reached my battle post, my fellow machine gunners were already there, positioned for action.

This was no drill! Air defense control had flashed a warning that a large flight of enemy planes had been picked up by sound detectors sixty miles off and heading toward Noumea. "Looks like the real thing, lads," the old-salt gunny said when the bugle blew the one-note shove-off.

The Marine gun crews were happy with the prospect of battle, and I was excited. From day one aboard, I had concentrated on the special training with the 20mms and my role in event of action. I was mentally prepared, I told myself, even for the worst eventuality—a kamikaze crash-dive. None of the "Mamie's" Marines had experienced or seen a kamikaze attack, but all had heard about the Jap suicide pilots.

I would not flinch, I vowed to myself. However, I could visualize Little Jeezus raising his eyebrows as if he had some misgivings about one more pledge of mine to stand fast. Maybe he had reason to doubt my will under so horrendous an attack?

The crews were then ordered to fall into the alert deployment, with one-third of each crew manning the battle stations at all times. Every day while at sea there were several calls to general quarters and air-raid attack drills. These drills were strict, serious, time-clocked.

The next morning, and every morning of the seven-day sweep, was greeted with the "sunrise serenade," as predawn general quarters is whimsically known. It was chilly and wet, and I was glad to be wearing my kapok life jacket.

From my housetop aerie I beheld in awe the mighty task force—two carriers, three battleships, one cruiser, and eleven destroyers—as it deployed into battle order, charging out to the open sea to confront Yamamoto's armada. A mighty task force it was, even if most of the big warships had been bombed or torpedoed out of action and rushed back into service before they could be fully overhauled and rebuilt.

The two flattops had a powerful punch, more than 150 warplanes: Wildcat fighters; Dauntless dive-bombers; Avenger and Devastator torpedo bombers; British Corsairs, Barracudas, Swordfish.

The USS *Massachusetts*, at point, was flanked by the two

sister battleships *Indiana* and *North Carolina*, the trio together shielding the ponderous flattops *Saratoga* and *Victorious*, which were also attended by the light cruiser *San Juan*, and eleven destroyers darting around sounding for subs.

The *Indiana* was a same-class ship as the *Massachusetts*, launched at Newport News and commissioned two weeks earlier. She had been dispatched directly to the Pacific to bolster our battle-truncated fleet. Both BBs had displacements of 35,000 tons, were 680 feet long and 108 feet abeam, with a full speed ahead of 27 knots. Each bristled with nine 16-inch and twenty 5-inch guns, and two dozen 40mm and three dozen 20mm antiaircraft machine guns. Each was manned by more than 2,500 personnel.

The *Massachusetts*, blooded in the Atlantic, had yet to see action in the Pacific; the *Indiana* had yet to taste enemy fire at all. The men of both BBs were eagerly awaiting the call to "Commence firing!"

The *North Carolina*, eldest of the three dreadnoughts, was commissioned in April 1941. The "Showboat" had supported the landings at Guadalcanal and Tulagi in August '42, and was torpedoed in mid-September near San Cristobal Island, some 150 miles off Guadalcanal. In that same clash the warrior *Wasp* had been sunk with the loss of some 200 men and fifty planes. But the *North Carolina* had been patched up at Pearl Harbor and had raced back to combat duty.

The carrier *Saratoga*, planned as a cruiser in 1920, converted into the Navy's first fast carrier two years later, was hit by a torpedo about a month after missing the Pearl Harbor fiasco. "Sara" flew the flag of Rear Admiral F. J. Fletcher in the Guadalcanal invasion, and her airmen had ended the career of the Jap flattop *Ryujo*. A week later, her fortunes were reversed; "Sara" was stricken by an enemy "fish" and had to be withdrawn for overhaul. So desperately short of carriers was the American fleet in the Pacific at that juncture that the *Saratoga* had to be pressed back into service before she could be fully reconditioned.

The flattop *Victorious* had been borrowed, after urgent

request, from the British Navy in the European theater, a case of lend-lease in reverse, to team up with the still wounded "Sara," filling in the place of the U.S. carrier *Lexington*, which was lost in the Coral Sea battle.

The *Victorious* was smaller than the American carriers, but her crewmen were highly skilled sailors and cannoneers, and had annihilated three Axis battleships off Italy. She later took several direct bomb hits from Hitler's Stukas, but had returned from repairs fit to fight again.

The light antiaircraft cruiser *San Juan* was a veteran of the Marine invasion of Guadalcanal, supported Edson's First Raiders on Tulagi, shot down a half dozen Japanese bombers, and had escaped serious hurt in its many darts into the maelstrom of the battles in the Solomons, until seriously banged up in the Battle of Santa Cruz some months earlier. But the *San Juan* was back for more.

The hastily assembled task force was not in top shape but nonetheless was ready, even eager, to run up against Admiral Yamada's air and sea armada.

I wondered: Were we heading for a Coral Sea standoff or a Midway victory? After all, our task force—so flew the latest rumor—was bearing down through the Coral Sea, where the carrier *Enterprise* had been sunk the year before.

Off the starboard beam, squadrons of bombers, screened by the fighters, shot skyward from the carriers, which were straining into the wind. One fighter failed to make the short breakaway and plopped into the sea. Without halt or hesitation, the succeeding planes sped off the flattops into the air, wheeling overhead into wide V's, like pelicans on the wing, then streaking off toward the aerial threat beyond the horizon.

At the same time, like an anxiously alert pup chasing after his master's thrown ball, one destroyer broke out of the escort formation and pounced on the floating pilot to rescue him before he could give his life jacket a fair tryout.

Aviators away, the warships of the task force began to deploy for the anticipated Japanese air attack. With ballet precision, the ships of the line zigzagged and crisscrossed, leapfrogged and abruptly changed course. Like gargantuan mechanical toys, the men-of-war turned and twisted and swerved: the battleships majestically; the carriers hulkingly; the antiaircraft cruiser jauntily; the destroyers prancing over the waves. It was a spectacular demonstration of U.S. sea power, perhaps more than our Navy was able to throw together at Coral Sea.

The first day out was clear sailing. All ships discharged their guns for last-minute checks, like opera stars clearing their throats before stepping onto the stage. The sixteen-inchers roared and shook the BBs as their shells blew off in gushers of red-orange-yellow.

The second day was chilly and wet, and I was glad to be wearing my Mae West. At sunrise I watched the dawn patrols zoom off the carriers, and followed their swift ascent by the flashes from their exhausts.

At about noon, the first enemy sub contact was made. The fleet smoothly maneuvered into a defensive pattern but did not shift from its main course forward. Big stuff like battleships don't bother with small stuff like subs—except when they have to evade and dodge the torpedoes. The Jap submarines—armed with torpedoes bigger, faster, longer-ranged, and more efficient than we had—were left to the destroyers.

Two of the American "cans" broke away from their protective positions and raced toward the suspected sub. A few minutes later, a series of concussions signaled that a succession of depth charges had been dropped on the contaminated area.

Sub contacts were often made, day and night, and one of the sonar blips turned out to be a school of blackfish. But with each alarm, a brace of destroyers churned over the suspected danger zone and dropped their depth charges. Meanwhile, the scuttlebutt flew aimlessly about the battleship that the American flotilla was heading for Bougainville, Rabaul, Truk—cutting off a renewed Japanese attack on Guadalcanal—setting a trap for Nips. . . . Oh, how we all hoped for action!

Third day at sea, official word was issued that our task force was sailing within range of Jap land-based bombers, and the unofficial word traveling almost as fast was that a formation of Betty dive-bombers and Kate torpedo bombers had been detected by our sensing devices 100 miles away. All hands were ordered to wear their life preservers at all times, even at chow. My hopes for battle rose, and the "Big Mamie's" band played with more gusto then at the customary afternoon concert, but the rumor proved to be false.

Little wonder, then, when the air attack alarm sounded on the fourth day, I thought: "This is it!" So did my compatriots and the gray-haired gunny sergeant. As we watched, dozens of our fighters zoomed off our carriers to confront the flight of "bogeys" racing toward our fleet.

It was exciting, all right, very exciting. We waited tensely, impatiently, for enemy assault.

But we never did see the Jap planes or warships—any of them—that day.

The attackers fled at the approach of our fighters thirty miles off, out of sight of the expectant Yanks and Brits, primed for a battle that never took place.

When "All Clear" was signaled, I and the Marine antiaircraft teams reluctantly quit our battle positions and cursed our bad luck. The leathery-faced sarge started humming "Sweet Lelani," as if to say, "I told you so."

There had been a slight distraction at the Marine gun section. Pfc. Edward J. Moore, of DeSoto, Missouri, had been lying in a sick-bay cot suffering from fever when the bugle sounded: "Man the Antiaircraft Stations!" Without thinking twice, the twenty-one-year-old bounded out of his bed and raced to his post in his hospital pajamas. Not until Sky Control phoned the station to get Moore off his ass and back to his sack did the reluctant gunner give up his post. Marines and sailors at nearby antiaircraft mounts broke into cheers for the spunky leatherneck.

The next day, the flattops' fliers were given a chance to blow off steam in a realistic demonstration of their skills. Scores of fighters, dive-bombers, and torpedo bombers rose into the sky to disappear behind the sun, and then come hurtling seaward, or overhead, to "attack" the maneuvering fleet.

The following day another mock battle was executed, and this time the antiaircraft gunners were given the opportunity to show their stuff, transforming the target sleeves into sieves. Our guys were deadeyes!

One of the observation planes from the "Big Mamie," which had been towing the aerial targets—a risky business—was lost when the brisk wind and choppy surf whipped over the pontoons of the small craft as she landed alongside the battleship. Once again, a watchful destroyer sped out to the rescue.

During my spare moments, I knocked out short pieces about the leathernecks aboard. It was a simple matter coming up with a feature angle.

The Lydecker identical twins, for example, caused a lot of confusion throughout the ship. Bert and Bill, aged thirty, were alike in build, looks, manners, and apparel. Each weighed 175, stood five feet ten and a half inches, and presented a ruddy complexion. Each was blond, and losing hair on the same part of the scalp. They even talked alike.

One day a bluejacket paid Bill $5 he owed Bert. That made up in part for Bill's having been punished with ten hours of extra police detail the day before for Bert's violation of a rule.

For a period, both served as orderlies for the skipper of "Big Mamie." Each orderly stood a four-hour watch. After a week's duty by the twins, Captain Glover approached Bert—or was it Bill?—and sympathetically asked why he had to stand watch for eight hours instead of the regulation four. That's when the skipper discovered that the brothers followed one another on watch.

The Lydecker twins hailed from Long Island, New York, where Bert sold sewing machines, and Bill delivered milk. They joined up together after Pearl Harbor and baffled the drill instructors at Parris Island and Norfolk, Virginia, Sea School. Like some of their gunmates, they had already earned three campaign ribbons and one for battle.

Then there was a natural story to write about Pfc. Edward LaPort, great-grandson of Feudin' Randall McCoy, a sure

shot of the West Virginia–Kentucky hills. The twenty-year-
old fourth-generation McCoy was a sharpshooter too, but
with the machine gun on the "Big Mamie," aiming for Japs
instead of Hatfields.

LaPort grew up in Matewan, West Virginia, with Cabell
Hatfield—on different sides of the river—and they were high
school classmates, football teammates, and good friends.
Together, in March 1942, they had joined the Marines, and
gone through boot camp. After basic training, they separated. Hatfield opted for radio school. LaPort for Sea
School. I never did learn whether they met again.

Another hometowner sure to make the local papers disclosed that two of Admiral Davis's orderlies had moved with
the flag commander through the American, European, and
Pacific war theaters.

Sgt. Richard Boss, twenty-three, of Parma, Ohio, and Pfc.
Clevern L. Waugh, twenty-two, of Section, Alabama, had
seen action against Nazi sub wolf packs off Iceland, against
the German battleship *Von Tirpitz* in the Arctic, with the
Navy in the battle of Savo Island off Guadalcanal, and had
already earned three campaign ribbons.

There was a story to be found in every one of the Marines
aboard *Massachusetts*. I just plucked them and sent them to
HQ for distribution to the local papers drooling for hometown heroes.

The "Big Mamie" and the task force returned to Noumea
base May 28. I was let down for the lack of a sea battle, but
my spirits were lifted by the feeling that our Navy packed a
powerful punch. I reported to C-2 with a stack of stories
covering all ninety Marines aboard. My Hermes had seen
more action than some of the guns.

If I had stayed with the "Big Mamie," or on any one of
the capital ships in "my task force," I would have seen all
the action I craved, even more.

"Big Mamie" steamed off to take part in the Solomons
advances; in the carrier strike against the Gilberts; in the
shelling of Nauru; and in the onslaught at Tarawa. She bombarded Kwajalein and Truk, and cleared the way for the
landing in Hollandia. Then, her gun barrels burnt out, "Big

Mamie" had to return to Hawaii for rehab. But she quickly returned to trample Truk again, to bolster the battling in the Leyte Gulf, Okinawa, and Formosa; and to shell Japan's industrial centers until the surrender to MacArthur. The *Massachusetts* earned eleven battle stars.

The *Indiana*, after surviving a collision with the *Washington*, took part in the "Great Marianas Turkey Shoot" of June 1944 and blasted out an outstanding career in the Pacific. She won nine battle stars.

The *North Carolina* got involved in just about every scrap with the Jap navy, and was up to its gun turrets in action from Guadalcanal to the enemy surrender on the *Missouri* September 2, 1945. The "Showboat" was sunk three times—by Tokyo Rose—and acquired twelve battle stars.

The *Saratoga* teamed up with *Victorious* in November to carry out a brilliant, devastating aerial attack on the Jap cruiser flotilla at Rabaul, later participating in the storming of a series of Jap bastions, including Iwo Jima, where she was torn up by six Jap bomber hits, losing 123 men. She stayed afloat, got fixed up again, and wound up her glorious history by ferrying some 30,000 veterans back to the States after Japan surrendered. She won seven battle stars.

The British *Victorious* also joined the *Saratoga* in the assaults on Sumatra and Java before being recalled by the British admiralty.

The cruiser *San Juan* somehow managed to get into just about every fight and fray along the way to Tokyo Bay and wound up with thirteen battle stars, a record achievement.

And what about me? Oh, yes, I was pinned with the salt Marine Seahorse insignia.

CHAPTER 10

Rendova

Nourished and invigorated by the month at sea, I returned to Noumea and snooped around Intelligence, looking for upcoming battle action. I soon picked up scuttlebutt that an American offensive was in the works—the invasion of the New Georgia Islands.

This island cluster—designated by an English sea captain for his king—was the next target of the Allies' grand strategic plan to recapture the Solomons, the archipelago that spreads out southeasterly in two chains for some 600 miles from Rabaul, the anchor of the Imperial High Command in the South Pacific, to Malaita on the eastern and Guadalcanal on the western ends.

"Watchtower" was the code name for the master plan, but the dubious—in view of the limited resources of the Allies at the time—thought of the operation as "Shoestring." The faint-hearts proved to be wrong when the American forces seized control of Guadalcanal after six months of combat. The next link, the Russell Islands, was taken without a fight. The New Georgias comprised the third lap of the route to Rabaul. I obtained orders to participate in that upcoming campaign.

On June 19, after seven hours on a motor raft back-and-forthing between shore and ship due to a maddening screwup of orders, and the frenzied retrieval of my left-behind Hermes, I boarded the *Tryon*, a transport that served alternately as an evacuation hospital ship and as a troop carrier. Unlike the bright white traditional hospital ship invoking immunity—but not always honored—the gray *Tryon* was fair game for air attack like any other troop carrier. Each side had a crush on enemy personnel transports and crashed them from air, sea, and ground at every opportunity.

The slow vessel pulled out of Noumea harbor in a small convoy for the hazardous run through Torpedo Junction to Guadalcanal. The word was out that two Allied ships had been sunk along that sea-lane only two nights before, and the tension aboard was palpable, especially among the Marine replacements from the States.

The newcomers were a garrulous lot and loudly voiced their eagerness to get into the thick of battle, bragging about what they would do to the "yellow-bellied Japs." They were young, fresh, confident.

The veterans who had undergone the savage foot-by-foot fighting on Guadalcanal and the adjacent islands of Tulagi and Gavutu were a grim-looking lot, appearing older, whatever their age. They said little, reticent about relating their chastening experiences in combat.

Some of the newcomers, even while boasting of action tomorrow, were already showing signs of homesickness. But to the leathernecks who'd been through the mill, nostalgia was by then a deep inexpressible ache.

The greenies prattled about their quick victories to come. The Guady graduates were acutely conscious that it had taken six torturous months to drive the fanatical Jap forces from their entrenched defenses, and they wondered how long, "how fucking long," it would take to reach Tokyo. They knew by then that it would be a long, long, treacherous road exacting a high toll in casualties at each furiously guarded gate through the New Georgias . . . Bougainville . . . Rabaul . . . Kavieng . . . Truk . . .

The seasoned leathernecks kept their concern among themselves, however, and gave only assurance and encouragement to the bubbling novices.

The vets took good-natured advantage of the newcomers. Proponents of a bewhiskered gag rushed around the ship with a cloth-covered bucket, ceremoniously stopping every now and then to lower the pail and peer into it. The curious suckers, naturally, came up to ask what the excitement was all about.

"A seabat," says one of the pranksters.

"Izzat so?" exclaims the gullible newbie. "Say, let me look at it, will you?"

"Sure, Mac, have a look."

Whereupon the butt of the wheeze bends over to see the seabat, and . . . *whack, whack, whack* . . . from all directions hitherto concealed paddles descend with stinging force on the exposed rear of the duped victim.

The freshmen had an insatiable appetite for battle trophies and shelled out as much as $25 for a "genuine" Japanese flag, which the scammers fabricated from discarded parachute silk, coloring in the Rising Sun. Oh, yes, the mature Marines were a serious lot, but they couldn't pass up a little profitable flimflam.

On June 24, I disembarked at Guadalcanal, where the next invasion force was being organized, and learned that only a week earlier some ninety Jap warplanes bent on bombing Henderson Field had been destroyed by the reinforced and expanding American aerial fleet with relatively small loss in encounters over Lunga Point.

I reported to HQ MarForSol (Marine Forces Solomons) and was assigned to the Ninth Marine Defense Battalion, comprising the biggest long-range guns, the most potent antiaircraft guns, special weapons, and tanks. At the Ninth, I found myself paired with T. Sgt. Jerry Sarno, of Yonkers, New York, a Marine combat photographer, and member of a camera-clicking clan.

Jerry, tall and strapping, had been an all-around athlete at Yonkers High and had been shooting photos for the Macy Westchester papers. At twenty-four, he switched from Macy to the Marines.

Four of his brothers were already snapping shots in the military services: Army Captain Richard, formerly with the New York *Daily Mirror*; Marine Sergeant Henry, also ex-Macy; Marine Private John, out of International News Service; and Marine Private Arthur. A fifth brother, Tony, was New York society photographer for INS.

Jerry was a six-footer, broad-shouldered, long-armed, good-natured, and fearless, attributes that were invaluable for Speed Graphic snapping and speedy foxhole digging. He remained calm in all situations . . . well, in almost all situations. His reaction to the most perilous circumstances was a long, drawn-out "Ver . . . ry . . . int . . . ter . . . rest . . . ting!"

At the battalion bivouac we were greeted and briefed by the two CCs regularly attached to the Ninth: Bill Frank, at twenty-one, the youngest of Denig's Demons, and Jim McNamara, his cameraman. Jim was somewhat bigger and older, and both were endowed with lots of guts. They had worked on the Washington *Times-Herald* and had trained at Guantánamo, Cuba, with the Ninth, which reached Guadalcanal in December 1942.

When Sarno and I caught up with the Ninth Defense Battalion, the artillerymen and tank crews had already seen service for sixteen months—seven training in Cuba, two at sea aboard a transport, and seven on Guadalcanal.

The Ninth had landed at Koli Point, some twenty miles south of Henderson Field, to protect the rear of the airbase. During its beleaguered months on The Island, the battalion had had few contacts with the enemy, other than shooting down seven Jap warplanes and picking off several snipers. Some of the Ninth's disappointed artillerymen described their unit as "the lost battery."

During those months on the alert at Guadalcanal, the Ninth had nonetheless maintained its discipline and readiness by responding to daily air alarms, undertaking scouting patrols, drilling and practicing with their multiple weapons. Still, the battalion had suffered severe inroads from tropical diseases.

Although the Ninth's morale was low for the lack of intensive front-line action, those leathernecks had learned from daily experience how to cope with their hostile jungle environment. Their gun batteries were freshly armed with bigger, faster, more accurate weapons: long-range 90mm antiaircraft artillery, effective for ground fire as well; 40mm automatic antiaircraft guns, deadly against short-range attacking targets; twin 20mm guns, fast firing for incendiary and armor-piercing shells; and the 175mm "Long Toms," which could hurl huge projectiles more than seven miles with excellent accuracy.

Officers and men alike were impatient to show their stuff with their new weapons.

On Sunday, the chaplain held a simple service outside of the folli in which I had slept fitfully in between bouts of flailing at pesky lizards the night before. There was a big turnout, including many who were professed nonbelievers but who came just in case a prayer or two might prove to be beneficial.

Monday was a quiet day.

The invasion of the New Georgia Islands—Operation Toenails—was scheduled to be mainly an Army show, with the XIVth Corps due to lead the initial invasion on Tuesday, June 30, and the Marine defense battalion to follow the next morning.

I and my fellow Marines boarded two large LSTs, #395 and #354, "Green Dragons," the largest and most voluminous of the Navy's beach-landing vessels.

No sooner did I get myself oriented on #395 than I bumped into Capt. Lionel Pool, executive officer of SBD Squadron 142, the Munda Maulers, whom I had interviewed at Henderson airfield.

He had been reassigned to special service as an aerial observer for the Ninth's long-range artillery. It was a warm reunion, as if we'd been close friends for years. Such surprise meetings, no matter the brevity of acquaintanceship, were always glad and hearty in the battle zones. There was that sense of relief in learning that someone you knew had survived at least up to the moment.

Captain Pool brought me up to date on Squadron 142. In fifteen weeks' action, the dive-bomber team had earned decorations for eighteen pilots and gunners, he himself receiving the Distinguished Flying Cross. Pool was cited for leading his unit 180 miles through dusk and thick weather to join a flight of torpedo bombers in sinking four Jap warships.

He had never been shot down, Captain Pool said, although he'd been shot up by two Zeros during a Marine raid.

His rear gunner, Johnny Miller, knocked off one Zero; a Grumman fighter did in the other.

That first night on the LST, we Marines were pleasantly surprised by the special "night-before" dinner the skipper had laid out for the artillerymen—thick, fat-sizzling pork chops. Some of the more greedy diners—including me—went for greasy seconds, then spent most of the night rocking and rolling at the rails as the shallow-draft vessel pitched and tossed like a wild bronco with a burr under its saddle.

The leathernecks, in spite of their nausea—or was it because of the nausea?—champed to charge off their Green Dragon onto land . . . and to hell with the Japs waiting to shoot at them. The mass malaise would vanish the instant the Marines sprang off the dropped-bow ramps and flung themselves onto the beach.

On deck through the dark rain, I observed, with a sensation of wonder, the ominous column of Green Dragons emerging from the sea like fabled monsters trailed by luminous trains in their wake. The LSTs were simply huge compared to any other landing craft, 328 feet long—the length of a football field—50 feet abeam, each carrying 21,000 tons of tanks, tractors, bulldozers, huge guns, ammo, and provisions in its enormous hold and two decks, along with some 200 troops.

The LSTs ran up onto, or close to, the landing beaches and speedily spewed out their artillery and machines, in contrast to their slow diesel-powered passage at sea at nine knots. The slow LST (Landing Ship, Tanks) was called "Green Dragon" by some, "Green Snapper" by some, and "Large Stationary Target" by more than a few.

LST #395 ran into a sandbar, so that we Marines unloading its mammoth interior had to work in hip-deep water in the torrential rain. By nightfall, despite the blinding downpour, all the Green Dragons had dumped off their precious cargoes: Marines' guns, machines, supplies.

At about 10:30 that morning, a slew of Bettys and Zeros ripped in, bombing and strafing, and a free-for-all broke out in the sky. It was raining not only buckets, but pilots as well. I counted five planes shot down, flame and smoke marking the trails as they plummeted into the water, but I couldn't make out which parachutists were ours.

Two American pilots were pulled out of the sea by the crash boats: Army Air Corps 1st Lt. James E. Parker, twenty-seven, of Compton, California, and Marine 1st Lt. Milton N. Vedder, twenty-four, of Los Angeles.

Lieutenant Vedder, who had joined the Corps on his twenty-third birthday, had two Jap fighters to his credit. This was the second time he'd had to take to his parachute. The first time, in May, in the lower islands, he landed in a tropical wilderness and wandered around for four days before being found and canoed back to base by friendly Melanesians.

It was the first forced jump for the blond Army aviator. He had quit his plant nursery to join the Army Air Corps nine days after the attack on Pearl Harbor. Parker had scored two Zeros on an earlier patrol.

Both fliers, unknown to each other, made the identical comment when I talked with them: "We love the crash boats!" they exclaimed. I responded in each case—speaking for the crash boats and all us groundlings—"We love the fliers!"

Unlike the incursion of Pavuvu, in which the leatherneck scouts had cased the enemy defenses for only two days and even then were unable to radio back the information gathered, the invasion of the New Georgias was preceded by a twenty-day, thousand-mile reconnaissance of three principal islands by a First Raider Regiment team, an extremely dangerous mission, with the odds 7,000 to 12—that is, the 12 Marines spying on terrain held by an estimated 7,000 Japs. There was always the dire possibility of ambush, such as befell the Goettge patrol on Guadalcanal.

The prize, though, was well worth the gamble—a viable course of action to seize the key enemy airport at Munda.

No sooner had the American armed forces secured the undefended Russell Islands than a dozen of the hardiest Raiders were picked to penetrate the Japanese positions on the New Georgia group, sixty miles northwest of the Russells, and find the best potential approaches.

Over the three weeks, these leathernecks played hide-and-seek with the unwary Japs, sketching coastlines, shooting pictures, and even watching American warplanes bomb the enemy airfield.

Time and again the scouts were almost exposed, but good camouflage, good jungle tactics—and good luck—brought them through each ordeal unseen and unheard by the enemy.

One reconnaissance patrol was led by a thirty-two-year-old Nicaragua campaigner, robust, levelheaded, mustachioed Lt. Col. Michael S. Currin, whom I had met with the Third Raider Battalion in the Russells. He had forged his way up from the ranks to the command of the Fourth Raider Battalion. His wife, Barbara Jane, lived in San Diego, California, with a ten-month-old daughter he had not yet seen.

Armed with light weapons and carrying one month's field rations, the patrol was flown by amphibious plane to a secret anchorage in the middle of the three islands to be surveyed. The landing by daylight was daring, with a half dozen Wildcats hovering solicitously overhead, while the Catalina discharged its passengers and their equipment.

The seaplane was unloaded at top speed, and although one enlisted man toppled into the water with all his gear, he and his equipment were recovered. Hands shaken, the Catalina and the Wildcats took off. The patrol faded into the jungle for the night, after arranging for guides with the cooperating natives.

The next dawn the patrol broke up into four teams, each to make a detailed report on potential beachheads, airfield sites, roads passable by jeeps; and on Jap concentrations and installations, emplacements, depots, observation posts. All this was to be accomplished without being seen or heard by the enemy, without giving the foe an inkling of the plotted Allied offensive. The scouts were under strict orders to engage in battle only if cornered with their lives at stake. HQ Command wanted live info, not dead foe.

As the patrols quickly discovered, the terrain of the New Georgia Islands is harsher than that of Guadalcanal. The jungles, trackless for the most part, run right up to the water's edge or into mangrove swamps. The terrain is steep and rugged, without any coastal plain or clearing. The conditions made the going slow, but proved to be beneficial for camouflage and concealment.

The three-member teams traversed their designated areas mainly at night by canoe. They slept by day, surveilled Jap positions, sketched maps, and took photographs. Sometimes it was necessary to travel by day, and in preparation for this probability, the men had let their beards grow to prevent the tropical sun from glinting off their faces. The Marines also hid themselves under palm-frond mats while the Melanesian guides paddled their dugout canoes slowly past any Jap outpost as if they were going someplace in no particular hurry.

When the scouts had to move overland by day, the natives followed behind, obliterating foot tracks so as not to leave any suspicious clues for Japanese patrols.

Lieutenant Colonel Currin, with Cpl. Robert Tharp, twenty-six, of Shamokin, Pennsylvania, and Pvt. Salvatore Gatto, twenty-one, of Albany, New York, skimmed through the southern half of New Georgia Island. Once they barely ducked their canoes among the spider-limbed mangroves as two Jap search planes flew overhead; and once they almost ran into a Jap barge. Gatto later said he had the time of his life snapping scenes virtually under the noses of the Jap sentries.

Capt. Lincoln N. Holzcom, twenty-three, of Greensville, Illinois, and Michigan State University, started on the mission as a lieutenant and learned on return he'd been promoted to two bars and leader of Q Company. He reconnoitered the west coast of New Georgia, including the Munda sector, where the prized airfield was located. Together with Cpl. Alvin T. Maxwell, twenty-two, of Sleepy Eye, Minnesota, and Cpl. Jack S. Fuller, thirty-six, of Montrose, Colorado, a former state game warden, he pushed within a few miles of the enemy airport.

"What a thrill it was to see our planes dropping their loads on Munda, hearing the explosions and enemy ack-ack," commented Captain Holzcom. "It was a wonderful feeling."

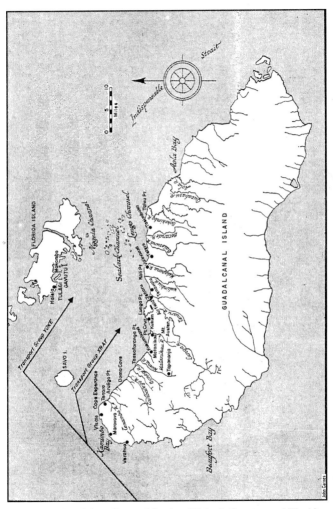

Guadalcanal and the adjacent islands of Tulagi, Gavutu, and Florida.
U.S. Marine Corps

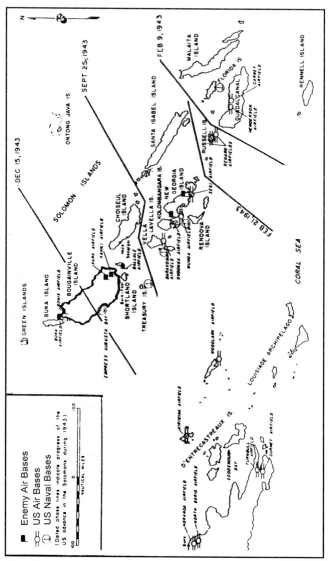

Guadalcanal, **Russell Islands, New Georgia Islands** (Rendova and Munda). *U.S. Marine Corps*

Training at Marine Corps boot camp, Parris Island, North Carolina, to use the butt of my rifle as a weapon in close quarters. (USMC)

My buddy Sgt. Al Lewis (right), beaming, and I in a publicity shot taken at Marine Headquarters, Arlington, Virginia, following our graduation from boot camp. August 1942. (USMC)

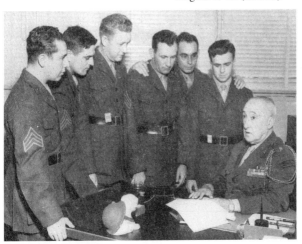

Six of the first Marine combat correspondents get their marching orders to the Pacific theater of operations from Brig. Gen. Robert L. Denig: (left to right) Al Lewis, *Washington Post*; Art Mielke, *Washington Times*; Paul Long, *Chattanooga Times*; John Black, *Philadelphia Bulletin*; Sam Stavisky, *Washington Post*; Joe Alli, *Buffalo Courier Express*. October 1942. (USMC)

The Green Dragon, LST 195, which took me to Rendova, New Georgia Islands, June 30, 1943. Taken by combat photographer Jerry Sarno of Yonkers, New York. (USMC)

Landing beach at Rendova a couple of days after the invasion, with Long Tom artillery being hauled off the Green Dragon. July 1, 1943. (Jerry Sarno, USMC)

Long Tom 155mm cannons, on Rendova, about to be fired at a Jap airfield on Munda by the crew of 9th Defense Battalion. July 1943. (National Archives)

A wounded Marine being treated where he fell during the Battle of Suicide Creek, Cape Gloucester, June 1943. Photo by Sgt. Bob Brenner, Brooklyn, New York. (USMC)

Helmet on my lap, I'm seated on *Aces 'n' Eights* (the dead man's hand!), PT 157, off Munda. To my left, with field glasses, is Lt. Comdr. Robert G. Kelly, leader of the "Mosquito Fleet" in the New Georgia Islands. July 1943. (Jerry Sarno, USMC)

A Marine tank blasts a path through the jungle as infantrymen watch for snipers. (USMC)

Combat correspondent Jerry O'Leary of the *Washington Post* (left) and I, lost in kunai grass behind enemy lines in Cape Gloucester, are startled to stumble upon three freshly killed Japs. Combat photographer Bob Brenner was also surprised, but he recovered fast enough to get the shot. (USMC)

Marine Pfc. George C. Miller, Jersey City, New Jersey, carries his machine gun down a rain-soaked jungle trail from Hill 660, after twenty-three days of battle. (Bob Brenner, USMC)

(above) Another graphic shot taken by Bob Brenner of the men of 3rd Battalion, 7th Marine Regiment, coming down from Hill 660 on Cape Gloucester. (USMC)

(right) Col. "Chesty" Puller, executive officer of 7th Marine Regiment, Cape Gloucester, and commander of the Itni Patrol. (*Marine Corps Gazette*)

A day's rest on the three-week Itni Patrol has me shoeless (in white shirt). Next to me are combat photographers Al Monteverdi, Los Angeles, California, and Bob Brenner, Brooklyn, New York, my teammates on Cape Gloucester. The man with the camera is unidentified. (USMC)

In fresh uniform, back in the States, I am ready to go on a Liberty Bond drive following campaigns in the Pacific. (*Boston Globe*)

T.Sgt. Jerry Sarno, Yonkers, New York, Marine combat photographer. My teammate in the Rendova campaign.

Once, their canoe slid by the Japs within 400 yards of the shore guards, the trio concealed under the woven-leaf mats. Another morning the three hid knee-deep in a swamp to spy on the activity of a Jap camp at Masi.

"The Japs were swimming nearby, and peering into the camp we could see who had taken the trouble to shave," the captain remarked.

Southwest New Georgia and the island of Vangunu were the objective of Lt. Harold B. Schrier, twenty-seven, of Corder, Missouri, also up from the ranks. Together with Cpl. William T. Jolly, twenty-three, of Albuquerque, New Mexico, and Pfc. Howard W. Schmid, twenty-two, of Milwaukee, he had to take refuge in a putrid cave to avoid detection one day; on another occasion he had stumbled in the dark within ten feet of an enemy launch.

"After a week's reconnaissance, I commented that we hadn't seen any Jap patrol planes yet. One of the boys urged me then to knock wood. And five minutes later two Zeros swooped over us. We ducked just in time," the lieutenant recalled.

At Viru, his team came upon a Jap radio shack, the operators asleep. "We could have slit their throats, but decided against the slim possibility of their raising an alarm," Schrier revealed.

Closest brushes with the enemy were made by Capt. Edwin B. Wheeler, twenty-five, a Williams College grad from Port Chester, New York; Lt. Philip A. Oldhand, twenty-nine, of Rye, New York, brevetted from platoon sergeant during the scouting mission; and Sgt. George B. Lewis, twenty-four, of Linden, Alabama.

This team got within one and a half miles of the Munda airport, and had to scurry in daylight by canoe through Blackett Channel, the main waterway for the enemy's transport traffic.

The Wheeler detail also could see the Munda airfield being bombed. One day they watched some 100 American bombers and fighters, returning home from a raid on Bougainville, detour long enough to drop a few on Munda. Later they saw an equally large fleet of Jap warplanes take off from Munda to attack our Solomons bases.

It was hard going for the three scouts who traipsed and canoed through 430 miles of enemy territory. They hit a squall one night, and soon after were trapped between the shore and a Jap barge flashing a searchlight around them. Most fortunately, the Japs failed to spot them.

Their most anxious day, according to Captain Wheeler's log, went like this:

"A party of eleven Japs was reported by the natives to be heading toward our camp. We watched them approach. All were armed with rifles; their officer, a major, with a sword; and one man carried a camera. They stopped 50 feet away on the other side of the river.

"We could see their features plainly. . . . They looked over to our side . . . chatted . . . then looked over toward us again. They made as if to cross, and we took off into the bush."

The next day, the log read: "I'm afraid the Japs are on our trail now."

The enemy patrol had seized a lad from a village hut and was holding him hostage until his parents appeared for questioning. The kidnappers left a note behind signed "from your friends, the Japanese Army." The youngster, however, escaped the next day and said he had been questioned about Americans or British in the area, but that he had feigned ignorance.

The Melanesians considered themselves to be not only our friends but also our allies, all four patrols reported. The locals spoke with pride of the American bombers as "our planes." They described the P39, the Army's Aeracobra fighter, as "long-nose fellow"; the SBD Wildcat dive-bomber as "two-fellow plane," the B-17 Flying Fortress as "big fellow too much."

They liked the Raiders and composed a song about them, the theme of which is the freeing of the Solomon Islanders from Japanese bondage by the Marines. They took every opportunity to show their appreciation. In the villages, the chiefs feted the patrols with chickens and fresh eggs. In the jungle, the natives brought oranges, lemons, pineapples, sweet potatoes, and watermelons. The guides would go off and return with fresh fish they had just speared, and—we couldn't believe it!—lobsters.

The flabbergasted scouts in turn shared their ration packs and smokes with their benefactors.

Several times the Raiders found themselves close by, unable to help, when Jap patrols pillaged a village, grabbing everyone and everything in sight. The plunderers tried to force the local populace into labor squads, but the natives escaped sooner or later. Once, a Jap patrol set up camp on the very ground the Marines had used the night before, but the site had been cleaned up so well that the Japs were not aware of it.

The Melanesians were deeply religious, the patrols found, most either Seventh-Day Adventists or Methodists. They held frequent services with hymns and sermons, and in the villages the call to prayers was beaten out on their drums.

"I sit here at twilight amazed, listening to the natives hold church service and singing," Captain Wheeler recorded in his journal. "The four-point harmony is magnificent."

On the appointed day, the four patrols rejoined at the rendezvous point and radioed a message to HQ: "Chickens . . . returned . . . to . . . roost!"

The Catalina glided in and flew them back to home base without incident.

In the interim, another reconnaissance had been made of Rendova, largest of the New Georgia group, and the principal objective of the Georgias campaign.

On June 30, the Barracudas of the Army's 43rd Division poured onto the initial stepping-stone of the Central Solomons offensive, Rendova Island, which was only six miles from the key enemy airfield on Munda. The GIs were followed—and sometimes led—by the first echelon of the Marines' Ninth Defense Battalion, commanded by Lt. Col. William J. Scheyer, a smart, aggressive leader.

The GIs and Marines met stiff resistance but not as stubborn as anticipated, an unanticipated boon, inasmuch as the littoral quickly became clogged with Allied guns, machines, and supplies, barred by dense jungle from being shifted quickly inland.

The Ninth was also prevented from placing its big guns at vantage points by the virtually impenetrable rain forest quagmire. The artillerymen were continually harassed by snipers, hidden in the leaf-shrouded trees, some strapped to their posts and certain to be killed when spotted. Tojo struck hard at the invasion with hordes of bombers and fighters, of which scores were shot down by the Yank squadrons that rose to meet the enemy head-on. The Jap air force nonetheless inflicted severe damage before being driven off, and clobbered the *McCawley*, the AP—assault personnel—transport that was serving as Rear Admiral Richmond Kelly Turner's flagship. The vessel, though still afloat, had to be abandoned.

To get off the beaches—where they stood out like a fat bull's-eye for enemy bombing and strafing—the jungle-wise leathernecks of the Ninth hacked, chopped, and slashed a path through the brambled, scrambled underbrush, through the tangled mesh of vines, through spiked boughs locked in arm-wrestling grips, through thorn-leafed branches coiled around one another like boa constrictors, past mean spiders big as a man's hand.

They slapped, smacked, and cursed a path through clouds of aroused, angry mosquitoes, chiggers, and other vengeful vermin. They were stung, bitten, and bled by flying and creeping beasties. They were nicked and pricked by needles and nettles. They sweated and stank through their sodden fatigues, or bared their arms and torsos to the pelting rain. They would halt their strenuous labors momentarily to flip a swig of tepid water from lukewarm canteens or to take a dribbly yellow piss where they stood.

No one joked; no one yacked; no one bitched. They just hacked it.

Marine and Army engineers and Navy Seabees, working feverishly, hewed down regal coconut trees and chopped and sawed them into common logs for menial service as a corduroy road over the mire.

Then, dismantling their heaviest armament into movable

components, the Marines tugged and dragged, pushed and carried the massive gun sections to selected spots, where they quickly reassembled the works into ready-to-fire posture. The newly acquired 155mm Long Toms were designed to be hauled by their own tractors, but the mechanical movers proved to be incapable of pulling the enormous, fifteen-ton eight-wheel cannon through the intractable terrain. The tractors' pulling power had to be helped by the straining shoulders of the fifteen-member gun crew. But the Marines interrupted their own panting struggles to cheer when an enemy plane was shot down, or when a Navy crash boat sped out and plucked a Yank flier from the sea.

The very first day ashore, June 30, the antiaircraft crews of the Ninth Defense Battalion quickly set up their guns, long range and short range.

The honor of shooting down the first enemy warplane went to two crews that had lugged their .50-caliber machine guns through knee-deep mush to set up firing positions. At 2 P.M. a Zero dove on the beach, spitting death. But the gunners simultaneously zeroed in and demolished it. Officers of the Ninth confirmed Strike One. The crews paid a high price for their prize, as one of their gunmates was mortally wounded.

One crew was made up of Cpl. Paul V. Duhamel, twenty-three, of Millis, Massachusetts; two civilian life chums, Pfc. George D. Clancy, nineteen, a fellow townsman, and Pfc. Ernest E. O'Brien, twenty, from nearby Milford; Pfc. Fred Hanba, of Rome, New York; and Pfc. Nemo Hancock, twenty, of Tipton, Indiana.

The second team was composed of Cpl. Carl Fredericks, twenty-seven, of Washington, Iowa; Theodore W. Pierce, twenty-three, of Oneida, New York; Pfc. Clinton R. Watson, twenty-one, of Lyons Falls, New York; Pvt. Phillip Patrick, nineteen, of Richmond, Virginia; and the slain member, whom I was not permitted to name, as in most cases of combat deaths. The general rule required that the kin of the war dead be notified first before the names were made public.

At noon of July 2—Black Friday—the Jap air fleet blitzed the American beachhead. Ceiling zero between Rendova and the Allied air bases on Guadalcanal and the Russells gave the enemy the rare opportunity to slip in from the murk above without aerial opposition. The Jap foray, streaking in from Bougainville, bombed and raked the harbor and beaches, raced away, and left devastation behind.

That Black Friday, American losses in men and matériel were heavy because the antipersonnel bombs pelted the beach with shrapnel. The Ninth was severely hurt, splattered with shards of iron and steel, some killed outright, some fatally ripped, some flesh-torn, bone-fractured, bloodied.

I sensed rather than saw the bombers. I was sitting on a large chunk of driftwood, fingering away at the Hermes on my lap, when I became aware of the distinctive dishwasher-machine whir of the Japanese Bettys. I carefully closed the typewriter case, squeezed on the canvas cover, and only then, with Little Jeezus screaming "Cover yer ass, stupid!" even as I heard the bombs exploding along the beach, did I cast around for shelter.

Not a foxhole, nor dugout, nor trench to be seen!

Desperate, I spotted two Alligators—amphibian tractors— to my front, a bulldozer to my right, each about twenty yards away. I grabbed my Springfield and Hermes and lunged for the bulldozer, hoping to shield my body from the showering shrapnel if the bombs didn't fall too close by. I lay there trembling in tempo with the vibration of the beach as the shells burst, exploding ammunition dumps and fuel depots, fortunately well away from where I lay.

I became aware that two other men had pitched into the sand beside me when one let out a gasping cry of pain. I never did learn who the wounded victim might be, because when the raid was over, uncontrollable fright overcame me. I crawled away, and ignoring the vehement pleas of Little Jeezus, I abandoned rifle and typewriter and tore wildly toward the jungle to hide from the overhead terror.

My chest agonizing for breath, my leg muscles gripped in spasm, I tumbled into a gumbo-gucky gully. Convulsions of nausea and retching took over. The violent seizure was relieved only when I passed out.

I was roused from the comatose sleep by Little Jeezus rattling my brain, accompanied by a rude shaking of my shoulders. I foggily recognized the insignia of an Army chaplain. "Where can I find a doctor?" the padre pleaded. "We need doctors. The Seabee dispensary is blown up. The Marine dispensary is swamped." I could only shake my head dazedly.

I tried to pull myself together, and with Little Jeezus clamoring in my pulsating, aching head, I was now beset by feelings of guilt and shame for abandoning my two companions. Discarding the rifle is a cardinal sin—as Little Jeezus kept reminding me—but I could easily replace it from the scattered weapons on the battered beach. But losing my compact portable was a catastrophe. Where could I obtain another in Rendova—or, for that matter, in the Solomons?

Sick to my stomach, legs wobbly, I forced myself to stagger back in search of my two weapons. The Alligators had been splattered with bullets, and one was still burning. The bulldozer was still there, unbelievably unharmed, as were my rifle and typewriter, which I reclaimed with a prayer of thanks.

I managed somehow to stow the portable into the hollow of a tree trunk, slashing an *S* on the bole so I could find it later, and, hanging on to my rifle, shakily hurried to join the stretcher lines carrying Marine and Army casualties from the bombed beaches to the LSTs for evacuation.

Most of the evacuees were badly wounded or dead; some were bleeding through bandages hastily wrapped around cuts and gouges on faces, arms, torsos, bellies, legs. Some of the wounded were crying out in pain as the desperate corpsmen ran from one to another to administer a quieting shot. There were some, too, who had suffered no physical harm but had cracked up and fallen to pieces under the tensions and bedlam of the slaughtering aerial attack.

There, among the litter bearers, I found Sarno. I was distraught, but he straightened me out with an avuncular bear hug, glad to see me alive. And was I happy to see him! Bless his huge dimensions and comforting arms!

Sarno, between rounds of stretcher hauling, was shooting movies and stills of the corpsmen, medicos, litter bearers, and of the carnage and chaos on the beach. He complained he had suffered some bad luck during the raid. He'd been up to the Long Toms, taking shots of the new 155mm artillery being fired for the first time by the Marines, when the enemy bombers roared in and went for the battery that Sarno was snapping. The long-limbed photog didn't hang around for the intruders, but leaped into a foul-smelling ditch to find himself sharing the refuge with a dead cow. He later denied the rumors that he had fallen into a pile of cow shit.

I fell into the line with him, lifting the wounded, some moaning piteously, and the dead, some blotted with gore, onto makeshift stretchers. Tears welled up in the eyes of some litter bearers; others cursed aloud, swearing vengeance on the "yellow bastards." They were sickened by the gaping wounds, missing limbs, mangled bodies of their buddies, of the same guys they had joked with only hours earlier. Some of the Marines vomited. I had thrown up earlier in my frenzied flight and had no more to heave. Only the corpsmen seemed to be unshaken; they had been through disaster before.

The sun broke through, and I glanced up to see fluffy sheep and lambs lolling in the azure sky, oblivious to the carnage below. But the perverse scene of serenity was quickly obliterated by a bank of black cloud.

The Green Dragons had been transformed into emergency hospitals, and the Navy surgeons, having to make the anguishing decisions of triage, were already operating on the most critically wounded. We kept the stretcher line running into the openmouthed LSTs until midnight.

A blackout went into effect as night crept in, but a ghastly glow was cast over the shore by the blazing dumps. The evacuation proceeded at top speed, the able-bodied anxious to get the LSTs away with their stricken compatriots before the whining Mitsubishis made another call.

The rescue operation over at last, Sarno and I were too exhausted to seek belowground shelter and fell asleep on the beach, stretched out next to a prone GI, whom we discovered to be dead when we awoke at sun-bursting dawn. The sun and strong coffee revived us. Then Sarno strode off to capture the devastation of Black Friday. I went after a different story. I wanted to write about the pill pushers, the naval surgeons and twenty-one corpsmen who were attached to our Marine outfit, and who had so coolly, so caringly carried on during the bloodbath of the day before.

By then, I had begun to understand the ambivalent relationship between the Marine Corps and the Navy. The Marines at the command levels resented being overruled— "pushed around"—by the Navy's superior authority in decisions affecting Corps combat operations. This reaction trickled down into the ranks, creating a shadow of friction between the two branches of military service.

However, the Marines on the line had a high regard for the Seabees, who side by side with them built bridges and roads while under fire; for the crews of the vessels, big stuff and small fry, that carried them into battle; for the sailors who manned the machine guns with them aboard the warships. And they loved the naval doctors and corpsmen— held them in high esteem—because they had guts . . . because they had balls . . . because they were there when needed, even before the cry went up for "Corpsman! Here! Corpsman!"

On the Rendova beach, under attack every day or night, the Navy's medical team was led by Lt. Comdr. Miles C. Krepela, of New York City, and Lt. Nathan I. Gershon, of Atlanta, who heedlessly exposed themselves to the very dangers besetting the Marines and corpsmen.

The battalion medics had to carry the brunt of the emergency assistance in the first days of the invasion and occupation of Rendova, because a bomb demolished the only other field dispensary. The surgeon and his aides fell to with the inspired, cold passion of a Marine platoon storming an enemy entrenchment. The Marines did it with rifle and bayonet; the medics did it with hypodermic needle and scalpel.

Although the beach in Rendova harbor had been a prime target of the Zeros and Bettys, Lientenant Commander Krepela and his team refused to move the Marine dispensary to a safer location inland because the deep mud and lack of roads made transportation of the wounded very difficult. On the beach, they argued, the dispensary could be quickly reached by ramp board, and after emergency treatment, the wounded could be easily carried onto the evacuation vessels.

The Marine dispensary was kept in operation on the beach even after a bomb's steel fragments spattered around it and felled Pharmacist's Mate First Class Clyde E. Henley, twenty-three, of Pensacola, Florida.

The remaining pill pushers nonetheless scattered out to give first aid to the wounded and bring them in, as Pharmacist's Mate Second Class Vincent Yamaitis did when two leathernecks were hit by shrapnel on either side of him. The twenty-six-year-old Yamaitis had signed up for the duration from Wilkes-Barre, Pennsylvania. I told Yamaitis I admired his guts. He replied: "When a Marine goes down, a corpsman goes up."

And there were instances when the corpsman left his patient long enough to man the vacated gun post, as was the case with Pharmacist's Mate Second Class Francis G. Peters, twenty-one, of Elizabeth, New Jersey.

It is fairly simple to estimate the number of Japs a Marine platoon kills in the course of an engagement. Add up the bodies. It is impossible to add up the number of lives the medical platoon saves in the same action. But then, it doesn't take statistics to understand why the leathernecks consider the corpsmen to be fellow Marines. And that's the highest tribute a Marine can pay.

The Fourth of July, 1943, was celebrated on Rendova with fireworks of a different kind. "Murderers Row" went into action, and I was there to see for myself the destructive firepower of the Big Toms, two of which had been disabled in the Black Friday bombing but were already restored for action. A single blast from Murderers Row catapulted the explosive fury of a flight of dive-bombers against the Japanese.

These 155mm cannon were under the command of wiry Lt. Col. Archie O'Neill, a thirty-seven-year-old Naval Academy graduate hailing from Williamson, West Virginia. From his post at fire direction control, he picked the target and delivered the order to fire. Then, bracing for the tremendous backlash roar of the guns, he nodded in approval as the shells swooshed Munda-ward in deadly precision.

After finding a suitable stand for his batteries, Lieutenant Colonel O'Neill dispatched Maj. Robert C. Hiatt, of Indianapolis, Indiana, to reconnoiter the area and pick out the best point available for the artillery observation post.

The OP as a rule is set up forward, ahead of the guns, but with the Japs holding the ground and the islets fronting the batteries, Major Hiatt had to pick an OP location on a hill behind the guns. He found a good place, all right, but had to kill a sniper in his way.

The OP was little more than several boards hammered into the precariously swaying top of a 150-foot-tall leafless casuarina tree, providing a clear view of Munda six miles off. The Melanesian bearers, usually eager to help, refused to climb the odd-looking leafless tree with its drooping reedy limbs, protesting that the casuarinas were too high and too dangerous for them to climb and build on.

Four members of the recon group volunteered, and using ropes, lifted one another through the bare branches, then improvised a platform steady enough to bear the weight of the 300-pound telescope they raised with ropes from the ground. The scope had been taken as booty from the Japs on Guadalcanal. Like much other battle equipment, the Jap optical instruments were superior to our own, a recognition quickly exploited by the omnivorous Graddick on Rendova.

The OP builders were four enlisted men who swung through the branches with monkeylike ease: 1st Sgt. Ernest Smith, thirty-four, of Washington Courthouse, Ohio; Pfc. James Lee, twenty-two, of Madison, Tennessee; Pvt. Rocco D'Angelo, twenty, of Rockford, Illinois; and Pvt. Eugene Feeley, of Brooklyn, New York.

I, of course, simply had to scale the 150-foot tree to the OP platform to see for myself what there was to see, and for me the ascent wasn't monkey business. Oh, sure, I was in good enough shape to manage the climb, and wooden slats had been nailed one above the other to create a makeshift ladder, but as I discovered, the rungs were too far apart for my short limbs, so that I had to stretch to the utmost on my toes and jump in order to get a grip on the next strip up. I had to utilize the ropes, too, to pull myself laboriously to the top.

Once up there I saw that there really wasn't much space for me, and I didn't really enjoy the uncontrollable swaying of the OP in the breeze. Nor was I in the mood to enjoy the scenic view, because I wondered what I would do in the event of an air raid.

"So what do you observers do in an air raid?" I asked one, casual-like.

"Nothing to it," responded the OP officer. "We just scramble down the tree and duck away into our foxholes. You needn't worry. We'll find a place for you below."

My arms and legs aching from the climb up, his offer of hospitality below was not truly appreciated. If I "just scrambled" down, I'd break my neck. Oh, I got down later, to be sure, but it was a slow, painful process.

Up in the platform with the observer—Lt. Col. Edward Hanna Forney, of Chevy Chase, Maryland, also an Annapolis grad, who signaled the shots for the artillery—I can testify to the uncanny accuracy of the Big Toms. I was there just when Colonel Forney spotted flashes of light emanating from a small house on a hill on Munda Point. He concluded that the hilltop structure was serving as a signal tower for the Jap defenders' cannons. Lieutenant Colonel Forney fieldphoned the essential target data to Lieutenant Colonel O'Neill at the fire control center, who issued the order to fire. The volley of a single Long Tom battery liquidated the pinpointed target before my eyes. The exploding shells sounded like distant thunder.

That same day, July 4, Sarno and I turned up at the Big Tom firing center to get a photo story of a bomb disposal squad gingerly digging out a dud that had plummeted into the earth between the trail legs of a 155mm cannon but had failed to detonate.

"Can the dud go off?" I asked, trying not to show my qualms.

"Sure as hell can," replied the disposal squad leader, Lt. Mike Taylor.

I didn't quite hear Lieutenant Taylor's added comment: "But probably won't."

I didn't even hear Little Jeezus screeching, "Cover yer

ass, stupid!" I was already racing for cover, but I was behind
Sarno's long strides. We found a vacated foxhole on an ad-
joining hummock, from which we could watch Dauntless
dive-bombers pounding Munda and simultaneously keep an
eye on the delicate dud disposal activity below.

Then a third sight caught our attention. A formation of a
dozen Bettys ran into withering fire from the ground. We
peered from our knoll-top dugout and watched with pride as
long-range 90mm antiaircraft guns of Battery E permitted
the twin-engine Mitsubishi marauders to fly within dead-
duck range. Then the battery opened fire and destroyed
every one of the twelve bombers. I later confirmed that the
armada annihilation was executed with a record burst of
eighty-six rounds of ammunition in sixty seconds.

It was an incredible spectacle. The very first round destroyed the lead plane, from which a flaming chunk rammed
a second bomber, which then also disintegrated. The rest
were blown up aflame, as I verified later with the battery
commander, Capt. William N. Tracy, twenty-five, of Green-
wich, Connecticut. He credited the sensational performance
to the quickness of Staff Sgt. Robert Merritt, twenty-two, of
Clearwater, Florida, who operated the altitude reader and set
the firing gauge to a dead-right 15,000 feet.

The gunners who fired the remarkable shots included Pfc.
John Warren, twenty-two, of Savannah, Georgia, who stuck
by his post despite burns from the hot shells; Pfc. Evan
Evans, twenty-two, of Richmond, Virginia; Pfc. Fred. V. Pa-
ley, twenty, of Road Fork, Kentucky; and Platoon Sgt.
Robert Wattles, twenty-seven, of Chicago.

First to spot the Mitsubishis was Pfc. Francis M. Kerns,
twenty-five, of Charlotte, North Carolina. Like Warren, another crewman, Floyd Noonkester, twenty-six, of Canbria,
Virginia, was painfully scorched but stayed fast until the
battle was over.

Even as ground fire destroyed the twelve bombers, our
Wildcats knocked down four escorting Zeros.

After the spectacular Fourth of July shoot-down, Sarno
could restrain himself no longer. He jumped out of our nest
and, thrusting off my attempt to restrain him, dashed down

to the harbor arm—later designated Suicide Point for its attraction to enemy bombers and strafers—to snap pix of an
exploding ammunition dump, which had been hit by a jetti-
soned bomb. A Navy cameraman had been blown to bits trying to take a similar photo on July 20, and I knew it. Sarno
knew it, too! But then, Sarno was not only courageous, he
was also foolhardy. He was there to take photos, wasn't he?
Sarno got his pictures.

Later, when I rebuked him for doing something so
dangerous, Sarno merely said, "Ver . . . ry . . . int . . . ter . . .
rest . . . ting."

I returned to the Long Tom firing center to find the disposal crew patiently gouging away for the dud lodged within
the trails of the cannon. The eight-man team, starting at the
stovepipe-shaped hole punched by the shell, had been pick-
axing down through the resisting coral four at a time, each
quartet relieving the other every half hour, and catching
whatever sleep they could. Since they had not had the time
or energy to dig a foxhole for themselves, they slept one
night in the pit they were digging. And since it was raining
most of the time, the hole kept filling with water, so that the
excavating had to stop for the bailing out.

At eleven feet down, the digging went from tough to
worse, when water began oozing *up*. The diggers passed up
noon rations and, fatigued as they were, somehow drew up
the strength to pour it on, and soon after, at twelve feet deep,
reached the dozing missile.

Then Lieutenant Taylor and Cpl. Bill Waters carefully—
very carefully—examined the bomb where it lay and decided to blow it up. Ten pounds of dynamite obliterated the
dud and the pit. The "Big Toms," which had continued their
thunderous bombardment of Munda during the digging, ignoring the peril of the unexploded bomb, ceased firing for
the few minutes of the disposal explosion and then went
back to work.

Lieutenant Taylor, twenty-seven, of Carlsbad, New Mexico,
and Corporal Waters, nineteen, of Solvay, New York, had
volunteered for bomb disposal duty and said they liked the
assignment. An alumnus of New Mexico State College,

Lieutenant Taylor taught Navajo and Acoma Indians and had been a high school teacher. Corporal Waters had been working in a defense plant.

The six other bomb burrowers, all privates first class, were Edgard G. Honaker, eighteen, Norfolk, Virginia; James N. Johnson, twenty, High Point, North Carolina; Curtis Westbrook, nineteen, Detroit, Michigan; Samuel J. Lerose, twenty, Old Forge, Pennsylvania; Harry N. Langworthy, eighteen, Buffalo, New York; and Thomas R. West, nineteen, Youngstown, Ohio.

The Ninth Defense Battalion's other disposal teams extracted and exploded some seventy-five duds that day—a routine performance on a routine day.

The Fourth of July celebration ended spectacularly that night with a "brilliant" naval bombardment of Munda that shook us awake for hours, but it was worth it.

After the spectacular Fourth, next day Sarno and I chose a spot 500 yards inland, among the coconut trees, to chop out a deep and wide foxhole and make it relatively comfortable. We needed to get out of wet, filthy fatigues and dry our wet, filthy bodies.

By chance—well, not entirely by chance—we built our new dugout adjacent to the motor pool, which proved to be a sure source of the most edible rations and freshest rumors around. Little Jeezus beamed in recognition of that savvy example of covering ass and using our "haid."

The first night in our new shelter, July 5, a detachment of rookie Marine replacements, on unloading detail, holed up close by. Because their noncom had left them on an urgent errand and had not yet returned, the newbies became panicky when Condition Black—prepare for invasion—was sounded. The tension mounted with the approach of darkness, and I, a newborn convert to panic control, suggested to Sarno that we act to reassure the nervous Nellies before one of them blew his stack and kicked off a stampede.

Sarno, a four-stripes sergeant, and I, a three-striper, moved in among the jittery replacements, and Sarno's commanding presence calmed them down.

When the absent leader failed to show—forbidden to

move around in the dark—Sarno and I, as senior noncoms present, ordered the detachment to build a bunker as a defense against the anticipated shelling from the sea. We then selected a large bomb crater and put our new charges to work digging, filling sandbags, chopping down two trees and cutting them into logs to cover their collective refuge. All through the pouring rain of the night they toiled, and by dawn they had created a sturdy shelter. They were ready for the assault from the sea.

The anticipated naval bombardment failed to materialize that night. Sarno and I nonetheless felt good because we had done a good night's work. I had another reason for feeling my good-deed glow. I felt that I had atoned somewhat for my own panic-stricken reaction two days before.

At Sarno's suggestion that there was a good story to be unearthed at Suicide Point, we took off for the little peninsula extending into Rendova Harbor, which had become the hottest spot since the landing, having undergone two severe bombings and one strafing raid.

On D day, June 30, a Nip fighter pelted the palm groves of the cape and was nipped by Marine antiaircraft fire. A second time, Black Friday, July 2, a large flight of Mitsubishis, breaking through our aerial cover in the cloudy sky, literally rained bombs on Suicide Point, destroying two ammo and fuel dumps and inflicting heavy casualties.

On the Fourth of July, sixteen enemy warplanes stormed in, and though all were shot down, six managed to drop their missiles on the point, setting off another ammo depot, causing more deaths and injuries.

Nonetheless, Suicide Point wasn't abandoned, even though it was strewn with the wreckage of blasted ramp boats, plantation huts, and coconut trees, bare, black, and forlorn. The cape area was pitted with bomb craters and looked like the face of the moon. One wheel of a bomber, chunks of engine, and fusilage were scattered over the beach, mute evidence that one Mitsubishi had followed in the wake of its missile. And crudely decorated graves already marked the place where several Marines had died at their posts.

The leathernecks there, still holding on, were a grim, weary bunch. They hated the point, but wouldn't let go.

There I found Pfc. Jerry H. Grueter, thirty, Cincinnati, Ohio, still by his light antiaircraft gun. He and his buddy had been eating chow when the bombers first sneaked in. Grueter dived into the gun pit to start firing away when a bomb burst behind him, seriously wounding his gunmate.

A few yards away, a 500-pounder struck close to another gun crew, killing one, injuring five, who had to be evacuated. Alert at their gun mounts, I found Pvt. Richard T. Driver, twenty-three, of Cherokee, North Carolina; Pfc. Raymond C. Willits, twenty-two, of Detroit; Pfc. John A. Nolan Jr. twenty-three, of Pawtucket, Rhode Island, and Pvt. Clifford M. Borchers, of Crescent Springs, Kentucky.

At a third antiaircraft post, when a bomb dropped only five yards away, only one member of the eight-man crew escaped injury. The lucky fellow was Pfc. Richard E. Newbold, twenty, of Richmond, Indiana. Hit by shrapnel but still carrying on were Pvt. William C. Carpenter, twenty, Marshfield, Massachusetts, and Pfc. Reginald H. Connors, nineteen, of Livermore Falls, Maine. Only his rosary escaped destruction in the collapse of the shelter of Sgt. John M. Trusz, twenty-four, of Ludlow, Massachusetts. Three of the men had to be evacuated when two bombs struck near a fifth gun.

I found Suicide Point to be aptly—unhappily—named.

Next I wanted to check out a potential story that had been nagging me since Black Friday. What had happened to the crews of the two shot-up amtracs?

I had been aware that three Alligators had been trampling through the muck and mire beyond the beachhead delivering ammo, medicine, and food to front-line units unreachable by wheeled vehicles, most of which broke down or stalled in the doughy turf.

The Alligator—Landing Vehicle Track (LVT)—had been originally designed for the Everglades swamps by Donald Roebling, son of the engineer who built the Brooklyn Bridge, and had been adapted by the Marine Corps as an amphibian tractor for beachhead logistical support. The paddle treads of the Alligator gave it mobility in water and mud. Most of the amtrac's steel body was devoted to its cargo hold, leaving just enough space aft for the motor. The mounted machine guns were available for both defense and offense, as needed, and the strong hulks could be planted in streams to support pontoon bridges.

In the Rendova landing only three Alligators were available at first: *Tootsie, Gladys,* and *Frances*, their three-man crews working around the clock. On Black Friday, a bomb struck nearby and destroyed *Gladys*, leaving it ablaze. Two of the crew were wounded by shrapnel and one was killed.

The Marines on *Tootsie* were luckier. Manning that Alligator when the Jap warplanes blasted the beachhead were three twenty-two-year-olds: Cpl. Dominic Bove, of Wilmington, Delaware; Cpl. William C. Coker, of Palmetto, Florida; and Pvt. Mitchell Tydryszewski, of Trenton, New Jersey. Corporal Coker described what had occurred:

"We were arguing if they were our bombers or the Japs'. I said they're not ours. I got the last word in, I guess. An explosion blew me off, ripped my jacket, and caved in my helmet. I found myself under the amtrac, and still don't know whether I crawled under or was blown under.

"Dom and Mitch were also under, as well as a wounded corpsman. Nobody knows how he got there."

The *Frances* was gassing up at the fuel dump several hundred yards away. "All I remember," recalled Pfc. Otha W. Kirkland, twenty-two, of Fort Myers, Florida, "is that we were arguing about the identity of the planes, when a terrific explosion knocked me down into the cargo compartment."

Cpl. Keith W. Randall, nineteen, of Napa, California, remembered more: "A bomb landed plumb in the middle of the gas dump. I was blown off the tractor and under it. First thing I remember was that I was saying my prayers. I'd been hit by a piece of shrapnel, but it wasn't much. When I finally got up, Jackson wasn't to be found. We were scared, I tell you. We'd thought he'd gotten it. But he'd been dazed by the concussion and had wandered off down the beach."

Leader of the crew, Sgt. H. C. Jackson, twenty-one, Columbia, South Carolina, recovered from his shock but was stricken with malaria a couple of days later and had to be evacuated.

I never did find out what happened to the driver of the bulldozer beside which I had sought refuge before taking off like a lunatic.

CHAPTER 11

aces 'n' eights

Like nocturnal winged predators of the jungle, the Mitsubishis sprang up every night to pounce on their quarry on Rendova. Unlike the stealthy avian prowlers, the sound of the clattering two-engine Betsys heralded their approach.

The Betsys bombarded the American troops and positions on Rendova several times a night—my aching eardrums reverberated to eleven raids one night—despite heavy losses to ground fire. The blasts played havoc with American personnel and destroyed a lot of supplies.

Sarno and I were also awakened out of our snatches of shut-eye several nights by mysterious flashes and explosions at sea. Curious, we checked with Intelligence and learned that Navy PT (Patrol Torpedo) boats were running nightly strikes against the Tokyo Express, the Jap troopships and barges bringing reinforcements to their defensive lines and the escorting destroyers that sneaked up after dark to fire on U.S. installations on Rendova.

The PT boats were the most exciting and most hazardous wing of Admiral Turner's Task Force 31 supporting the Army-Marine invasion of the New Georgias. The "Mosquitoes" had carried out urgent missions in the Marine invasion of Guadalcanal and in the current drive up the Central Solomons, dropping off scouts into enemy territory, flitting in supplies, flitting out casualties. Camouflaged gray, the PTs blended into the low visibility of their dusk-to-dawn sallies to prey on enemy shipping and harass enemy destroyers. The PT boats had already sunk at least two warships, and had lost a number of their own craft—and men—to the much more potent Jap counterfire.

Of course, informed and misinformed by the latest scuttle-butt, the jungle-locked grunts on Rendova knew all about the Mosquitoes, and they admired and envied their sea-skimming compatriots. Here, the infantrymen were digging endless muck and hacking endless coral; there, the PT crews were sporting around in sparkling seas, speeding out and shooting up *dihatsus* (Jap supply barges), slinging torpedoes at enemy destroyers, raising hell in high water.

Here, they were grubbing it down on the gooey ground; there, they were grooving it up on the bracing breezes. Here, they were miserably slogging it out through relentless rain; there they were zipping jauntily through the speckled waters.

Here were the ordinary joes who'd joined up in patriotic fervor; there were the golden-spoon scions who'd been weaned on yachts and teethed on high-priced, high-jinks powerboats.

Oh, what a beautiful way to fight the war!

Well, there were a few kernels of fact in the grunts' glamorous vision of life on the PTs, but very few.

The PT crews were having the adventure of their lives, it is true, for they were a wild bunch, daring and at times even reckless during their dusk-to-dawn operations. And many of the skippers were as familiar with the wheel of their speed-boat as with the wheel of their sporty auto back in the States. But they had to have guts, too, to seek out enemy supply ships and warships, and maneuver close enough to spurt torpedoes at them.

However, it was the rare fish that hit the mark, because it was hard to see in the dark, because it was hard to fire accurately at a fast-moving target in the rolling sea, because too many of the PT torpedoes were aged, defective, undependable.

As for the gossip about giddy "torpedo juice" (absolute alcohol used to fuel the fish) parties, they were the exception, and were said to leave bigger, throbbinger hangovers than the concoction distilled from medicinal alcohol, the witches' brew of the grunts who could lay hands on the stuff.

The PTs sailed out of their nests every night, but some mornings not all returned, and not all of the crews came back unhurt, if they came back at all.

The PT motor torpedo boat was light, forty-five tons; streamlined, seventy feet stem to stern; swift, top speed fifty knots; driven by three Packard 1,200-horsepower engines. The fourteen-man crew could throw lethal punches from the PT's two or four torpedo tubes, four .50-caliber machine guns, and a 37mm deck cannon. The Mosquitoes were supposed to hit and run and, if lucky, to survive to hit and run another night.

But the essential need, swiftness, deprived the PTs of armor and left their fragile mahogany plywood frames vulnerable to enemy bullets and shells. The engines were sensitive to dirt, heat, and overuse, at times forcing the speedboat to slow down even when being hotly pursued by the Jap destroyers.

The Mosquitoes often found themselves outgunned even by the Jap troop *dihatsus* that they hunted. And, by comparison, the enemy destroyers were armed with overwhelming firepower, and the newest class could even outrun the worn PTs. Caught in the daylight, the PTs were gone geese for Zeros and Vals, and even during their night patrols, the motorboats were easy victims for Jap floatplanes that spotted their rooster-tail wake in the phosphorescent waters.

Then there was the irregular threat of the Black Cats, Army PBY Catalinas, unable in the pitch blackness of a moonless night to distinguish friend from foe. And whenever the Mosquitoes nosed around the poorly charted shores and lagoons, there were coral reefs lying in wait to snatch and ensnare them.

Sarno and I, digging around, also learned that the Lilliputian flotilla of Task Force #31, comprising a dozen PTs in Squadron 9, was led by Lt. Comdr. Robert G. Kelly. In the predawn of July 3, Squadron 9 had ripped into a skulk of ten Japanese marauders—the cruiser *Yubari* and nine destroyers—creating confusion and fleeing the infuriated response.

We quickly agreed that we would pay a call on Kelly,

whose bantam armada was snuggled in at Lumberi, an islet adjacent to Rendova. This base was named Todd City after Leon E. Todd Jr., the first PT crewman killed in the Rendova action.

Neither Sarno nor I had ever met Kelly before, but we knew who he was. Everybody knew about Kelly, one of the first nationally acclaimed heroes of the war in the Pacific.

Kelly had skippered one of two patrol torpedo boats that had delivered Gen. Douglas MacArthur, his family, and his key staff from Corregidor after the onrushing Japanese had invested the Philippines and locked MacArthur's underarmed, underfed, undermanned defense force into Bataan Peninsula.

When Washington determined that Bataan would have to surrender, plans were hastily drawn at the highest level to extricate General MacArthur, against his wishes, from the doomed last stand at Corregidor.

The American position was hopeless. Three days after wiping out Pearl Harbor, Jap aerial might fell on the U.S. Navy base and Army airfields in Manila Bay and obliterated warships and warplanes alike. Just about all that was left of the American military might were the six PTs of Squadron 3, led by Lt. John D. Bulkeley, a New Jersey descendant of a Navy family going back to the Revolution and as fearless and daring as John Paul Jones. Lt. Bob Kelly, a New Yorker, also an Annapolis Naval Academy grad and likewise daunting, was his executive officer and captain of PT #34.

Squadron 3 was just about the very first of the PT boats to get into action in the Pacific and had already knocked off two enemy ships when called upon to deliver General MacArthur from Corregidor to a safe way station on Mindanao.

The night of March 11, 1943, four Mosquitoes—two had been lost in operations—commanded by Bulkeley, undertook the perilous voyage. Bulkeley's #41 took on General MacArthur, his wife, Jean, and infant son, Arthur. Kelly's #34 carried Rear Admiral Francis W. Rockwell, who ran the Philippine naval base, and several MacArthur advisers. Other chosen aides-de-camp boarded #32 and #35.

The four Mosquitoes, their usually roaring engines muffled, stole out under a gray cloud cover of the murky night, threading through an obstacle course of mines, through a bristling blockade of watchful warships and intervening island sentinels, through violent, sickening seas, whitecaps cresting some twenty feet, through tumultuous Mindoro Strait, aiming for the safe haven 560 miles away on the island of Mindanao.

The tiny fleet was broken up by the rampaging winds and waves, and at one stopover point, PT #32 had to be abandoned and its passengers transferred to Kelly's motorboat, nearly foundering during one lap of the voyage. PT #35 went astray and made port later. Bulkeley and Kelly, PT #41 and PT #34, reached the safe port at Cagayan after three agonizing days and nights. The grateful General MacArthur, beat but not beaten, himself awarded the Silver Star, for gallantry, to Lieutenant Bulkeley and Lieutenant Kelly, and later proclaimed his famous vow:

"I shall return!"

The PT heroes were given a tremendous welcome in the United States, complete with a ticker-tape parade down Fifth Avenue, to honor them and to give a needed boost to America's low state of morale.

(Lieutenant Bulkeley was accorded the Medal of Honor and sent to the European Theater of War for secret, hazardous duty. He rose to the rank of admiral.)

Brevetted to lieutenant commander, Kelly was awarded the Navy Cross, and called to the South Pacific to direct the operations of the expanding PT fleet in the Solomons campaign.

We also had learned that Kelly had been credited with at least two torpedo bull's-eyes against a couple of Jap warships in the Philippine sector of the war, and was running PT operations in and around the New Georgias.

What we did not know at the time—and only later learned—was that it was Kelly and six of his Mosquitoes that had sunk the *McCawley* in Blackett Channel, twenty-four hours after the transport flagship of Admiral Turner had been torpedoed by a Jap destroyer and left dead in the water.

It seems that because of a communications snafu, Kelly was confident the target of his six PTs that black night was the "enemy."

Oh, well, the admiral and the men of the *McCawley* had already been transferred to other vessels, and Admiral Turner, vexed no doubt, took the blooper in stride. Yes, we knew about Kelly, but had never crossed his path in our chase for the stories.

Before sunup, Sarno and I hitched passage on a lighter to Todd City. We found Kelly—lean, lanky, reserved—aboard PT 157, which he had chosen as his flagship for the upcoming night's outing.

He and his crews had lit out every night on patrol since the June 30 invasion of the New Georgias. Each night, the squadron commander designated a different Mosquito to serve as his flagship. Inasmuch as the PTs ran into unfriendly encounters virtually every night, Kelly was sure to be in the middle of the action. That's what he wanted.

Each PT boat boastfully flaunted its name in large letters and figures. PT #157, flagship for that night, defiantly proclaimed itself to be *aces 'n' eights* in large lowercase letters, with the two-pair poker hand showing two aces and two eights and the seven of spades, and embellished just below: the deadman's hand! Aces and eights and the seven of spades were the cards clutched in the mitt of "Wild Bill" Hickok, the notorious Wild West marshal who had been shot in the back and murdered at the table stakes in Deadwood, Dakota Territory.

Sarno and I made our pitch to Lieutenant Commander Kelly.

He politely but firmly turned down our request to take part in the sortie scheduled for that night. "Too dangerous," he said. "You'll only be excess baggage and in the crew's way."

The commander had a point, to be sure. The night before, Jap planes dropped two bombs 200 yards off the starboard beam of PT #157. Two nights earlier, Kelly's PTs had been beaten up badly in a deadly bit of give and take with four of the Imperial Navy's destroyers. The PTs had observed orange shellfire several miles away, had darted to the scene to investigate, and had run into the destroyers engaged in pasting an empty sector of Rendova.

Lieutenant Commander Kelly, in the lead PT, charged his speedboat head-on at the first destroyer, and veering sharply, launched two "fish" at the adversary. The second PT, racing behind in the wake of Kelly's craft, was unable to fire its torpedoes. The third, *aces 'n' eights*, held back momentarily, swung around and away, then, plunging in, hurled two torpedoes at the fast-moving targets, also missing.

The hunters, now fleeing for their lives—no match for the destroyers' guns—didn't have time to assess the damage they had caused, though some of his sailors believed they had possibly made a hit.

We pressed Kelly for more details, and he reluctantly filled us in.

"We found ourselves trapped. Two of the Jap cans, new and fast—faster than our tired engines—had cut across our path and boxed us in. We were caught between the crossfire of the destroyers, which were so eager, they were shooting at each other half of the time.

"We were hemmed in for thirty-five minutes, and hit a few times, but somehow we slipped through them with only a couple of minor casualties."

Two of his speedboats, including #157, had taken hits but already were repaired, their crews ready to go out for more that night.

Despite our pleas, Kelly refused to relent on letting us participate in that night's sally. Instead, he invited us to join him on *aces 'n' eights* that morning.

"It will be," Kelly assured us, "a quiet ride."

Little Jeezus instantly rang an inner warning bell. Nonetheless, I ignored the alarm. Why should I pass up a swanboat sail because he was nervous? Anyhow, what did a DI who couldn't cross a Parris Island stream know about the kaleidoscopic sea around Rendova?

On a nod from Kelly, the skipper of *aces 'n' eights*, Lt. (j.g.) W. F. Liebenow, twenty-three, of Fredericksburg, Virginia, an alumnus of Randolph-Macon, skimmed PT #157 over the surface of the harbor, the three engines purring contentedly.

Only then did Kelly let us in on his "sudden" change of plans. He wanted to take a look-see at two of his PTs, #153 and #158, which a few days earlier, on a moonless night, had run into a coral outcropping off Kundukundu islet, within firing range of the Japanese batteries ensconced on Munda Point.

The Munda Point sentries had spotted the marooned Mosquitoes and had spattered the reefed patrol boats with shot, killing one sailor and wounding several others. The crews had had to jump into the shark-infested water and keep swimming, for hours, until they could be rescued.

Kelly said he hoped there still might be some chance of retrieving the two abandoned craft, and was willing to risk the danger of a probe. He ordered his flagship to run up to within 300 yards of the coral trap and, fortifying himself with a tommy gun, the commander pushed off to the pinned PTs in a skiff manned by two crewmen, Q/M First Class Robert C. Link, twenty-two, of Valdosta, Georgia, and Radioman 2nd Class Sam Koury, twenty-five, of Leesville, Louisiana.

While the skiff was bouncing toward the reef, *aces 'n' eights* scooted back and forth in irregular turns and twists, all eyes aboard anxiously scouring the hostile Munda Point shore, at the same time keeping anxious watch on the three rowers. The skipper had his eyes glued to the binoculars and snapped out his orders sharply, but otherwise kept his cool. Lenny was that kind of a fellow. He could contain himself under the direst conditions.

The men manning the twin .50-caliber Brownings in the turret, and the two .30-caliber Oerlikons on the deck poised at their stations, alert for command to fire. A couple of the crewmen held on to rifles. I held on to my rifle too, but must admit I didn't know what to do with it except hang on.

The attention of all was momentarily interrupted by an outburst of Jap antiaircraft fire at a U.S. fighter patrolling up ahead, so that we were caught short by the abrupt blasts from the Jap shore guns.

The booming shells fell within 200 yards of our PT boat,

and I instinctively hit the deck and hugged it for a few seconds. I quickly realized there was no place to hide and that I should grab a life jacket. But I didn't want to get in the way of the crew, so I stayed put and peered around to see what was going on. I was too intent on fixing the scene in my mind to think about ugly consequences of a direct hit on the PT or of having to leap into tropical waters said to be the playground for crocs, snakes, and sharks.

I looked around for Sarno.

There was the big lug coolly shooting his camera, murmuring "Ver-ry int-ter-rest-ting!"

And out there was Kelly—who had started to climb into one of the forsaken PTs—hopping and skipping over the slippery shoals in an effort to return to the bobbing skiff, as the shells whistled and threw up geysers around him. It looked like a scary reel in the weekly serial films I gawked at in the dime movies when I was a kid. Except it was real, and instead of hollering in excitement along with the audience at the peril confronting the hero of the melodrama, now I looked on in rapt silence. So did the other spectators on #157.

As Kelly pulled himself into the flimsy dinghy, a swell overturned it, and only then did the crew break the tense silence, uttering a collective cry of dismay.

Commander Kelly had picked experienced men to accompany him, and together the three quickly uprighted the skiff, then pulled on the oars as if their lives depended on it through the swash of shellfire, as Skipper Liebenow, outwardly unruffled, directed the flagship as close to the rowers as he dared in the shoals, paying no attention to the shells exploding around us.

We could see Commander Kelly shouting to us through his horn-cupped hands, but not until he was more than halfway back could we hear him.

"Keep the bow to the shore!" he was yelling. "Don't give the bastards a broad target!"

Once the soaked trio was eagerly grasped aboard, PT #157 raced swiftly out of range of the Munda batteries. Kelly, soaked but relaxed, looked around, and noticed Sarno, still snapping away, and me, trying to look nonchalant.

"You guys still here?" Kelly inquired with a grin. "I told you it would be a quiet ride."

Then he added scornfully: "Hell, those bozos couldn't even shoot straight."

I couldn't help but wonder what would have happened if they could shoot straight.

The return to the PT nest was uninterrupted. Sarno and I thanked Commander Kelly, Skipper Liebenow, and the crew, too, for the quiet ride. I expressed aloud my admiration for their skill and discipline under enemy fire, and then to myself added the ultimate words of praise:

"Little Jeezus would approve!"

Did I mention that Lieutenant (j.g.) Liebenow was cool? Here's his log report for July 9, 1943: "Anchored in 15 fathoms PT Base Rendova 0800. Mustered crew at quarters, no absentees. 0852 underway for reef of Kundukundu I. Com MTB Ron NINE aboard. 0926 lying to off PTs 153,158 aground on reef. Com MTB Ron NINE went to beached boats. 0950 Com MTB Ron NINE came aboard with shots from enemy shore battery landing 200 yards short. Underway for PT base Rendova and anchored in 15 fathoms at 1015. Laflin, R.E., TM 2/c, reported aboard for duty. Made daily inspection of magazines and all other inspections required by current security orders. Conditions normal."

I was not aware at the time of my visit that Squadron 9 included PT #109, commanded by Lt. John F. Kennedy, the future president of the United States. Kennedy was audacious, and earned a reputation for pushing his PT just a bit harder on his patrols.

On the night of August 1, a spread of PTs zipped out into Blackett Strait and took a swipe at three Jap destroyers. Liebenow's #157 fired two tubes, missed, and scrammed. Kennedy's #109 fired two more and also missed but did not get away. The forty-five-ton speedboat was literally sliced in two by the prow of the 2,500-ton *Amagiri*. Several crew members died in the collision. Lieutenant Kennedy led survivors, including the several wounded, through a haunting week of swimming from island to island, until found by an Aussie coastwatcher and rescued by Lenny Liebenow's *aces 'n' eights*.

The day after our whiff of sea and woof of shell, I came down with an attack of malaria. I refused to turn into sick bay for treatment, because I knew that all cases of malaria were being immediately evacuated along with the cases of crackup. I argued with Sarno that I had come too far to beat it before reaching Munda, and I dosed myself heavily with Atabrine.

The onset of malaria can be foretold hours, even days before, by a frequent sufferer. It begins with a headache and shooting pains in the neck and back, followed by acute nausea, retching, the runs, and an urgent desire to urinate. The spleen swells and becomes rigid. Chills set in, teeth chattering and bones aching, followed by high fever. A short period of the sweats brings temporary relief, and the victim is left weak and limp but feeling somewhat better. This chain of reactions repeats itself one, two, three times or more, depending on the virulence of the attack. Each attack leaves the victim increasingly enervated.

Through five dismal days and nights, eating little or not at all, I clung to my foxhole, sleeping most of the time. All the while Sarno hovered over me as nurse, companion, and protector.

After one of my bouts with high fever, Sarno commented that I was in the wrong profession. "Should have been a songwriter," he remarked. Puzzled, I asked him to explain.

"During your last delirium, you were singing out song titles, like 'Moon Over Munda,' 'Rain Over Rendova,' 'Come to Kolombangara,' and other silly stuff."

Well, I must admit that some of the endless nights I would try to lull myself to sleep composing Tin Pan Alley titles for the mellifluous name places of the Solomons—Vella Lavella . . . Vanga Vanga . . . Kokenggolo . . . Kukurana . . . Kundukundu . . . Lumbaria . . . Lambete . . . Nusulavata . . . Tambusolo . . .

I had never discussed this count-the-sheep game with Sarno, but in my delirium let the secret out.

When I got to feeling better, I pecked at my keyboard and turned out a few short pieces about some of the unusual individuals I had met.

There was, for instance, Master Technical Sergeant Oscar Niles, "official" safecracker. The Tennessee native had earned many medals since joining up some twenty-four years before, but his high repute came not from the accuracy of his rifle but from the efficacy of his blowtorch. He had forced open more than a hundred strongboxes accidentally locked at Marine quarters or deliberately locked at overrun enemy camps.

Another was Lt. (j.g.) Norman Porter, a graduate of the City College of New York. He wore a Marine uniform and held Navy rank, but was neither. He was a commissioned officer of the Coast and Geodetic Survey, on detached duty with the Marines, and wore both both insignia: eagle, globe, and anchor of the Marine Corps and the triangulation station of the Geodetic Survey.

So what did the guy do? He made maps. Now and then there was a lull for battle, but none for map-making. There are never enough maps of enough places to meet the needs of the Marine forging into strange terrain. Porter was a wanted man.

Then I simply had to write a squib or two about Lt. Harry E. Ralston, twenty-three, of Dallas, the X-X-X man, the camp mail censor. He read some fifty letters a day from Marines to their parents, wives, friends, and girlfriends. He exed out any word, phrase, or sentence that would give the enemy a useful clue about U.S. forces, but the grunts had no clue about what he had rubbed out until they heard from the mystified folks back home.

Although he got no thanks for his diligence, Lieutenant Ralston's extra duty gave him access to the latest scoop and poop, and made him privy to the private lives of the company members. He told me that his own letters had to be checked out by another censor.

I also wrote an item that General Denig had specifically cited as the kind of hometown news he was looking for from his CCs. If the Marine is boxing champ of his battalion, write the story, the general urged. So I wrote a piece about twenty-two-year-old Burrell W. Smith, Iowa's Golden Glove welterweight champ of '42, whom I found throwing leather for the leathernecks. "Smitty," an Oskaloosa policeman, joined up in July and fought in the ring for the Marine boxing team when he wasn't in the line fighting Japs.

It was during this spell of the bug that a mail call brought me an envelope from the United States with newspaper clippings of the story I had dispatched from Pavuvu about the tropical diseases taking down the Raiders. I was feeling too rotten to appreciate the irony.

CHAPTER 12

Munda

On Rendova, the enemy kept bombing away at night. The daylight raids, after the memorable Fourth, were limited to quick in, quick out. But come the darkness, the Mitsubishis and Zeros roared in at full parade, until one night our searchlights caught and trapped them as illuminated targets. After that, the night forays were confined to dashes in and out by the "low-flying Higgins boats," as the Washing Machine Charleys were now derisively referred to on Rendova.

Army's 43rd Infantry Division, which made the incursion onto New Georgia Island, northeast of Munda Point at Zanana Beach, and later took Laiana Beach against fierce opposition, was only two and a half miles from the coveted airfield at Munda Point.

The beachhead was seized only after seven U.S. destroyers hurled hundreds of high-explosive projectiles against the enemy fortifications on Munda. No sooner did the warships end their barrage than 200-plus Allied bombers—virtually every machine that could carry a bomb—followed up the battering from the sea. Then the Marines' Murderers Row unmuzzled its guns and the Army's shorter-range howitzers chimed in to the cannonade chorus for an hour or more.

I saw and heard that day the mightiest outpouring of American firepower in the Solomons since the Marines first hit the beach on Guadalcanal nearly one year earlier. Immediately following the bombardment, Army infantry advanced—exactly 400 yards—in hand-to-hand combat.

We were lambasted from the air every night in the New Georgias, so that a full night's sleep was impossible, but there were short periods when the jungle was quiet. Not a silent quiet, but a stillness that resounded with a cacophony of strange noises: soft squealing of lizards ... gossipy jabber of the mynahs ... raucous screaming of the cockatoos ... mooing of wild cows ... sawing of mosquitoes ... rustling of palms ... plopping of coconuts falling to the ground ... pattering of the rain on the logs over my foxhole ...

I discovered another explanation for the Japs' tenacity in a reconnaissance of the Munda lines with Capt. Bob Blake, twenty-five, of Canton, Ohio, a Notre Dame graduate, commander of the Marine light tank platoon that had spearheaded the 172nd Infantry GIs inching forward on the Laiana beachhead.

We halted before a mound of coral rock and coconut logs, its camouflage of jungle brush and palms torn away where the tanks' armor-piercing shells had busted the thick breastwork of the Jap pillboxes. A sickening stench revealed that the fortification had become a tomb for the gunners in it. The pillbox was a miniature fortress, cunningly blended into the jungle colors and plotted to cover the approach to its adjacent bunkers, many of which were connected to one another by a warren of brush-disguised trenches.

Blake's Raiders had rolled ashore on the jungle-choked beach five days before. They were restrained from action for two days, then called upon to break up the Japanese Maginot Line of pillboxes. The entrenchments were holding up the advance of the Army infantry and could be taken by the GI grunts only at heavy cost in lives.

The platoon of Stuart tanks moved out in two columns, one led by Captain Blake, the other by thirty-eight-year-old Gunnery Sgt. Charles L. Spurlock of Charlotte, West Virginia.

Blake's team included Cpl. Thomas J. Hoban, twenty, of Croton-on-the-Hudson, New York; Pfc. Eugene P. Amurri, twenty, of McClellandtown, Pennsylvania; and Pfc. James Thelford, nineteen, of Oaklyn, New Jersey.

Flanked by foot soldiers, the section rumbled into a riverbed toward the concealed Japanese defenses. Blake related what happened next:

"I spotted a black oblong slot in the brush on the far side of the streambed. That was a pillbox, and we opened up on it.

"Soon we saw another pillbox, and it developed we were in the middle of a pillbox concentration. Keeping formation, we smashed into the whole lot of them, and running into a bivouac area, we showered it with canister shot.

"Heavy machine-gun fire was thrown at us for fifteen minutes before we could find the source of the fire. Their shells rattled off our tank, some fragments penetrating and rattling around inside. We could smell the burnt lead, and the tank walls became scorching hot.

"Then we caught the bubbles of light from the muzzle of a machine gun, and we charged into it, only to discover two tremendous pillboxes confronting us.

"Our bullets had no effect on those little forts, so we battered them with armor-piercing shells and then hurled in high explosive, with excellent results.

"After four hours of continuous battle, we returned to our base, having liquidated eleven pillboxes for sure."

Meanwhile, Gunny Sergeant Spurlock and his column had concentrated on eight bunkers defending an adjacent hill and had wiped them out. Spurlock suffered a broken leg during the melee and had to be evacuated by his crewmen: Pfc. Eugene A. Hall, nineteen, of Arlington, Virginia; Pvt. James E. Golden, twenty, of Chicago; and Pfc. Roy K. Ballou, seventeen, of Omaha, Nebraska.

The next day the captain's tanks again ground along the coast and ran into five more buttressed machine-gun barriers. The Japs lashed back and pinned down the GI infantrymen when the "treadnoughts" became entangled in the tall thick kunai grass.

"We were, frankly, lost," recounted Blake, "and afraid to shoot lest we fire on our own soldiers. That gave the Japs a chance to close in on us, and they pummeled us with everything they had. One dropped an explosive on the lead tank. We got jarred but we were unhurt. We checkerboarded the area with canister shot.

"The Japs respect the tanks, but they're not afraid of

them. We can vouch for that. They went after us with anti-tank guns and explosives, and we had a helluva time of it. We were crippled, but after using up all our ammunition, managed to crawl back to our rear."

The second file of Stuarts, now commanded by Staff Sgt. Douglas Ayres, twenty-three, of Los Angeles, again drove onto the Jap hill bastion.

"We got stuck in a Jap trench for about fifteen minutes, and had a hot time of it," recalled Sergeant Ayres. "But we broke out in the clear and went ahead to hit nine pillboxes."

He and his team—Pfc. Arnold McKenzie, eighteen, of Los Angeles; Pfc. Joseph LoDico Jr., twenty, of Sharon, Massachusetts; Pvt. Noel M. Billups, twenty-one, of Columbus, Ohio—came through roughed up but without serious injury.

The following day—the third—the light Stuarts still capable of operating went into battle as a single force under Captain Blake. The Japs were apparently expecting them to return, and had taken to the trees with flamethrowers, spraying the armored caterpillars with an oily liquid as they trundled by.

"We were in tight spots before, but this was the worst," Captain Blake said. "Imagine how we felt when we saw the Japs in the trees, spraying us with brown liquid from hoses. We knew they were flamethrowers. Luckily, the liquid failed to ignite, and we cut down the Japs before they could get the stuff working."

One Nip sneaked up on a tank commanded by Cpl. John J. Fickett, twenty-four, of Oaklawn, Illinois, and planted a magnetic mine under the nose of the driver. The blast tore through the armor plate and the driver, Private Hall, suffered a severe concussion, yet withdrew his tank to safety. Fickett was wounded by shrapnel.

Shortly after this struggle, a squad of Japs, filtering into the rear, attempted to sneak up through the bush to attack the tank guided by Pfc. Alexander B. Nobile, twenty-one, of Asbury Park, New Jersey.

"We saw those Japs in the nick of time," said Blake. "We took care of them with a burst.

"The fighting lasted thirty minutes, but it felt like ten hours, for we were at it every second of the time."

All the Stuarts made it back, despite the severe pounding they took, and, according to Blake, all but two were ready to return to the action after quick repairs.

Two days later, another newly arrived Marine tank platoon, from the Tenth Defense Battalion, led by 1st Lt. Albert E. Bailey, twenty-three, from Pasadena, California, smashed at the gateway to Munda Hill, overlooking the enemy airfield, in an effort to breach a gap for the tired but willing GIs.

Tanks and troops failed to take a key ridge, which was fortified by a web of camouflaged entrenchments deeply dug into the steep slope of the jungle-choked hill. The Stuarts piled into and crumbled thirteen pillboxes together with their guns and gunners, but the infantry advance was halted halfway, because the tanks couldn't churn farther up the clifflike rise and jungle-covered terrain. The Army soldiers and the Marine tankmen had to take heavy losses for every foot of advance.

Two of the crews had to abandon their crippled machines and were rescued by GI riflemen. It was at the very limit of the day's drive that one tank was set on fire by a magnetic mine dropped on its rear end. The other tanks and a squad of grunts moved quickly to provide cover for the crew.

The tank commander, Corp. Paul Cirtaus, twenty-one, of Houston, Texas, suffered a burned hand. The driver, the radioman-gunner, and the loader—Pfc. Robert L. Wooten, twenty-five, Marshall, Texas; Pfc. Roy L. Hust, nineteen, Magnolia, Arkansas; Pfc. Robert M. Lowe, Kalama, Washington—were jolted but otherwise unhurt. For Lowe, it was his twenty-first birthday and first battle. A fourth tankman, Pfc. Edward Myers, twenty-three, of Eureka, Illinois, tried to tie a pullout cable to the abandoned vehicle but was laid low by enemy fire.

Another Stuart was lost when a burst of Jap bullets shot out the vision slits. Cpl. William Gorforth, twenty-two, from Chicago, and his buddies kept fighting but had to fall back because of sniper infiltration. Our own grenades destroyed the abandoned tanks so that they would not fall into the hands of the enemy. All of Blake's tanks were riddled and pitted by bullets.

Blake's Raiders stayed in battle until every one of their tanks was knocked out of action by enemy grenades, Molotov cocktails, magnetic mines, or flamethrowers. It was impossible to keep the machines in repair and running, because enemy bombs had blown up the spare parts depot.

For days, the Allied beachhead contained so little depth that the line commanders feared that a strong Jap counterattack would drive the Yanks into the water. At night Jap snipers stole down to the beaches, killing and maiming our troops, or crept into the Americans' foxholes along the front, stabbing and slaying. The nights were hideously long for both GIs and Marines.

On the Laiana beachhead everyone was worried that the nonstop barrage of Jap 90mm mortar shells would land on the beachhead where the Yanks were dug in instead of blowing up beyond, into the water. There was also the dread of being killed by the high-angle shells launched from our own mortars, which at times fell short of their enemy targets.

Once, when two projectiles struck the beaches and killed several of our men, it turned out that the shells had been fired by American howitzers. The inexperience of the GIs and the fierceness of the fighting made the jittery soldiers trigger-happy; sometimes they ended up shooting each other in the confusion created by the night-prowling Nips. None dared to leave his foxhole during the night, not even to respond to the urgent demands of diarrhea. You did what you simply had to do in the foxhole.

Some of the Army infantrymen went bananas during the terrible nights. The evacuation vessels, which pulled out of the beachheads each day for field hospitals in the rear bases, were loaded down with "combat fatigue" casualties. In close quarters, under acute conditions, combat fatigue was a contagious infection, like an outbreak of mass hysteria.

As to nervous Nellies with overanxious trigger-fingers, they were not confined to the GIs. The antiaircraft gunners of Army, Navy, and Marines sometimes developed itchy fingers and more than one shot down an Allied plane. Nor were the aviators free of the taint. Some nights, the PT crews swore, their major menace loomed in the sky, when U.S. pilots mistook the Mosquitoes for enemy craft and raked them with machine-gun fire. For their part, the PT boats were sometimes blamed for firing at our own air patrols on moonless nights.

On the Zanana beachhead, the GIs had been having a rough time not only trying to advance but also stopping the Jap banzai counterattacks. Probing that sector for story stuff, I was tipped off that two Marines of the Ninth Defense Special Weapons had slain some 100 Jap raiders attempting to capture the Army's command post the night before, on July 17. The enemy maneuver, if successful, would have seriously endangered the 47th's operation, I was later informed by Marine officers.

I had heard of similar extraordinary feats on other fronts, but all had proved to be exaggerated. In this instance, the exploit was authenticated by 1st Lt. John R. Wismer, twenty-six, of Trenton, Michigan, Marine gun group commander on the Zanana beachhead, who said that intelligence confirmed the extraordinary encounter.

The bloody bodies of some 100 enemy soldiers were found that very morning within an 800-yard sweep of the two machine guns positioned on a ridge overlooking the Army command post and manned by Cpl. John Rothschild and Pvt. Joseph J. Wantuck.

Private Wantuck, in his twenties, from Elmira, New York, was found dead, pierced by two bullets and his chest deeply slashed by a saber.

Corporal Rothschild, thirty, a Wall Street employee from New York City, was still planted at his gun post, but out of his head, screaming epithets at the unseen foe. A Japanese soldier, slain and battered, lay beside him, killed by the Marine in a hand-to-hand struggle. Four more blood-spattered corpses were sprawled around the machine guns.

I tracked down Corporal Rothschild, cut, bruised, still suffering from aftershock, and I patiently pieced together his account of the gory night of horror. With fixed eyes, uttering his words with difficulty, Rothschild recalled the harrowing details:

"My buddy and I are attached to the Marine special weapons unit guarding the beach . . . we're attached to an antiaircraft gun . . . when two volunteers were asked to man the ridge machine guns . . . we decided to take over . . . we knew how to handle those guns, too.

"We were told there were a number of Japs in the area . . . beyond the outpost line of resistance . . . and the two machine guns were placed . . . to block the avenue of approach to the ridge . . . by the infiltrating Japs.

"We took over the guns . . . each of us joining a soldier already there . . . We didn't even introduce ourselves . . . We started digging an emplacement for the light machine guns . . . about ten yards apart . . . It was a full moon . . . almost as clear as daylight.

"About a half hour later the *ping* of Jap machine-gun bullets burst overhead . . . We didn't fire . . . We just ducked and checked our ammo . . . There was no firing unless we could see what we were firing at.

"Maybe it was an hour later . . . maybe it was longer . . . when we observed a column of Japs . . . about thirty of them, I'd judge . . . approaching the trail from the west . . . in suicide fashion . . . in file about five feet apart . . . We could see their bayonets glistening in the moonlight . . . You know . . . your mind turns somersaults when you see a sight like that . . .

"We gave them a burst . . . and the leader went down . . . The others scattered . . .

"After a few minutes . . . the Jap patrol tried it again . . . we opened up again . . . eliminating them . . . until they gave it up . . .

"For the next half hour or so it was quiet . . . You know, that noisy jungle quiet . . . Then another Jap column approached . . . from the same direction . . . We waited until they came close . . . and opened up both guns on them . . .

"Again we eliminated some . . . and dispersed the rest . . .

"The next spell of quiet was broken . . . when a Jap dived

into our emplacement. The doggie stuck by the machine gun and I went for the Jap. I shot him once with my rifle . . . and then beat him over the head with the butt . . . up against the barbed wire . . . Anyhow, he was eliminated. . . .

"Later, a third Jap column tried to sneak up the trail . . . We let them approach to within twenty yards of us . . . then mowed them down. An officer . . . I could see his saber . . . and four men tried to close in on the gun . . . but we eliminated them, all right . . . What Japs were left formed some kind of skirmish line . . . and kept firing away at us . . . trying to filter through and behind us . . .

"But the infantry on the line stopped most of them cold . . . The infantry had gotten into firing on the three patrols . . . after we opened up on the Japs.

"Not until morning did I discover my buddy had been killed . . . He was still by his gun . . .

"I'm not sure what happened to the two soldiers, whether they were killed or evacuated. I don't think I was in condition to remember . . ."

Rothschild's account was the first I had heard that two GIs had participated in the heroic episode. None of my Marine informants had mentioned the presence of the two Army grunts in that night's action. Maybe they didn't know, or simply forgot under the wild circumstances. I tried in vain to determine the identity of the two GIs, and was unable to learn whether or not either had survived.

(Rothschild and, posthumously, Wantuck were later awarded the Navy Cross.)

In the New Georgia Islands campaign, I sent my dispatches, along with Sarno's photos, to Noumea HQ every which way I could find. On July 21 I put a large envelope of stories and four dozen negatives aboard LST # 343. Later that day, a Jap air raid caught me in the buff taking a rare soap-scrub in a clear, fast-running stream. I crouched in the flow seeking cover against the embankment rocks, but the bombs fell far from me. However, LST # 343, filled with wounded, was severely damaged. The casualties, their nerves shattered, rebelled when shifted to a second outbound Green Dragon, yelling about being sent to "another death trap." But the Navy officers and petty officers master-fully calmed down the emotional insurrection and shooed the frightened evacuees onto an alternate relief ship.

Only weeks later did I learn that my envelope of dis-patches and photos had been salvaged from the wrecked LST # 343, and sent on to Noumea. Amazing! Especially since some of the stories I sent by normal channels never got through.

Sarno, on fresh orders, departed for Guadalcanal on July 25, after having taken fifty-five dozen still photos for Intelligence, Ordnance, and for my stories.

"One bit of advice," I urged Sarno on parting. "Don't take so many chances with fate."

Sarno gave me his signature bear hug and responded with his winning smile:

"Ver-ry int-ter-rest-ing!"

The next day, while returning from Rendova to Zanana beachhead on Munda Point, I was horrified to see an Army observation plane, relaying info to the howitzers, shot down in flames. From afar, I had witnessed other American war-planes blown out of the sky, but this disastrous dogfight, so close overhead, made an unforgettable impact on me, and kept recurring in my snatches of sleep that night. For the first time I felt a personal sense of outrage against the Japanese.

The following day, when the Jap line erupted with machine-gun fire, I dived into an Army machine-gun nest on the flank for refuge from the hailstorm, and automatically thrust my-self into the prone position. Through the sights of my rifle I took careful aim at two Japs scrambling from one pill-box to another. To myself I whispered: "Steady . . . aim . . . fire"—or did I hear the command from Little Jeezus?—and fired at the running targets.

I had fired my rifle before in action, but only enfilade, across a staggered line of enemy soldiers charging into our wire fence. This was my first opportunity to shoot at a spe-cific moving target. I let fly two bursts. One of the running figures dropped.

Did I hit the bull's-eye?

Or did I miss?

Did I hit one, or did he throw himself into the brush?

I made a quick judgment call. I had come through boot camp rifle training as a marksman, the lowest passing grade, it is true, but nonetheless as a marksman. So, I reasoned, I must have hit the Jap.

For a moment, the thought made me feel proud of myself. I DID IT!

Then I threw up.

On July 31, only five days before the Army took the Munda airfield, I received radio orders to return to my base in Noumea.

As I was boarding the outgoing LST, a heartwarming incident took place. We were watching our bombers drubbing Munda, when a flight of Zeros zoomed in to intercept our warplanes. Our fighters responded to the challenge, and broke up the attack into a swirling spate of dogfights.

A Marine dive-bomber was fatally hit. The pilot, preparing to abandon, swung his plane over Rendova harbor, and slowly circled the craft to give his rear gunner an easy parachute jump. Even as the pilot did so, six Army Warhawks popped out of the clouds and opened an umbrella over the stricken Dauntless.

As the rear gunner floated down, one of the P-40s followed him down to make certain that no Zero would slip in and machine-gun him, as had been done on past occasions. The Marine pilot, meanwhile, set his controls so that the stricken plane was still gracefully spiraling when he parachuted from it, escorted down by a pirouetting pilot.

A crash boat was already racing to the scene as the dive-bomber plunged into the sea. Only when the speedboat had picked up both gunner and pilot did the Army fliers wheel off to rejoin the fighting over Munda.

Ashore, the servicemen who witnessed the comradely gesture broke into cheers.

So did I.

CHAPTER 13

"St. Louis"

So there I was July 31, 1943, aboard LST # 395, leaving on the same Green Dragon that had deposited me onto Rendova exactly one month earlier. I was not happy having to leave before the Munda airfield was wrapped up—a few days after I departed—but I must admit it was with a feeling of release that I left behind the unceasing rain, unending mud, and the repeated air raids.

The LST pulled off the beach just before dark, and we'd no sooner cleared the harbor than the Washing Machine Charleys showed up for their twilight game of seek-and-hide. The ship's crew immediately jumped to battle stations—a dozen .50-caliber and six 20mm antiaircraft guns—but we passengers were merely onlookers at the evening's contest. From our railside vantage point, we would admire the arching tracers and the flitting fingers of the searchlights weaving shifting patterns, reminiscent of the musical fountain that had danced so gaily at the New York World's Fair.

It was good to have the feel of a hard, smooth deck underfoot instead of prickly coral and clammy mud, and I reveled in the steamy shower before sitting down for dinner, by invitation, at the captain's mess, for my first savory meal since hitting the beach at Rendova. In return, I regaled the table with anecdotal accounts of the battle ashore.

Before I turned in, the skipper asked me what I would like for breakfast. Anything in his larder would be available to my desire. Without a second's thought, I replied, "A rasher of real ham and real eggs!"

The next morning the hot plate burned my eager fingers, the hot food tingled my tongue. I knew that it was gastronomic crime to bolt down so delicious a dish, but I couldn't restrain myself. I asked for, and received, a second helping.

The LSTs were renowned through the New Georgias for their generous hospitality. Just as the Green Dragons opened wide their gigantic jaws to disgorge cargo, so too did they open their galleys and shower stalls to the work gangs, with piping-hot coffee, piping-hot chow, and hot-piped water. If the LSTs had to lay by overnight, the unloading details, who otherwise would have to fend for themselves on the beach in improvised shelters, were invited to a night's rest in the vacant bunks topside.

Commodore of the shallow-draft fleet was a dynamic red-snapper sea dog, Capt. Grayson B. Carter, a big Californian whose hearty voice boomed encouragement throughout the day to the sweating haulers. Sometimes he loudly praised them; sometimes he gently razzed them; but always he spurred them on. And during a raid, he'd move agilely around the flagship cheering his "chicks," the gunners.

Captain Carter, forty-five, a silver-haired Naval Academy graduate from San Diego, had served on the heavy cruiser *Salt Lake City* in the Battle of Cape Esperance. He then was chosen to lead the newly constructed LSTs through sub-harried seas from the East Coast into the Pacific war waters, and he'd been in hot water since. He was in command of a flotilla of fifteen LSTs that poured machines and men onto the invasion shores of the New Georgias.

His original flagship had been plastered by a Betty's bomb with a loss of ten dead and thirty injured. But his chicks had given a good account of themselves, knocking down twenty enemy planes. Even so, the first flagship had to be abandoned. Commodore Carter then raised his ensign over LST #395.

One of the ship's officers confided to me: "The Commodore drives himself with such fury, you'd think he'd drive himself to a frazzle. But instead, he works everybody else to a frazzle."

The skipper of #395, Lt. (j.g.) Bertram W. Robb, twenty-eight, of Detroit, had been seafaring since the age of thirteen, earning a law degree at Wayne University to boot.

After entering the landing beaches and unloading, he turned his LST into a mother ship, dispensing fuel, food, water, to the brood of small craft—PT boats, Higgins boats, ramp boats, tank lighters, and other small fry. Damaged boats were hoisted aboard for fast repairs by the ship's carpenters and machinists.

It was becoming evident even to me at the time that the development and mass production of the LSTs and kindred smaller landing craft were giving the American forces in the Pacific a much-needed more efficient means of getting the big guns, tanks, and personnel from ship to shore.

The Green Dragons, although slower than the destroyer-transports and the converted liners utilized as cargo and troop carriers, delivered larger loads, heavier and more massive machines, and dumped them directly onto the beaches instead of having to transfer personnel and freight via the launches. With their aid, it was possible to off-load men and supplies in a matter of hours instead of days.

The small-fry craft, manned by three or four Navy or Coast Guard seamen, had already established their worthiness to amphibious warfare at Guadalcanal. The little boats were essential for landing troops and matériel from transports and destoyers; for beaching through reef-studded waters even from the LSTs; for setting up communications and supply transmission lines among coastal units and islets. Harassed constantly by Jap strafers, the crewmen—many in their upper teens—manifested pride in their dangerous duties.

As soon as the LSTs were emptied, they were transformed into evacuation vessels, hurrying to pull out at night with the wounded and the dead. A Navy surgeon assisted by a team of corpsmen was attached to each of the vessels. The medics tended the wounded until they could be released to a rear-base hospital. Often surgery had to be carried out even as an aerial attack was in progress.

Emergency scalpel treatment was required for one sick Marine on #193. Pvt. John Edward Maloney, a Philadelphian, came aboard with acute abdominal pains. The ship's surgeon, Lt. Stanley E. Drennan, twenty-six, of Oklahoma

City and Oklahoma University, diagnosed the trouble as appendicitis and operated on Maloney using a dining table in the officers' wardroom. The eighty-minute procedure was successful.

I enjoyed the comforts aboard LST #395 for forty-eight hours, then disembarked at Koli Point, Guadalcanal. Returning to The Island was a visual jolt; an amazing change had taken place since I had last reported from The Island seven months earlier.

The once turbulent island that had seethed with fire and smoke was now smart and neat, like a regulated military base in the States.

The main highways, once furrowed through the mud and coral only yards behind the advancing grunts, were now second-class roads reminiscent of rural Maryland. Drainage canals paralleled coastal Highway 26—equivalent to U.S. 1—like the grooves of a bowling alley.

Once a vehicle-jostling, body-punishing ride requiring the entire day, we jeeped from Koli Point to Kokumbona, a distance of forty miles, in an hour and a half.

Koli Point is the beach where, in an effort to break the Marines' hold on Henderson airfield, the Japs landed behind the Marines early in the battle for Guadalcanal. Kokumbona is the village where the Japs made their last stand. Highway 26 connects the two milestones.

It was a scenic route by August '43, even though blackened and blasted trees gave testament to battle, even though four bombed and stranded enemy transports still bared their rusted hulks to the tides. And here and there the ugly, crushed remains of pillboxes and gun mounts caught my eyes.

The wreckage seemed out of place among the military-trim depots, among the geometric fighter and bomber strips, among the long straight lines of telephone poles and neatly printed road signs.

The coconut groves and the fields and the beaches through which Highway 26 winds had been swept of debris. Permanent bridges had replaced the pontoon spans. The bridge across the Lumba had been built of solid mahogany, they said, worth a quarter of a million dollars. Ain't that som'pin?

Where once strict blackout reigned from sunset to dawn, lights glared brazenly and nightlife—outdoor movies, band concerts, and amateur shows—invaded the dark.

Guadalcanal had doffed its filthy mud-soaked jungle clothes, taken a hot soapy bath, and donned fresh gray-green herringbone twill uniforms. The Island had assumed the languorous lifestyle of a rest-and-recreation center to the rear of the action.

I was barracked at the new base at Camp St. Louis, tucked in a hollow among the wrinkled mountains, named after a nearby mission.

For Marines passing through the Solomons, all roads led to Camp St. Louis. Everybody stopped there for a few days or weeks: replacements bound for the battle zone; military transients heading north to Guadalcanal, the Russells, or the New Georgias, south to New Zealand, west to Australia, east to the Fijis, Samoas, Hawaii, and the States.

Transient camps of all three services had notoriously poor reputations for accommodations and food. St. Louis was no worse than the average, but it was bigger than most, so that the chow line was longer, red tape more snafued, patience shorter, griping louder.

The replacements were anxious to join a permanent outfit and get into battle; the veterans were anxious to get away. Except for camp policing and ship unloading parties, there was little work for the hundreds of men awaiting transfer, so time hung heavy, and esprit, the backbone of Marines in action, ebbed to a low.

While waiting for transport to Noumea, I began visiting the Raider battalions, recuperating at St. Louis, which had made strikes into Mbaeroko, Viru, Tiri, and Rice Anchorage in the New Georgias while I was covering the Rendova campaign. I found much to write about and send back to HQ. Here's a sampling of the dispatches I sent:

"BRING 'EM BACK!"

The platoon leader called for six volunteers. His instructions were brief. They were to penetrate the Jap field of fire, find the wounded, and bring 'em back.

Any questions?

No questions.

The six had started out on their mission, when word flashed down the line that the platoon was ordered to retire to a more defendable position. The platoon—according to the drawback command—was in danger of being trapped. No one said it out loud, but everyone understood that the casualties out there in no-man's-land would have to be left as they were until the withdrawal had been effected.

Reluctantly, the lieutenant recalled his volunteers, but three had already disappeared into heavily wooded marshland.

The trio—Pfc. Warren M. Lambuth, of Pueblo, Colo.; Pvt. John J. Vannatter, of Flint, Mich.; and Pvt. Gordon E. Yancey, of Paducah, Ky.—were buddies, platoonmates from way back. They'd trekked in the four-day Raiders' march from Segi Point to Viru Harbor to surprise the enemy from the rear. They'd fought together at Enoghae. Now they were confronting the Jap pillboxes at Mbaeroko.

The platoon had already crossed the big swamp and was approaching the edge of a thicket, when a sudden outpour of machine-gun fire stopped the outfit in its tracks. Not only was the platoon pinned down, but soon the Raiders were fighting desperately to prevent the enemy from enveloping their right flank.

The skirmish continued into dusk, with the Marines unable to dislodge the cunningly entrenched foe. It was at this point that volunteers were bidden to bring in the wounded platoon members lying out there in the no-man's-land separating the Yanks and the Japs.

The three leathernecks, unhearing or ignoring the callback, slowly creeping out, spotted a fallen comrade. As they crawled forward more quickly, a bullet drilled through Lambuth's helmet, in from the back of it, out through the right side of it, grazing his scalp.

"The bullet rang like Major Bowe's gong," Lambuth told me later. "I lay there, half-dazed, half—scared to death. I played possum so that the sniper wouldn't fire at me again."

Yancey was not so lucky. A bullet slammed into his arm, leaving the limb paralyzed, but he urged his pals to go ahead. "I can get back alone," Yancey whispered. He did, too, and discovered he had escaped death by a freak. The slug had pierced his shoulder and passed through his chest without touching his heart or lungs.

"How about you?" asked Vannatter of Lambuth.

"Okay, I think," the latter responded.

"Good," said Vannatter. "Here goes!" And heaving a primed grenade that exploded ahead of him, he plunged forward, Lambuth right behind. They got within six feet of a prostrate figure, and recognized their friend, Pfc. Sidney Davis, of Franklin, N.J., who had been severely wounded.

"Christ!" cried the stricken Marine. "Get down and get out of here! You can't get me out of this!" As if to underscore the warning, a Jap machine gun fired furiously over their heads.

The two rescuers knew what they had to do. They had been trained to deal with such a predicament. One feinted and drew fire from the machine gunner, the other detected the muzzle blast and silenced it with his tommy gun. Not always so easily executed, but this time the tactic worked.

"What say, pal, can you crawl?" Vannatter asked. Davis nodded, and painfully pulled himself forward, dragging his ruptured leg. The other two then laid themselves down along each side of their friend, eyes and guns alert. A few inching yards forward and they came upon another bleeding Marine, moaning in agony from a mangled foot.

"For God's sake," he cried out. "Don't leave me here!"

Lambuth and Vannatter exchanged glances. What to do? They both felt instinctively their first allegiance was to their platoonmate. "We'll be back for you," they tried to reassure the other wounded youth. The two buddies then tugged Davis some 150 feet and rested him behind a sheltering tree trunk, where he would be shielded from snipers.

Vannatter then hurried off to bring assistance, and Lambuth slipped back into the killing ground to the help-less leatherneck. Throwing the tommy gun onto his shoulder, Lambuth raised the stricken youth, who screamed from pain. A hail of Jap bullets tried to shut him up. Lambuth, not much bigger than his burden, staggered on for about twenty-five feet before tripping over a clump and tumbling on to the treacherous ground.

Exhausted, Lambuth fell prone beside the groaning gyrene, praying that Vannatter would quickly return. Vannatter didn't get back, but he sent help. Another platoon member, Pfc. Calvin D. Fields, 18, of Louisville, Ky., crept up, followed by Pharmacist's Mate (3/c) Stonewall E. Sparlin, 22, of Bemidji, Minn, who injected the sniper's victim with a pain-easing shot of morphine. Marine and medical aide then improvised a litter out of a poncho and two sturdy branches, and carried the unknown Raider away. Private Davis, too, was later found and rescued.

HOW TO GET LOST AND FOUND IN JUNGLE

It took me two days to pull together the harrowing experience of Pvt. Thomas "Jinx" Powers, a 23-year-old from West Springfield, Mass., lost for four days in the jungle.

Powers had been last seen staggering off to get aid for a wounded companion. Search parties found the comrade, but not Tommy. He was given up for dead, somewhere in the jungle morass.

Tommy was not dead; he was lost, but he didn't panic. He was a jungle-tried, battle-tried vet of Tulagi and Guadalcanal. His platoon had fought its way out of ambush in that all-night battle on Bloody Ridge. His Raider unit was nearing Tiri in northeastern New Georgia Island when a bullet tore his rifle from his hands and three other bullets hit his leg.

Simultaneously, Pvt. John W. Conley, 21, of Brooklyn,

N.Y., was cut down by enemy fire. The two Raiders gave
each other morphine shots to ease the pain. Then Powers
dragged Conley, who couldn't move by himself, ten yards
over a rise and out of the line of fire. Moments later, Pfc.
Clarence J. Mobely, 19, of Miami, Fla., slipped over to
them and offered to stick by Conley while Powers,
wounded but ambulatory, squirmed back for help.

"The trail back to the battalion command post was only
about a hundred yards, and despite my wounds, I thought
I could make it," Powers told me.

"I left behind my cartridge belt, canteen, compass, and
knife, figuring I'd be back in a few minutes. Luckily, I had
borrowed a pistol and six-round clip, and had a bar of
chocolate and packet of K rations tucked away inside my
dungarees jacket.

"I must have been dizzy from the loss of blood and the
morphine, because when night came—I'd left the others
about 3:30—I still hadn't found the trail. I slept in the
roots of a banyan tree that night, but not until the next
morning when I climbed a hill and could see nothing but
jungle did I realize I was lost.

"Well, I figured the best thing I could do was try to find
the shoreline. I planned to eat one square of chocolate a
day. There was six in the bar, you know. For water I had
the swamp. My leg was stiff, but I could walk on it."

His first day alone in the jungle, Tommy came across
two dead Marines, their lacerated corpses stripped. He
peered at them trying to recognize them, and heaved at
the horrible sight. He had to pull himself away. Later on
he stumbled upon six dead Japs, but had no reaction. That
night he again hid himself in the cleft of a tree trunk, feeling secure until a Jap patrol set up camp for the night
nearby. It was a hot, humid night, but he shivered through
it for fear of being discovered.

The second day of wandering, Tommy almost floun-
dered into an enemy bivouac, retreating after hearing the
rattle of mess gear. The third day Tommy became aware
he had been walking in circles when he came across the

dead Japs again. Later that day he startled a Jap sentry, shot him point-blank, and dived back into the jungle. He got away.

"I tried twice to get up a hill to look for the shore, but each time I was driven off by machine-gun fire," Tommy recalled.

He was awakened the next dawn by the whistles and explosions of mortar shells. He had no idea which side was firing. Then he heard the bursts of machine guns virtually on both sides of him. He lay still and heard the movement of men shuffling through the brush.

"I waited, pistol cocked," said Tommy. "They didn't see me, and I let them pass. Then I heard a voice . . . the voice of Mobely. I yelled out: 'Don't shoot! I'm a Marine!' " The buddies hugged each other.

Powers was convalescing in a field hospital when I chatted with him. I meant to ask him why he was nicknamed "Jinx," but I forgot.

CAIN'S SWORD

Several Raiders urged me to write a story about Cpl. William F. Cain Jr. The 22-year-old from San Francisco had been shunted to quartermaster service and wanted to get into battle action.

"I'd just as soon be in the WACs for all the fighting I'll get," the clerical aide pleaded with the CO of the crack Raider battalion. The Old Man liked the mettle of the youth and had him transferred to his outfit. Cain trained hard and worked hard and quickly proved to be an outstanding squad leader.

Came the invasion into New Georgia Island, with the battalion as spearhead into the northeast sector. The Raiders worked their way into the Tiri jungle, Cain's squad leading, Cain out front, and suddenly they were faced by five Jap soldiers, one an officer. Without a flicker of hesitation, Cain fired fifteen rounds from his carbine and killed them all before they could react. For this feat Cain was awarded the sword of the officer.

In five days of battle, Cain took his unit into four fire-fights, wiping out an enemy machine-gun nest. At Enoghae Point, heavy resistance was met, and the Marine advance was balked.

Cain and his men were assigned to destroy the enemy's focal gun emplacement. They sized up the situation and charged from the flank . . . only to be swept by a hitherto silent machine gun. Cain was killed. Within 24 hours, Cain was avenged when both machine-gun nests were destroyed by fellow Raiders.

The company recovered Cain's sword and carried it into battle as an inspiration. The Marines planned to send Cain's sword home to his folks as a symbol of his courage.

HOW TO TELL IF THEY'RE DEAD

A couple of Raiders took the oath in telling me of their encounter with three dead Japs. The battle of Enoghae was under way, and Sgt. Jack F. Tracy's unit was standing by for an expected counterattack, while two of his men were flushing out the snipers.

Pfc. Howard R. Schultz, 20, of Norristown, Pa., and Pfc. Harold H. Loeffel, 22, of North Bergen, N.J., were suspiciously poking into the brush when they spotted three Japanese soldiers huddled inert in the mud. They approached cautiously.

"Bet you a Coke they're not all dead," wagered Loeffel.

"It's a bet," assented Schultz.

Sneaking up to the nearest body, Loeffel gave it a sharp kick and jumped back, set to shoot. The body didn't react. Loeffel then kicked the second figure. Again no reaction. When Schultz toed the third in the ribs, the corpse bobbed up and raised his arm to throw a grenade. The grenade, which failed to detonate, was still in the Jap's hand when the two Marines certified his death with blasts from their ready weapons.

Loeffel won the bet, but he had to wait a long time to collect it.

THIS CIG LIGHTER WORKED

Wherever the Marines fought there was always one particular place that was so bloody it was spontaneously labeled "Suicide Beach," "Suicide Point," or "Suicide Hill," etc. In the jungle of Mbaeroko it was Suicide Ridge where the Raiders underwent a brutal day of fighting and a terrible night of suffering.

"The fighting was so intense and furious," related the leader of a first-aid unit, Pharmacist's Mate First Class Stanley E. Thompson, 25, of Esparte, Calif, "that we ran out of bandages and dressing. So we ripped up undershirts and jacket sleeves and dungaree legs, and used them to cover the wounds.

"For hours there'd been no water, and when night fell, there was still no water for the wounded and able-bodied alike.

"Those who could sucked water out of the jungle vines. Others scooped out holes on the beach and drank the vile seawater that seeped in. It took a cast-iron stomach to hold the stuff down.".

There was no way to evacuate the wounded that night, so they lay out there in the night chill and the jungle terror side by side with the dead. For fear of a Jap counterattack, even the wounded who could move at all were brought into the line to fill the gaps left by their slain compatriots.

Pharmacist's Mate Third Class Woodrow Thrapp, 31, of Nevada, Mo., took over the account:

"We collected the ponchos from the dead and ablebodied, converted them into stretchers and blankets for the wounded. Some of us crept into the dark night jungle and, relying on the sense of touch, administered morphine, blood plasma, and sulfa drugs.

"Three of the boys were badly hurt, needed urgent attention. So we treated them by the hand-cupped flame of a cigarette lighter."

The night chill was capped by a predawn rain, when litter bearers arrived with water and medical supplies. Dawn also brought relief.

REUNION AMID CARNAGE

Sometimes, not often, something pleasant takes place in the carnage. It happened on Vangunu, one of the New Georgia Islands. Raymond Lajoie, 25, had been called up with the Maine National Guard. A year later, brother O'Neil, three years younger, joined the Marines.

Fighting side by side, the leathernecks and GIs moved forward seven miles and then ran into blistering fire from cleverly placed and camouflaged machine guns. At a riverbank, the crossing was made at heavy cost.

When the battle was ended, Cpl. O'Neil felt a tap on his shoulder. He turned to face Cpl. Lawrence Harvey, a school chum back in Augusta. The latter revealed that Sgt. Ray Lajoie was somewhere around with his Army unit. O'Neil managed to locate his brother for a brief but "wonderful" reunion.

"THE LEAST WE COULD DO"

As told by 1st Sgt. Herbert N. Rapson, 25, of Lynn, Mass., the Raiders left two crude graves behind on Vangunu: The Marines had to ford a river in the Vangunu fighting, but only one company made it through the heavy machine-gun fire. Pfc. Frank T. Kelley, 21, of Pittsburgh, Pa., a squad leader, "and a good one," tried to get around the enemy flank with two of his men. The three shoved out, but only Kelley got through, with his tommy gun blazing.

The Raiders tried to silence the Jap machine guns with rifle grenades but couldn't get the range. The sergeant continued:

"Then from the other side of the river we heard the voice of Pvt. Ray Costello, who had been hit in our first attempt to cross, yelling directions at us, even though he was lying only 15 feet from the Jap machine guns, giving away his own position. We fired the grenades, but they failed to explode. If we had hit the gunners, we probably would have killed Costello too, and he must have known it when he called out to us.

"We lost Costello. Kelley was still alive when recovered by our corpsman, but he was picked off by a sniper as he was being carried back to our line."

The corpsman was Hospital Apprentice First Class Leonard J. Pelton, 19, of Tacoma, Wash. Costello was found with his tommy gun clenched in his fingers, the 50-round magazine empty, and two dead Japs near him. Kelley and Pfc. Ray F. Costello, 18, of Morse, Ill., were buried where they died, their graves marked with bamboo crosses.

"It was the least we could do," the sergeant said.

HELP PDQ FOR TRAPPED PBYs

At Rice Anchorage, PBY Catalina bombers had to be called in to take out the casualties. Three of the huge Navy flying boats had landed in a lagoon, but were kept some 40 feet from shore by outcroppings of coral. The wounded had to be rowed to the seaplanes in small rubber boats carrying two wounded at a time.

The unexpected delay compelled the hovering fighter escort to withdraw for lack of fuel. No sooner did the Grummans fly away than two Nipponese "ducks" raced over the lagoon, strafing the PBYs. The Catalinas couldn't take off but roared around the surface of the lagoon desperately firing back at the enemy floatplanes.

Word of the seaplane duels reached the battalion in the jungle, and scores of enraged Raiders rushed to the shore, putting up a barrage of fire from their hand weapons and from a couple of newly captured machine guns. One U.S. pilot was hit by the Japs, but the three hospital PBYs got away with their wounded passengers.

TOMMY THE PIRATE

Lt. Tommy Pollard could always be counted upon when special attention was needed for a sudden problem. So when the drinking water problem became acute, the 21-year-old platoon leader was ordered to break through or sneak around the enemy position at Enoghae to see if water was to be found out there. Tommy and his detail infiltrated through the Jap line but failed to find water. He did find sake, and that helped for a little while to slake the thirst, until water could be obtained.

When machine guns pinned down the Raider advance, Tommy was given the word to take a few men and do something about it. His waist bared to the rain, his head wrapped in a blue bandanna, his camouflage jungle "zoot suit" spattered with mud, he "looked like a bloody pirate."

Tommy and five volunteers attacked, and two of his men went down. A machine-gun bullet tore the carbine from the lieutenant's mitts and bowled him over by the force of the blow.

Then, according to Tommy's company commander, himself a jungle combat vet, "occurred one of the most remarkable things I've ever seen.

"Tommy fell on his back and, without a break in the movement, rolled over the body of one of the dead Marines, grabbed up the dead man's BAR (Browning automatic rifle), rolled onto his feet like a football player and, spitting lead, covered the 25 feet between himself and the machine gun in a single lunge.

"It was all over in a matter of seconds.

"Tommy took the gun over the bodies of seven Japs."

I took time out to pay a visit to Noumea, a long way from Camp St. Louis, and saw that the Paree of the Pacific had swelled in importance. Our military engineers had broken the logjam of cargo vessels in Noumea's spacious harbor by rapid construction of landing and unloading facilities. Noumea was by then more than the titular headquarters for ComSoPac (Commander South Pacific); it was a tremendous arsenal, depot of supplies, and troop reservoir.

Just as Camp St. Louis had become the crossroads for all Marines moving through, so Noumea had become the hub of ship activity in the South Pacific.

Military brass hats and civilian bigwigs could hardly sidestep Noumea in their hop-skip-jump quick-see to the "lines." Arrangements for the VIPs were made in a degree and style proportionate to the dignitary's rank or position.

Most military visitors were whisked in and out of the battle areas, being there just long enough—according to the wiseacres—to become technically entitled to add another campaign ribbon and battle star to their dazzling chest collections. For civil personages, the bumblebee itinerary guaranteed a half column of newspaper print.

The tours of inspection by the VIPs were inspirations neither to the command nor to the rank and file, for each visit involved a lot headaches in the way of preparation, not only in the matter of safety but—war or no war—in the matter of personal comfort expected by some of the VIPs.

The undercurrent of resentment against important but not-really-welcome visitors flared into an underground outpouring of wrath when Eleanor Roosevelt, wife of the president, made her memorable goodwill tour in the late summer of 1943.

Not that she was to blame. Circumstances combined to make her the main target of cloud-darkening resentment. The First Lady, I believe, never realized that the goodwill she engendered in New Zealand and Australia was more than matched by the ill will she created among the Marines.

In the Marine Corps, Mrs. Roosevelt already had been bad-mouthed long before the inspection tour. The Marines had a lingering grudge against the First Lady, a grudge based on a strong, recurrent belief that she had slandered the Marine Corps. The First Lady, it was alleged, had stated that the Marines fighting in the Pacific should be interned and isolated on the West Coast for six months before being allowed to associate again with decent American womanhood.

I first heard of the First Lady's reputed remark on Guadalcanal but thought nothing of it, since the individual who made it was a loudmouth who hated all the Roosevelts because they were "nigger lovers" and the First Lady especially so.

I heard the charge repeated, in a slightly different form, in the chow line of the Third Raiders on Pavuvu. I questioned the youth who casually passed on the allegation. He first maintained he had read it in a newspaper, but then admitted he had picked up the story from another Marine in another company, but couldn't remember who or where. I chased the widespread rumor all over Pavuvu but failed to find a single individual who would demonstrate to my satisfaction that he was not shooting his mouth off with the nasty piece of scuttlebutt.

Again and again the allegation kept popping up, like mushrooms in the jungle, but not once could I find confirmation. I did trace the rumor back to 1940, to the Marines stationed at Guantánamo. Several of the old-timers I nailed remembered first hearing the slander there, where it was prevalent at that time.

In Cuba, the accusation was somewhat different. Mrs. Roosevelt, it was claimed, had called for internment of Marines who had served in banana republics of Latin America.

I was convinced the charge was malicious hearsay without substance, but the vicious tale was repeated in the Corps as if it were an unassailable fact.

The First Lady had become the Marines Corps's bête noire.

"Why would she say such an awful thing?" I asked around. And always the same answer: "Well, wasn't she responsible for letting the niggers into the Navy and into the Marines?"

Until World War II, the Navy and Marine Corps had barred U.S. blacks from their branches of the U.S. military service, although the Navy accepted some blacks as stewards.

When President Roosevelt ended the ban in mid-1941, the angry reaction of the old-boy cadre of senior officers and noncoms was heaped on the First Lady, because, they charged, she had persuaded the president to do it.

Mrs. Roosevelt's Pacific tour of inspection, intended as a morale builder, also became a pet peeve of the Army, despite her graciousness and sincerity.

Here the arguments were that her visit consumed fuel at a time when the gas shortage was being blamed for the slow progress in the field; and that her comings and goings necessitated extraspecial otherwise unnecessary details of troops to provide for her safety. For example, it was averred that when the First Lady arrived in New Caledonia, her plane landed at Tontouta Airport, forty-five miles from Noumea. Every few yards of the coastal highway from the airport to Paree an armed GI had to stand guard ... for hours ... in the rain. Or so it was said and believed.

As soon as word filtered out that Mrs. Roosevelt planned to visit such and such a camp or hospital, the CO immediately ordered a frenzied flurry of cleanup. Nor did the troops feel especially gratified with the holiday menus served when the First Lady showed up. It was hardly worth the trouble, they bitched, and anyhow the special chow was giving her a distorted view of camp food.

The sad truth is that Eleanor Roosevelt made few friends among the troops, and these were the officers and men who had had the opportunity to witness at close hand her acts of kindness.

She made a friend for life of CC Sgt. Al Lewis, my pal of happy newspaper days and unhappy boot camp days. When the First Lady appeared at a Marine bivouac in Melbourne, Sergeant Lewis—as was his ingenuous way—approached her, introduced himself, and asked for a favor. Would she, on returning to Washington, get in touch with his girlfriend there and ask her why she had not written him?

Mrs. Roosevelt did—as all of America read in the papers—but the girl didn't.

In contrast to the First Lady, President Roosevelt retained a high degree of popularity among the men in all the services, as far as I could determine. Although not completely forgiven by the Navy and Marine traditionalists for insisting that black Americans be given equal access and opportunity in both branches, his edict was looked upon as a matter of wartime exigency—and a natural willingness to lend his ear to what were, you know, his spouse's ideas.

After all, ran their reasoning, Franklin Delano Roosevelt had always been a Navy booster, and as Secretary of the Navy, an advocate of Big Navy; and since by law the Marine Corps constituted 20 percent of Navy personnel strength, the stronger the Navy, the stronger the Marine Corps. Who could argue with that rationalization? And if one could, who in the Marines would listen and be swayed?

By that time, that is, after the uncertain battle for Guadalcanal had been won, after the rampaging Japs had been stopped in the Pacific, even his loudest critics in the military—and in the Marines—were willing to admit that the president was running a winning war out there. And nothing mattered more than winning it!

I boarded the Liberty ship *Crater* bound for Australia August 4. My orders had been changed. I was ordered to join the First Marine Division, which had stopped and turned back the Japanese juggernaut on Guadalcanal, and which was recuperating and reorganizing in Australia for its next mission.

CHAPTER 14

Melbourne

I got away from New Caledonia on September 9 and with three stripes, holding highest rank among them, took charge of twenty-five Marines boarding LST # 170, fresh from the States and manned by a Coast Guard crew. This voyage was scheduled to carry personnel, not tanks, to Australia.

The Coast Guardsmen went out of their way to be nice to us Marines, especially in indulging us with flavorsome food. All that was asked of us in return was to keep our own compartment clean and to help man some of their guns, which we did with alacrity.

The congeniality between our two groups was typical of the friendly relationship between the two adjuncts of the Navy. A strong feeling of empathy draws the two together. Both organizations are small, possess a high esprit de corps, and feel at times that the parent Navy treats them like stepsons in a marriage of convenience.

Both supplements to the Navy, and the men in them, smart under their dependence on the "whims," they contend, of the Navy's high command. The Coast Guard in peacetime is an independent service, tucked into the Department of the Treasury, and its members never missed an opportunity to tell anyone who would listen that they were in the Navy only for the duration of the war. The Marines, of course, had no such fallback position, but argued just as passionately that the Navy's main reason for existence was to carry the Marines to amphibious invasions.

At Guadalcanal, Tulagi, Gavutu, the landings were made in Higgins boats manned chiefly by the Guardsmen, a rough and dangerous task that endeared them to the Marines. In turn, after seeing the Marines fight the Japs, the Guardsmen forgave the leathernecks their "big talk." It was a case of mutual admiration.

A similar feeling of reciprocal respect was bonded in the battle zones between the Marines and the Seabees, who built the essential airfields, bridges, and roads that permitted the Marines to advance. The Navy construction battalions often worked side by side with the Marine pioneer and engineer battalions. Under that arrangement, the Seabees could, and did, wear the Marine uniform, with their own distinctive markings.

There was a spirited rivalry between the Seabees and the Marines. The former would tell one and all it was the Seabees who were first to land, not the Marines. And in one section of the New Georgias, at least, the Seabees indeed were there first. The airfield building specialists, through a not uncommon mix-up of schedules, had come ashore in the belief that the Marines had already landed and cleared out the enemy. The Seabees razzed the Marines for their late arrival but shivered in their wet boots thinking what might have happened if the Japs had been there to greet them.

A favorite gag among the Seabees is the one in which a Marine commander pleads with the Seabee commander to cut out the business of destroying Jap pillboxes with Marine bulldozers. It was taking money out of the Marines' bank!

The undercurrent of irritation between the Marines and the Navy has a long history, but ask any leatherneck whether he'd rather fight under the Navy or under the Army, and the reply will be an unequivocal vote in favor of the Navy. Remember, at the time, the Marine Corps had been griping about the Navy for almost 170 years.

Even from the sea, Australia radiates the impression of a vast continent. Five days out of Noumea, we sighted through the dawn haze a mountainous rock island; then we passed through the Great Barrier Reef and sighted sawtooth mountains, peaks vying with one another for the sky. Our ship sailed into a huge bay and up a river whose shores reminded me of the New Jersey flats. We docked at Pinkenba, nine miles below Brisbane.

We were given liberty that first night, so we dug deep into our seabags for the most presentable uniforms, and likewise retrieved stowed funds or borrowed what we could. We took the tram to Brisbane with nary a care that we hardly looked like the spit-and-shine Marines required by the regulations.

Ah, well, truth is we didn't care about our appearance. It was a good feeling to be riding on a streetcar again, even if it did remind us of the Toonerville trolley. It was a cheery feeling, too, to be free to whistle at the girls and see them smile back. It was a comfortable feeling to amble around the crowded streets, to shop at the store windows, to mingle with the Aussies stepping briskly on their errands or simply sauntering along.

We packed the food shops. Most of the Marines in my group ordered milk by the bottle or ice cream by the quart. But desirous as I was for both, I passed them by for a basket of fresh, big strawberries. I must have looked silly walking down Brisbane's streets with a box of berries under my arm, nibbling every step or two. But those strawberries represented to me all the comforts and luxury I had missed during the months in the jungles.

Next day, we Marines were transferred to Camp Doomben, a racetrack that served as the Army's transient center. There were only a small number of Marines in Brisbane at that time, inasmuch as the First Marine Division, which had quartered there after pulling out of Guadalcanal, had found the cantonment uncomfortable and had transferred to a more congenial bivouac in Melbourne.

Doomben was more developed than most transient camps; however, for those of us who had served for months in the tropical belt, the chilly climate proved to be uncomfortably raw and we covered ourselves at night with all the blankets we could drum up. But at least it was dry.

Truth is, we Marines were none too happy to find ourselves in an Army camp, for we had been subtly infused with the Marine tradition that considers the Army, except for some units, inferior to the leathernecks as fighting men. In part, that attitude stemmed from the belief that volunteers, who made up the bulk of the Marine Corps, were better fighting men than draftees, who made up the bulk of the Army. In part, the attitude stemmed from the belief that the Marines had to undergo more rigorous training and preparation for warfare.

On Guadalcanal, this posture of superiority had been fed by circumstances. Although most of the Marines who landed on The Island were not fully trained or quite ready to undertake the invasion, the National Guard troops who succeeded them there were not at all trained or ready for jungle combat. Marines snidely repeated stories of the GIs leaving the lines to go to chow and returning to find the Japs manning their guns; of the dogfaces who landed on Guadalcanal with fixed bayonets, long after the leathernecks had mopped up the area. Many a Marine felt that the reason for their long weeks and months on the front was the Army's inability to take their places.

The scuttlebutt had it that the 164th Army Regiment, comprising the Dakota National Guard, whose fighting later won the praise even of the Marines, had petitioned the president to have its name changed to the 164th Marines.

Fuel was added to the smoldering antagonism between the two services on the New Georgia Islands, where the Marines and soldiers rubbed shoulders against the enemy.

Intertwined, there lingered the Marine Corps's feud with General MacArthur, who in the affections of the leathernecks stood only one rung higher than the bottom one reserved for the First Lady.

At that time, General MacArthur was regarded by the Australians as the savior of their country, and in the United States, still thrilling with the saga of his escape from Corregidor, as a hero. But in the Marine Corps, MacArthur was regarded as an arrogant SOB who failed to show proper respect to the leathernecks in his domain.

So it was, in the early, fateful days on Guadalcanal, when the Marines had little or no air support, that they blamed MacArthur. Guadalcanal veterans will tell you that MacArthur had plenty of planes at Port Moresby but that he refused to let them go. The Marines had the facts all screwed up, but the facts had no impact on their opinion.

Tales, mean tales, filtered back from the Marines who'd escaped from Bataan and Corregidor that General Mac-Arthur had not given appropriate credit to the leathernecks of the 24th Regiment trapped there with the Army. To the contrary, it was charged, the general hogged all of the credit for his soldiers.

It was evident to me that in Australia, where they were under the overall command of General MacArthur instead of Admiral Halsey, the Marine officers were uneasy. They were suspicious of him and did not trust him.

I soon learned that the Navy didn't like MacArthur either, in part because of the rivalry between the Navy and Army over running operations in the Pacific.

Nor did the GIs love their five-star commander. They, too, felt that he was imperious, far removed, and out of touch with the ranks. General MacArthur was not a popular figure, not an idolized leader like General "Ike" Eisenhower.

Well, I must confess that my party of Marines were so well treated by the Army at Camp Doomben, we were embarrassed. We were outfitted with new Army uniforms, on which we sewed our Marine insignia and stripes. We were provided with modest funds, to be deducted eventually from our accumulated pay, but a generous act nonetheless, requiring the cutting of much red tape. We were also given liberal opportunity for liberty.

One evening, in a Brisbane hotel dining room, we Marines threw a party for "Pop"—Cpl. Paul F. Crippen, of Miami, Florida, who at the age of forty-five had tossed aside his business and joined the Marines in the hope he could catch up with his son, Don, a Navy corpsman attached to a Marine unit.

"Pop" ostensibly had enlisted for Stateside duty, like guarding depots, but by arguing and pleading had badgered his way to Noumea, where after weeks of wheedling, he'd had himself moved on to Australia. He had reached Brisbane and now was trying to get to Melbourne, where his son was with the First Marine Division. He had been assigned to his son Don's medical unit as a vehicle maintenance supervisor.

It was a jolly party, especially since as "war heroes" we Marines were permitted to buy bootleg liquor, albeit at exorbitant prices.

The next morning we entrained for Melbourne, a long ride over beautiful if rugged country, with a three-hour stopover at Sydney. All I remember about Sydney is that all the servicemen on the train got off to jam their teeth into the best steak this side of the Pacific at the American Red Cross canteen. Next we pulled into Melbourne . . . ah, that was a wonderful metropolis!

My stay in Australia was less than a month, and perhaps two weeks were spent in Melbourne, but it was long enough for me to observe the "Battle of Melbourne."

The First Marine Division never did get a star for the Battle of Melbourne, yet according to hearsay, as many casualties were counted from "Waltzing Matilda" as were suffered on The Island. The casualties resulted not from machine guns and mortars, but from epidemic-proportioned outbreaks of venereal diseases, malaria, and filariasis that followed on the heels of the hard, fast living. Melbourne was a land of milk and honey for the leathernecks who had fought for six months in Guadalcanal and who were keenly aware that they would have to return to the jungles to fight again. They gorged themselves with sensual delights—with wine, women, and song.

It was simply a "normal" case of a liberty port becoming licentious. Nine months in Australia—most of it in Melbourne—left the men in worse shape than when they arrived, or so they insisted.

The reaction of the men—and the officers as well—was a natural one. They'd all had a close brush with death, and they'd have to fight in one or more campaigns before they could return to the States, to their homes, to their loved ones. With such a pessimistic future, why not party?

The Marines, out of their dirty dungarees into pressed forest-green uniforms that fit their lean, lithe bodies, their leather and brass glistening, their caps ajaunt, captivated the

Australians. The Aussies opened their homes, their hearths, and their hearts to the Marines.

The Marines needed a refuge to heal their wounds, to rest from the long black nights of ceaseless vigil and fear; they needed a haven in which to relax and play, to smile and laugh again. Melbourne gave the Marines that place.

The bighearted, generous Aussies made the Marines feel alive again, clean again, and tolerated their excesses. But even more, Melbourne gave the Yanks affection, and the beautiful, busty daughters gave them love in equal measure. Melbourne's homes were opened to the Americans. The Marines saw linen tablecloths and flowered bedspreads, and experienced the forgotten smells of kitchen cooking. The farms were opened to them, too, and the Marines pitched in with gusto, piling up the hay, tending the sheep, doing the daily chores. The visitations filled a void for both hosts and Marines.

The Australian girls were snowed by the clean-cut Americans and their neat-cut clothes, by their racy slang and impertinent chivalry, by their ardent courting and extravagant wooing. In those days, as the American men saw them, the Down Under lassies knew little about dressing and makeup. Their apparel was old-fashioned and their makeup gaudy. But there was a natural beauty in their healthiness and vibrancy, in their sparkling laughing eyes, in their warm eager lips. They were lovely, lusty, loving.

The Yanks had accumulated the service pay due them in the long months on Guadalcanal, and in Melbourne they spent the lode like struck-it-rich miners. They filled up the hotel rooms, bought out the stores, hired up all the taxicabs and cars for rent, ate up the best foods, and drank up all the liquor.

The few young Aussie men around, and the diggers of the Ninth Australian Division who returned on short leave from years of combat in the Mideast, didn't like brash competition for lady loves at all. The Americans, though, had an unmatchable advantage in their pockets ... jingle ... jingle ... jingle. The Yanks had money and were quick with a buck.

So it had to happen that here and there a fight broke out, which might spread into a melee, which could lead to a free-for-all. After a few shiners and broken heads, the leather-necks were forbidden to leave the barracks with their heavy leather, brass-buckle belts when they went on the town.

Some of the brawls were exclusively Marine affairs. It seems, so it was alleged, that members of the Second Marine Division training in Australia had warned the unsophis-ticated females to keep away from any Marine wearing a cord decoration on his uniform. The cord, the kidders solemnly averred, indicated that the wearer had a venereal disease. So when the First Division returned from the jungle and dressed up with all their honors, including the four-ragère earned in World War I, the innocent young things were scared away.

The outraged Australian males claimed that a Marine had three standards of taste: (1) Could he eat it? (2) Could he drink it? (3) Could he sleep with it?

No, the Aussies of the female gender were not immoral. They were simply amoral. Their menfolk had been far away from home fighting with the Allied armies overseas against Hitler and Mussolini and Tojo. Their menfolk had been away for two and three years. They were lonely and over-whelmed by the passionate tactics of the love-starved Yanks.

In a single evening—imagine!—Joe or Mike or Tom would send Mabel a large bouquet of flowers, take her to a movie in a cab, then escort her to a posh restaurant. He'd tip the cabbie as much as she earned in a day at the office. And the amazing things he taught her about making love!

Virginity and chastity went by the boards, and in their place the Australian girls learned about romance and pas-sion and, not to be overlooked, about sex hygiene. Mel-bourne was no place for the professional streetwalker. There were plenty of dolls available, one-man girls; and of course there were Marines who could handle and afford two or three, depending on his pocketbook and his propensity.

Shacking up—marriages of convenience—became for many Marines and their girlfriends the practical way of life, so that the leathernecks grabbed up every available apartment within miles of Melbourne and there ensconced their sweeties.

Military authorities made no attempt to halt or break up the illicit relationships, not only because the officers themselves were indulging in the same kinds of behavior but also because there was really nothing unusual about the situation. So it has been with soldiers away from home since the first expeditionary army set out from some ancient country in prebiblical times.

Many of the common-law unions were legalized in the normal course of events, and there were, of course, a few shotgun weddings as well.

It is fair to say, I think, that of the Americans in Melbourne, only the chaplains were not happy. They worked much harder than they were called upon to do in the battle zone, for in their laps fell much of the grief from broken hearts.

The Marines taught the Aussie girls a few important things besides loving: drinking beer ice cold instead of warm ... mixing cocktails precisely *so*. The leathernecks taught their girls to swing and jitterbug ... and to imitate the Yanks' slang. The lovely ladies had a good time, too, and when the time came to say good-bye, they wept to see their Yank lovers go. The Aussie men, however, preferred to see it differently—that the girlies were simply sorry to see the jingle-jingle-jingle go.

Yes, the Australians were truly generous hosts to our boys. When the Marines landed on their continent, the gyrenes demanded and consumed huge quantities of steaks and fresh eggs. It got to be so that the restaurants automatically dropped a couple of soft-fried eggs on every order of steak, whether or not requested, under the impression that steaks were served that way in America.

Australia is a sheep-raising country, and the folks there eat a lot of lamb and mutton, but the American was a beef eater. The Down Unders never could quite understand why the Yanks turned their noses up at the finest lamb chops. The Aussies drank gobs of tea, at all meals, and in between served tea and tiffins. Many Yanks converted from coffee to tea mainly because the Aussie java tasted like muddied water. In fact, the rather civilized custom of midmorning and midafternoon tea caught on, and the practice was actually carried on in some of the camps.

Americans generally, I have found, entertain the idea that Australians, like the Texans, are tall and rangy. I did not find this to be so. The average height seemed to be the same for both peoples, but the Aussies were a hardier lot, for their country was still under development and the pioneering spirit was still with them. They lacked many of the comforts of life we had in America that made for softer living, like central heating, and with fuel scarce because of war rationing, the residents of Melbourne inured themselves to their extremely cold winters. Their women did not wear stockings even on freezing days. They found their chilly homes comfortable.

There was one characteristic of the Aussies that at first contact startled the Yanks—false teeth. Many of even the prettiest girls had poor teeth or a set of artificial dentures. The Aussies blamed their dental deprivation to something in or out of their water, as a price they had to pay to live in Australia. But part of the problem, at least, was the Aussie penchant for sweets—combination desserts, French pastries, chocolates. The Marine, after his initial shock, took it for granted that his blind date would be good looking, but would she have her own teeth?

The Americans liked sweets too, of course, but many of them brushed their teeth twice a day or more, a habit seen by our antipodal cousins as a silly fetish.

For the most part, the Melbournians were friendly souls, and while there were a few Yankee-haters among them, they admired the United States, especially our industrial progress. The Australians, I found, are fiercely proud of their 99 percent descent from English-Scotch-Welsh-Irish forebears, even if some were unjustly branded as criminals by the royal magistrates. The Aussies were quick to come to the aid of the motherland in both world wars.

I also discovered in my own personal contact with them that the Aussies hold strong beliefs, often contradictory.

They treated the American black soldiers with the same generosity they afforded the whites but treated their own aborigines as second-class citizens.

They proudly looked to the day when their continental country would be peopled by tens of millions who would raise Australia to a seat with the principal powers of the world but placed strict limits on immigration to keep their population Anglo-Caucasian.

They were staunchly independent of rule from London but ready to defend the motherland when called.

Hundreds of American military men took Aussies for their brides, and before leaving again for the front, added a little to the continent's population. Hundreds of other Yanks helped raise the census figures without bothering to make it legal.

I felt that the generosity of the Australian people, the attractiveness of the girls, the vastness of the country, and the opportunities to build would draw Yanks by the thousands Down Under when the war ended, and they would help build Australia to its destined greatness. That would be, I surmised, America's repayment for Australia's unconditional hospitality to the Yanks.

In Melbourne I was reunited with some of the combat correspondents who had crossed the Pacific with me on *Juan Cabrillo*, and although the pubs closed down at 6 P.M., we found other spots for wassail and auld lang syne. I denied all reports of being missing or dead, but had some difficulty in gaining acceptance of my insistence that I was neither jungle-happy nor coconut-wacky, and if I did appear to have the thousand-yard glaze in my eyes, it was due to the watered scotch, nothing more.

I joined up with the Eleventh Marine (Artillery) Regiment in Ballarat, a onetime gold-mining town grown into a provincial city. The mines drew less attention from the Marines than the cricket grounds, especially after the moon came up.

The Eleventh had spread out in a comfortable camp laid out in a park, which was already in the process of being dismantled when I showed up. We moved out of bivouac by truck and train to Melbourne, remaining there for several days before boarding our designated Liberty ships, which were to carry us to the battle staging area.

Before Marines board, they usually have to load the vessel with their gear, guns, and supplies, and this time was no exception. For three days and nights all enlisted men below the two highest pay grades worked on the docks at hard labor. For two of those days, the first two pay grades loafed as was their due. Since I had been promoted to technical sergeant—four stripes—and was in the first two pay grades, I lazed about, too.

On the third day, the adjutant decided the cricket grounds, on which we were temporarily bivouacked, ought to be cleaned up, and called out the first two pay grades to do the job.

Now, policing of the grounds consists of sweeping, raking, picking up trash, and the like; and "The Book," the Marine Corps Manual, states that the first two pay grades shall not be used for such labor except in case of emergency. Apparently, the adjutant thought the emergency had arrived.

Altogether, there were nine of us affected by the adjutant's decree, some of whom had twenty years of service. It was the first time these career noncoms had ever heard— they claimed—of such an emergency. Several of the old boys, wrathfully up in arms, wanted to go over the adjutant's head and take it up with the colonel himself.

But the senior noncom suggested wiser counsel. So we all swung our brooms, shovels, and like equipment to our shoulders, marched out into the streets, and started leisurely cleaning sidewalks and gutters. Under persuasion of the senior sergeant we made a great show of cleaning up right up to the entrance of the cricket grounds—where we hoisted our paraphernalia to our shoulders and in a column of twos, marched double-time off to the nearest bar. There we hoisted mugs of suds for a couple of hours, every so often toasting the adjutant's health. Fifteen minutes before noon chow, we marched back in good order to the stadium, turned in our accoutrements, and went to lunch with that beatific feeling that comes from having completed a job well done.

The Marines were sad to leave Melbourne and, on the docks, the girls and mums and daddies and kin, all were there, smiling, and laughing, and kissing, and weeping unabashedly to see their Yanks off to war again. I made a mental note to write a special story about that bittersweet parting.

CHAPTER 15

Goodenough Island

Early in October 1943, the Marine battalions departed Melbourne on Liberty ships, sincerely sorry to be leaving new friends but glad to get going again, some to bases in eastern New Guinea. I went along with the Eleventh Artillery Regiment to Goodenough Island, largest of the D'Entrecasteaux cluster, less than a hundred miles off the New Guinea coast.

The Marines' next objective was an official secret, of course, but it was a secret that everyone shared.

Despite all the big signs shouting LOOSE LIPS SINK SHIPS!, every one of the sweethearts, wives, and friends seeing the Marines off knew we were preparing to hit New Britain, the next big island fortification blocking the road to Rabaul after other Marine and Army combat troops had wrested Tarawa and Bougainville from the Imperial forces in bloody battle.

There was no way to put a stopper on the leaks, since they dribbled out of the lips of officers as well as of the rank and file, of civilians who handled train movements and ship loadings, and from a dozen other sources. So it was no surprise to hear Tokyo Rose announce the night we landed on Goodenough, some 2,000 miles from Melbourne, that Tojo knew we were there and, she exulted, walking into a trap.

Tokyo Rose, the cultured mocking voice of Radio Tokyo, instead of discouraging the Marines, was actually a morale booster. No one paid attention to her boasts or threats, but everyone enjoyed the swing and jive records she played, songs that had been popular when they had left home. Her digs about life back in Brooklyn were received with amusement rather than resentment. Then, too, the broadcasts from

220

Radio Tokyo came in more clearly than any American program at that time and place.

Like every other troopship I've been on, this one was crowded; and like every other Liberty ship, this one was doubly uncomfortable. But as the vessel drew north to warmer climates, I managed to find a niche topside where I could escape the hot, humid, fetid quarters in the hold and sleep comfortably . . . when it didn't rain.

Now surfeited with nearly a year of R & R and crowded into a vessel with very limited facilities, the Marines suffered from lack of activity. So, military regulations notwithstanding, gambling became the action at all hours day and night. And if some luckless Marine ran out of the real green, he could play for toilet paper—a commodity in great demand and short supply. Aboard my Liberty liner one gee-wizard with the cubes was reputed to have garnered 4,480 sheets, the equivalic of four and a half rolls. Hey, that's a high roller!

On this transport, for inexplicable reasons, dice was not the main attraction. Blackjack—21—was the game of choice; stud and draw poker were poor runners-up. Strangely, chess outdrew checkers, and I never observed a game of bridge.

There was little reading material around on the ship, mostly light literature, detective and adventure magazines of the "Doc" Savage variety. I noticed a rare few of my shipmates absorbed in the Bible. I nibbled away at my well-thumbed copy of *War and Peace*.

There was ample opportunity to write letters, and the Marines, thinking of the Melbourne they had just left, or Melbourne, Florida, which they had long left behind, poured out their feelings in a flood of correspondence that inundated the censor at the end of the voyage. I, too, wrote my Bernice long letters, also catching up on my own belated correspondence.

The chaplain held services on Sunday, and in a gesture of respect, all the gaming was called off until church was over. And every afternoon, the band would strike up martial and swing music, drawing a large and appreciative audience.

In anticipation of the next invasion, the Marines, ever the

riflemen, gave sharp attention to their new M-1 Garands, which were replacing their beloved Springfields. The Marines brought up on the 1903 single-shot weapon were reluctant to give it up, but soon got to accept the .30-caliber, gas-operated, clip-fed air-cooled semiautomatic Garand because the M-1 had less recoil and permitted consistent fire in a shorter period of time, and the sighting system was superior under combat conditions. Pulling the M-1 apart for cleaning and lubrication was simple, but the most important attribute of the new rifle was the increase in the rate of aimed fire.

I hated to give up my Springfield, and kissed the barrel a fond farewell when I made the exchange. As a penance, I worked out intensely on my eye exercises and convinced another shipload of Marines that I was a kook or cuckoo.

Fresh water was hard to come by but was available for a bucket bath or for a clothing wash if you really felt the need for either. Once out of port, the male's vanity gave way to the more deeply rooted desire for comfort, so that he had his hair cut short. Since the barbering aboard was purely amateurish, the scissors in the hands of a buddy achieved fantastic results. Some of the men simply had all of their hair shorn off, leaving the scalp clean-shaven. Others cultivated fancy mustaches and beards so they could send gallant, grown-up "Look, Ma!" photos home, but most got rid of those embellishments as soon as the perspiration became a nuisance in the prickly, sultry atmosphere, especially since the sweat-trapping adornments began to attract flies. My own experiment, with an Adolphe Menjou mustache, drew derision as well as flies; I shaved it off after three days.

For the sake of discipline, reveille was blown every morning, but only after the first sarge rolled out of his sack. On this trip, the Marines made up for sleep they'd lost in the past and were sure to lose in the near future. They followed up with an afternoon siesta. So did I.

Such was the daily routine aboard our Liberty ship, except when the wind whipped up the swells and the ship's passengers were seized with a sudden impulse to rush to the rails or to the heads. But why bring that up?

The diggers of the Australian army had already killed or

scattered the Japanese garrison at Goodenough Island. Then the Aussies had built an airdrome there. All the Marines had to do was carve camps for themselves out of the jungle. The U.S. Sixth Army also pitched tent on Goodenough so that in a few weeks a margin of the jungle was converted into a series of cantonments with long files of tents.

I was attached temporarily to headquarters and service company of the Eleventh Marines. Our campsite was pitched on a high fertile plateau thickly jungled and well streamed at the foot of a 7,700-foot volcanic peak. My own tent was thrown up in a native fruit garden, amid coconuts, papayas, mangoes, bananas, and figs; amid Yule red and green poinsettias and bright, purple- and red-leafed bougainvillea.

Lest you get the idea that we had found the garden Eve gave up for an apple, I must reveal that except for the coconuts, the fruit plants had been ravaged and ripped up by the Jap marauders. And just as in Eden, in our oasis we had to contend with snakes. Nonetheless, we did have palm trees and palmettos to shade us from the naked sun, and the high-stretching flowers bloomed and cheered up our canvas abodes.

The military malaria-control teams made some headway against the island's nasty mosquitoes by clearing out rotting vegetation and destroying their breeding grounds in the choked pockets of the stream and by providing the servicemen with fresh, cold, fast-running water from the hills, easily made potable.

To be sure, other malignant insects were glad to see or smell us, particularly the scorpions, which stung many victims.

We also discovered a new disagreeable denizen of Goodenough, "Spit in the Eye," a vicious-looking, sausage-size millipede. Its cylindrical body bulged half an inch in diameter and extended four to six inches front to rear. The intimidating crawler not only was capable of making a stinging bite but also, like a flamethrower, of squirting a venomous brownish-red liquid at all who dared offend it. The Spit's spewing distance was only a few inches, but he was uncommonly accurate, especially at night when he wiggled under the mosquito netting.

The more-than-a-mile-high peak towering over our camp was deceptively enticing, verdant with many tints of green, etched by glistening waterfalls. Many a Marine on first seeing the pinnacle naively declared his intention to climb to the top the first chance he got.

Some did try it. Oh, yes, the mountain could be scaled . . . in four days—with the support of fuzzy-wuzzy guides who were acquainted with the difficult trails.

The verdant vista that looked like a packed mass of trees cloaked an impenetrable jungle, and the light green vegetation that looked like grass *was* grass, sharp-toothed kunai, six to nine feet tall. And both views concealed the sheer precipices that had to be overcome before reaching the summit. Some of the more reckless Marines and GIs tried to go it alone, but after several fractured arms and legs from free falls, unauthorized sallies were declared verboten by the CO.

The airport was laid out on the plateau after swaths of kunai had been cleared, but it was declared to be an unsafe area for the camps when brush typhus broke out among the servicemen. Of all the diseases that beset the men who fought in the Solomons, brush typhus was the most dreaded. It struck stealthily, quickly, lethally.

The Yanks had been inoculated against louse typhus, also spread by rats, but we were susceptible to the different types of disease-bearing mites brushed off into the grass by the hordes of rats that barged in wherever the Marines and GIs broke new ground on a new island. At the time there was no magic bullet available to prevent or cure the infection. Some of the victims of the fever came through; some died. Rat-catching contests, a ghoulish but common amusement in the Solomons, made little inroad into the teeming population of rodent interlopers.

No sooner did the engineers start tearing up the jungle for roads, camps, depots, and the like than they created mud. It was jungle or mud. So we had mud.

The training routine was not arduous, since a practice schedule of sorts had been maintained in Melbourne. On Goodenough the Marines were simply acclimatizing again to the tropical weather and jungle terrain. There was ample time for recreation. The dangerous grass was cleared to make way for softball diamonds. Innocent trout were basking in the creeks for fishermen, and deep natural pools of cold water awaited the swimmers.

An outdoor movie theater was erected, and we watched reels of old-hat movies. However ancient the films, the movies, I can vouch, played a major role in camp morale, especially during the long and tedious nights.

Shortly after setting up on Goodenough, the first film shown was *Son of Fury*, starring Tyrone Power, who was later commissioned in the Marine Corps. The reel started to roll at 7:30 P.M., but while there was sound, the machine failed to produce the picture. The night was dry, but a torrent of catcalls rained on the hapless projectionist.

Son of Fury was rescheduled for the following evening, when the image appeared but the sound failed. That time the loud squawks of derision were laced with four-letter words.

On the third night, the feature was presented successfully, picture and sound in sync.

The projectionist denied that the colonel had threatened to throw him into the brig if the third attempt failed.

Back in our bunks, waiting for sleep to take over, we were courted by the love songs of the exotic birds in the jungle umbrella. The sweet sounds were interrupted at intervals by the heckling bark of the "laughing hyena"—the kookaburra, a bird of another feather.

After the chaplain somehow produced an armful of harmonicas, kazoos, and ocarinas, when the day was done the maestros of the mouth organs blew their favorite tunes without regard to the feelings of their jungle neighbors.

In our encampment we built two chapels, Protestant and Catholic. And two separate Christmas carol choirs were organized despite the efforts of some from both sides to create a single choral group. There seemed to be some irreconcilable problem between the chaplains, minister and priest.

In my war experience I came across few, very few convinced atheists. Almost every Yank had some religious background, and no matter how lax or tenuous his faith might have become, in the pinch he turned to his God and prayed, if only a few words of "save me" or of gratitude.

As to the chaplains, their impact on the men depended on their own character and personality. The leathernecks on the line demanded deed, not preaching. The Marines respected the sky pilots who moved up the line with the men to inspire them during battle; who passed the ammunition if need be; who consoled them when they were wounded; who eased them in their dying moments. But some chaplains required orderlies. Those men of God who demanded comfort if they were to give comfort were held in poor regard.

I found that for most of the Marines, feeding the belly was a greater concern than feeding the soul. On Guadalcanal and on the New Georgia Islands, hunger, stomach-wrenching hunger was a routine experience for the grunts when the C and K rations ran out, or when supplies were cut off, or when our relief planes dropped their food resupply in enemy territory.

Warm food, especially bread, was rare on the lines. But on Goodenough the cooks and the bakers went all out to provide the combat veterans with hot chow and especially freshly baked bread. The Marines, who had tried to quiet their growling guts with the hard, dry dog biscuits on the line, loved that fresh white bread!

All Marines, grunts and generals alike, held their division baker, Tech. Sgt. Leon P. Breaud—pronounced b-r-e-a-d— in high regard. He and his galley gang had arrived on the island along with the infantry, but could not get their ovens ashore for several weeks. So Graddick ... I mean Breaud ... tore down the bricks of the nearest plantation copra kiln, improvised yeast out of potatoes, and turned out 5,000 pounds of bread daily.

"I swear, not a crumb was wasted. The men loved the bread. They would come down from their tents and hang around the ovens waiting for the loaves to appear. Then they'd chew at the whole loaf as if it were a steak," Sergeant Breaud bragged.

"They like my bread not only because it's fresh," the chief

baker pointed out, "but especially because we use the ingredients that Mom makes it with at home—flour, yeast, shortening, salt, and sugar, and none of the vitamin junk that increases the food value but decreases the taste."

On Goodenough, the chief baker had fifty-four assistants, and when his standard field kitchen equipment was in operation, he provided 9,000 pounds of bread daily. The heat and humidity, the bane of just about everyone else, was a boon to the bakers because they speeded up the dough-making process.

I was too grateful to ask Sergeant Breaud whether he, like a few of my fellow trainees at boot camp, had failed his rifle tests at boot camp, but I did learn that he had first started mixing the dough on Parris Island seventeen years before, and had been baking in Haiti, China, and Guadalcanal. Sergeant Breaud, thirty-five, hailed from Alton, West Virginia, where his wife was the bread maker.

The Marines on Goodenough even got a glob of ice cream a couple of times a week, the equivalent of two Eskimo pies. The goodies were passed out not to tickle the palates of the leathernecks but to stimulate the appetite and make the hard tack and iron rations more palatable, according to the commissary officer, 1st Lt. Vinson A. McNeil, thirty-seven, also a West Virginian, from Fairmont. He explained:

"During the long months on Guadalcanal our diet was by necessity chiefly dry and canned goods. Appetites flagged under the monotony of the diet, and loss of weight inevitably followed. I broached the suggestion to produce ice cream under combat conditions to the command, and it was approved. After all, there's more nutritive value in a pound of ice cream than in a pound of spuds."

But where to obtain an ice-cream maker? Call in Graddick! Graddick combed the island and found an Aussie who had been an ice-cream manufacturer Down Under, and with his aid, the bakers jigsawed a Rube Goldberg contraption that delivered ice cream at the end of an intricate process. Trouble was, the end product came out lumpy instead of soft. Sticklers for perfection, the bakers renamed their concoction "frozen dessert," but the grunts took their lumps and liked it.

For those willing to get dirt in their fingernails, there was another source of fresh food on our island. First to start his own victory garden, as best as I could determine, was 1st Sgt. William P. West, twenty-five, from Rhine, Georgia.

"I vowed on The Rock," said the Guadalcanal veteran, "that if I ever again had to go into the jungle to fight, I would take along enough seeds to plant a vegetable garden."

Before he pulled out of Melbourne, he'd bought $5 worth of seed. Three days after disembarking on Goodenough, he rooted out the buffalo grass in a plot near his tent and planted a row of tomatoes—"those big red juicy ones"— iceberg lettuce, butter beans, cantaloupes, and watermelons.

"I plan to hold an exhibition with the first crop," the sarge promised, "and then auction off the produce. This'll popularize the idea."

The top proved to be right; cabbage patches began to spring up around the encampment even before his crop could be reaped.

Pet-loving Marines smuggled all kinds of pooches onto the transports. Marines at rest in the Pacific tended to find, feed, and train strange pets. On Guadalcanal, it was monkeys; in the Russells, it was lizards. On Goodenough it was baby wallabies. The wallaby is a half-pint kangaroo with the curiosity of a cat. A mama wallaby bounded into camp one day while taking her brood out for a pleasant hop-skippety-jump. Whether the Marines or the marsupial was more startled is a moot question, because Mrs. Wallaby bounded out again with a tremendous leap, and infant "Digger" tumbled out of his mama's pouch onto the ground. He was immediately adopted by Pfc. Robert H. Van Lundingham, twenty-seven, of Clarksdale, Mississippi.

A tiny fellow, Digger was fed liquid powdered milk through an eye dropper, and he liked to munch the grass. Like a puppy he would gambol around in the coolness of the early morning or late evening, and in between curl up for a nap in the snug jacket pocket of his step-papa.

* * *

Once a semipermanent base is established, the signs start popping up. Soon there were as many signs and posters flowering in the outskirts of the jungle as there were billboards outside a big city in the United States. But in the jungle no complaints were raised about placards marring the beauty of nature; no, because the markers brought a touch of civilization to our jungle base.

Reminiscent of the posters strung along the main U.S. highways meant to keep drivers awake and prevent accidents— or to sell Burma shaving cream—our roads were lined with exhortations aimed at preventing malaria. An example:

> Tall, Short, Fat, Thin.
> Don't Forget Your Atabrine!

Personal hygiene received special emphasis:

> Cleanliness is next to Godliness. . . .
> GET GODLY, MAC!

And of course, with the posted bills came the traffic signs:

> SLOW DOWN! 5 MILES PER HOUR . . .
> WE LOVE OUR CHILDREN!

Those who drove into the commissary depot were confronted with:

> WELCOME!
> TRANSACT YOUR BUSINESS AND SCRAM!

Even more explicit was the announcement at the camp toolshed:

> WE SHOOT EVERY FIFTH MAN
> WHO WANTS TO BORROW TOOLS.
> THE FOURTH MAN HAS JUST LEFT—SO!

Every camp had its own entrepreneurs. One tent advertised:

"Headquarters of Better Business Association of Mela Bela: watch repairs, art metal craft, novelty jewelry, engraving, portraits, tinting, and leather work. Business hours anytime, except when called to official duties."

In my own judgment, the prize for the posters went to the Australian pilot who designated the tea shack next to the fighter run "Strip Tease."

Perhaps the most significant signpost was the mile marker at the entrance to the Marine base:

WASHINGTON—11,673 MILES (arrow points east)
TOKYO—4,231 MILES (arrow points north)
JAPS—¼ MILE (arrow points to jungle)

The mileage was deliberately inaccurate, of course, to prevent the Japs from acquiring important information.

The men of one battery of the 11th Regiment were in need of replacements for their beat-up and torn fatigue dungarees and jackets, so they soon sprouted a new style of trouser, sartorially snappy and equipped with extra-deep pockets. The other Marines eyed their artillery cohorts with envy until the word got out that the trousers were the standard pants issued to the Army nurses in the field.

With time on their hands, the Marines started to prepare for Christmas. The production of the Xmas greetings sprang up spontaneously, spreading from one unit to another.

The general sentiment was expressed in the concluding quatrain of the verse composed by an amphibious tractor crew:

And someday in the future
When Christmas rolls around
May we have won our victory
And be happily homeward bound.

Outstanding among the Yule greetings was the card conceived and drawn by Vic P. Donohue, of Omaha, Nebraska.

The twenty-five-year-old Marine combat artist had been cartoonist for the *Omaha World-Herald*. Tinged with irony and hope, the card displayed a wary Marine patrol advancing through the jungle darkness toward the distant Star of Bethlehem, superscribed: "Peace on Earth—Goodwill Toward Men."

The first sergeant of a crack cited company carried with him at all times a miniature rubber hammer and a children's set of drumsticks. The irregular accessories to the noncom's camp attire came to the attention of the CO, who demanded an explanation.

"Well, sir, when a member of my company comes to me with a gripe, I don't have the spare time to listen to all his complaints. If I think he's a gum beater, I give him the drumsticks. If I think he's a breast beater, I give him the rubber hammer. As you know, sir, a Marine is happiest when he's griping. I like to keep my men happy."

There was another old-time "Banana" campaigner (veteran of the '20s and '30s "banana republic" campaigns in Central America) who nearly lost one of his hash marks when, against strict regulations, he fired a shot at a kookaburra that he believed was laughing at him.

That breach of camp etiquette brought the sergeant before the colonel, known as the toughest disciplinarian on the entire island.

"What have you to say for yourself, Sergeant?" the colonel asked.

"Sir, all I have to say is that this bird was barking up the wrong tree."

Would you believe that the noncom got away scot-free? He did, because the colonel's bark was sharper than his bite.

Oops! I neglected to mention the warning put up by the chief medical officer:

DON'T LET THE SUN FRY YOUR BRAINS

A week before we were to board yet another transport to join the convoy that would sail on to New Britain—another open secret—I got myself shifted from the artillery to the infantry. I had already served with the gun crews of the Ninth Defense Battalion on Rendova, and wanted to rub elbows with the infantry grunts. I managed to get attached to the Seventh Marines, First Division, the Guadalcanal-hardened regiment that had earned a reputation in the field for getting tough assignments done.

CHAPTER 16

Cape Gloucester

The invasion of New Britain was not just one more stepping-stone on the road to Rabaul, the ultimate goal of the Solomons campaigns. New Britain was the last redoubt protecting the principal air and sea base of the Japanese in the Solomons. General MacArthur had concluded that the Allies would have to eliminate Rabaul in order for him to return with an avenging army to the Philippines.

The drive to Rabaul had begun with the landing on Guadalcanal. The offensive had pressed on unswervingly, as the American forces took the Russell Islands, New Georgia Islands, Tarawa, Bougainville; and as the Anzac (Australian and New Zealand) troops recaptured the Jap seizures in New Guinea and the adjacent island groups. Those bastions overwhelmed, General MacArthur was ready to launch "MacArthur's Marines"—First and Second Marine Divisions, which had come under his Southwest Pacific command—against New Britain.

The First Marine Division, its ranks rested, rebuilt, and retrained, twelve months after it had stopped Japan's steamroller on Guadalcanal, was given the honor of leading the invasion of Cape Gloucester, with its Seventh Regiment in assault.

Cape Gloucester sits on the northwest corner of banana-shaped New Britain Island, some 300 miles from the northeast tip where the Japs had planted the main base in their expansion into the Southwest Pacific. New Britain is the largest island in the Admiralty chain, but it is also at the top of the Solomons chain; Guadalcanal holds the bottom.

New Britain is six times larger than Guadalcanal, and its

girth fifty miles wide. Just about all of the island is covered with swamps and mountains, impenetrable in some parts, mostly untracked, and towered over by two peaks, 6,500-foot Mt. Talawe and 3,800-foot Mt. Langila. Not only is New Britain larger than Guadalcanal, it is hotter, wetter, muddier, heavily infested with disease-bearing insects and rats, and lashed by monsoons.

Discovered and claimed for England by William Dampier in 1700, the island changed hands several times as the European monarchs played military chess to extend their empires, but New Britain was left mostly to the devices of the autochthonous Melanesians until early 1942, when Tojo pounced on Rabaul and converted the piddling port into a mighty military base.

Taken by the Allies, Gloucester would tighten the Allied necktie around Rabaul and clear the Dampier Strait bottleneck between New Guinea and New Britain, another chokepoint to MacArthur's advance toward the Philippines.

The Seventh Marines were led by a tough campaigner, Col. Julian N. Frisbie, and an even more famous second in command, Col. Lewis B. "Chesty" Puller, whose feats of leadership in battle had already established him as a Marine Corps model of leadership in the field.

When I checked into Intelligence HQ of the Seventh Marines, I caught up with Jerry O'Leary, my friend and fellow newsman from Washington, whom I'd last seen in boot camp. Jerry was the first of the combat correspondents to be sworn into Denig's Demons. However, he had been shipped off to a Marine base in the Caribbean and had languished there, as I had on Treasure Island. He had missed the Guadalcanal campaign but was destined to see more Marine action than any other CC.

Sgt. Jeremiah A. O'Leary, twenty-one, endowed with a big body and a big mind, an Irish temperament and wit, was pining for battle.

We were teamed up with two combat photographers: Sgts. Bob Brenner, twenty-one, of Brooklyn, New York, and Al Monteverdi, twenty-three, of Los Angeles. Brenner, who learned to master both rifle and camera after enlisting, had

had his baptism of fire on Guadalcanal. Monteverdi had been a photographer shooting in the Hollywood jungle before shooting in the Pacific jungle.

On Christmas Day, 1943, just before the sun quietly announced its arrival with splashes of orange-red-yellow, our cruisers and destroyers thunderously announced their arrival with blasts of orange-red-yellow to rouse and rout the Japanese defenders from the guns overlooking the invasion shore. A geyser of flame revealed a strike on a large fuel or ammo dump.

The destroyer-transport carrying B Company, 1st Battalion, maneuvered toward Yellow Beach #2, a quarter-moon sliver of sand on the edge of a forbidding jungle at Silimata Point in Borgen Bay.

It was 7:45 A.M. when I slid down the netting of the APD into the Higgins boats with the grunts of B Company, 2nd Battalion, veterans of seven battles on Guadalcanal, led by Lt. George S. Plantier, of Washington, D.C., a thirty-six-year-old banana-wars campaigner and the lone company commander below the rank of captain.

The four Coast Guardsmen coping with the unruly craft looked like teenagers yet to take their first shave but displayed more aplomb on their first invasion—forty-five minutes of rough riding through bucking surf—than the battle-seasoned leathernecks. The four sailors handling the Higgins were Edward D. Hand, of Hazelhurst, Georgia; Richard D. Hardesty, of Shinnston, West Virginia; Bernard J. Hartken, of Richmond, Virginia; and John Vogel, of Omaha, Minnesota. I wrote a story about them, but for the life of me I cannot explain how I managed to get their names in that jammed jerkily bouncing boat.

The intense naval bombardment, lasting more than an hour, was followed up by intense bombing from the Army's Fifth Air Force Mitchells, Liberators, and Havocs.

Even so, we couldn't help thinking of the fate awaiting the Second Marine Division men who had hit the beach at Tarawa only a month earlier. There the Japs had pulled back, had survived the Allies' intensive predawn sea and air bombardments, and had poured devastating fire on the surprised leathernecks as they waded ashore. We worried that the Japs on Gloucester would spring out of their holes and mow us down as we came ashore. In anticipation of the firestorm, I crouched down in the beaching craft.

But that calamity didn't happen. The Navy and Air Force pounding had been effective. There was *no* response—no bullets, no shells, no sweeping fire.

I breathed an audible sigh of relief, and I could hear "Thank God!" ringing in my ears from dozens of tightened lips around me when we jumped off the launches onto the strip of beach.

The eye-tearing, nostril-biting smoke billowing from our sea and air barrages blanketed the invasion zone with an obscuring haze that baffled the foes' gunners.

B Company did not halt after jumping off on Yellow Beach #2, but quickly advanced into the adjacent jungle . . . into an unexpected, unmapped swamp that reached to our ankles, then rose to our knees and higher, while we struggled to keep our weapons high, dry, and ready to fire.

I mentally congratulated myself for having made a reluctant decision to park my Hermes with the regimental headquarters staff in the long-shot hope I could recover the typewriter later.

The quagmire was a stinker, and treacherous. Submerged logs and trees tripped us. A misstep could wrench a leg. Worse, invisible sinkholes snatched down several of the grunts, who had to be jerked out when their own desperate, flailing efforts failed to free them. I got sucked into one of the pits, but I was more terrified than hurt when platoonmates yanked me free.

I was unnerved by the horrifying experience but didn't have time to dwell on it because B Company was slogging forward, and I had to keep pace lest I fall behind with the injured and the exhausted. Somehow, I kept my rifle dry enough to shoot; my Hermes would have been ruined.

Our column's immediate target was a rise of about 450 feet, which was named, naturally, Target Hill. Already A Company was plunging ahead to the juncture of the river flowing from Target Hill into Borgen Bay, and C Company was deploying to protect the right flank. Lieutenant Plantier unhesitatingly took B Company into the massive jungle to seize the hill from the rear.

As we shoved through a higher-ground network of deserted dugouts and met no opposition, a new disturbing thought loomed up. Were we heading into an ambush? Ordinarily, I'm not a worrywart, but the tension multiplied my fears. Besides, I sensed that I was not the only guy who had that possibility on his mind, although no one expressed it aloud. In fact, no member of B Company pushing through the swamp and jungle uttered a yap of complaint.

The sun was now completely veiled by the phosphorus fumes. I glanced up to catch shafts of ghostly luminescence emanating from embers glowing in the bomb craters on the hills and piercing the forest umbrella. The scene was unearthly, a vision of what hell must be like.

On reaching the rear base of Target Hill, Lieutenant Plantier directed one platoon to cover his right, the second to cover his left, and he himself led the third platoon straight up the steep slope. One side of Target Hill was sheer cliff, and the others could be scaled only by crawling and clawing on the thick grass and undergrowth. Not until we reached the topmost ridge, honeycombed with vacated foxholes and pillboxes, did we learn for sure that the double bombardment had compelled the defenders to flee Target Hill. Not until we reached the top could we squeeze the mud and water out of our boondockers or, as some of us did, remove the sodden boots and wiggle our aching feet for relief.

B Company took over five abandoned field guns that had been skillfully positioned to traverse the beaches in front and the valley to the rear. All of the weaponry was in excellent condition, and the emplacement was well stocked with ammunition.

Two of the weapons were Colt Browning antiaircraft machine guns manufactured at Hartford, Connecticut, and the ammo was labeled from the Frankfort Arsenal and the Remington Arms plants. The shell cases were dated 1932, indicating that the Japs had been accumulating American ammunition for a decade before the Pearl Harbor raid.

By noon, B Company made Target Hill secure. We supplemented the Jap guns with our own and dug in to prepare for the customary night counterattack.

Meantime, the Allies' aerial defense—Hellcats, Corsairs, Avengers—overpowered and outgunned the once dominant Japanese air force and blasted down some fifty Mitsubishis, Aichis, and Zeros. Nonetheless, several enemy bombers broke through the Allies' cordon and attacked our invasion vessels offshore. In the very same moments, a squadron of Mitchells was flying through the same area to soften up the Japs on Hill 660, a mile beyond Target Hill.

In the confusion of the crisscrossing air raids, the American ack-ack guns on the ships and beaches knocked off not only several enemy planes but also three of our own Mitchells. The Army Air Force fliers, apparently believing the enemy was shooting at them, strafed and bombed one of our own outfits—the Eleventh Defense Battalion, as it turned out. The tragic spectacle cast a pall over the glow of our taking Target Hill without loss.

That afternoon the rains arrived. Did I say arrived? The rains slammed in, driven by monsoon winds that toppled the trees weakened by the bombardment as if they were bowling pins, maiming and killing a number of Marines. We were deluged by torrents of water. Our foxholes, dumps, emplacements were swamped. We were soaked, but most of us somehow managed to keep our weapons in shape for the anticipated counterattack.

The Japs were waterlogged as well, no doubt, and did not counterattack that first night.

Except on the extreme flanks, the assault battalions had met little opposition on D day, but other elements of the First Division, aiming for the two airports eight miles to the east, had run into stiff resistance.

On the second night, the *banzai*-bellowing Japs, some yowling English-sounding gibberish, attacked, striking at the right flank of the 2nd Battalion. We in B Company held the line off the left of the counterthrust, and although "all hell broke loose" to our right, we withheld fire under strict orders from Lieutenant Plantier. He did not want to give away our location. We would hold fire until the Japs attempted to breach our section of the perimeter and then we'd surprise and clobber them.

We lay there fidgeting with nervous expectation, sleeping little that night since the battle might shift to our company line at any moment. We kept vigil there in monsoon-raging blackness, as ricocheting bullets bounced erratically around us.

Late into the second night, one of the fresh replacements in B Company cracked, and screamed in terror. We had to pull him back into his mushy foxhole and forcibly hold him down and keep his mouth shut for the rest of that night, until he could be quieted by a corpsman's shot. He wasn't the only one.

On the third night, December 28, Aichi Vals dive-bombed our sector, making a hit on another company, the bomb exploding uncomfortably close to our own line.

Soon after the bombing, a tremendous tremor shook through our area. It took some time for us to realize that an earthquake had followed the near-miss bombing. We couldn't believe it!

A monsoon, a bombing, and an earthquake, too! What next?

On the third night, too, the Japs counterattacked, this time on our left flank. Our perimeter had become thinly strung out and reinforcements were needed. Green replacements unloading cargo on the beach—"chickens" to the Guadalcanal vets—were rushed up to fill the gaps. We suffered severe losses that night in dead and wounded, especially among the unseasoned fill-ins.

One greenie who survived was Pfc. Harvey I. Wosika, of Ponca City, Oklahoma. He said he was nineteen but didn't look more than fifteen. An orphan, he had signed up along with his older brother, Joe, who had been switched to artillery. When I talked with him later, he was still recovering from the trauma of his first battle experience, sitting on his hospital cot, his hands trembling as he lit the cigarette I offered him:

"There were seven of us . . . I think. . . . We went out in

front of the barbed wire . . . to clean out the brush . . . to get a field of fire . . . when one of the boys . . . I don't even know the others . . . spotted a wounded Jap . . . about a hundred feet out front of our line . . .

"We went over to see . . . found one Jap dead . . . and two wounded. . . . One started moving around . . . and one of the boys got excited . . . and started firing at him . . .

"Just then a sniper opened up . . . and one of the boys fell . . . shot through the head . . . We flopped down into Jap foxholes . . . and one of the boys cried out, 'Watch out for the snipers!'

"I couldn't see the sniper . . . because he kept popping at my foxhole . . . so I kept my head down . . .

"Then I heard a lot of the Japs yelling. . . . They came rushing at us from over a ridge in front of us. . . .

"One of the boys near me . . . about ten feet away . . . was shot . . . and a Jap started to beat him over the head with his rifle butt. . . . I fired into him twice. . . . Another Jap stopped right in front of me . . . just looking . . . and I fired into him twice. . . . A third one came running toward me, and I fired two . . . three times . . . I can't remember . . . when the rifle jammed. . . . I only had eight rounds in the rifle anyway . . . so I threw it away and ran for my life . . . back to our lines.

"I don't know how I did it . . . or what happened . . . because I guess I was half-crazy."

I tried to question Wosika, gently but probingly, to elicit more details, but he became hysterical and a corpsman made me end the interview. I tried, futilely, to find other witnesses to the gruesome episode. I could not corroborate the survivor's account, perhaps because a dozen of the boys never made it through that night.

We'd taken along rations for a day and a half on the Target Hill mission, and stretched the food out for three days. That wasn't a problem for us, because in the excitement of impending battle, we didn't have much of an appetite. We did need water, but there was plenty of water in the sluggish streams and we could quickly purify it with the halazone tablets in our combat packs.

However, getting food and ammo to us through swamp

and jungle and up precipitous hillsides was an acute problem. But the ingenious Seabees attached to the 17th Marine Engineer Regiment resolved it by building a bridge, the width of a single log, and a pathway through the morass.

Meanwhile, a party from each of the platoons on the line was sent down to the beach to carry up cases of rations and bandoliers of bullets on their shoulders and backs. Since the log catwalk over the mire had to serve the goings and comings of the carriers, the moving lines mimicked columns of ants marching out to forage and marching back to their queen's sanctum with their top-heavy loads.

We had captured a couple of Jap supply dumps, but the smoked fish and powdered rice, the staples of Tojo's soldiers, were too rancid, too wormy for our more delicate stomachs. The booty, however, included boxes of canned heat, so that in the evening of the third day, for the first time, we had hot drinks with our tasteless dog biscuits. The heated beverages gave us a lift although the coffee was bitter, the tea acidic, the bouillon too salty. We even drank a toast to the foresight of our benefactors.

There was no way to keep dry in the monsoon downpours, which continued for twenty-three days—stopping only for short intervals. We did what we could to cover ourselves but were wet most of the time, and had to put up with it, officers and men alike. We scratched, rubbed, massaged ourselves, and lived in and slept in our ponchos. A fortunate few scrounged up canvas and hung hammocks in the trees. We were all uncomfortable, but the constant wet was not as bad as being clipped by a Nambu sniper or clopped by a falling tree. Some of the guys found it less wretched to face the elements bare-chested, notwithstanding the omnipresent, omnivorous bugs.

Through all the drenching misery there was one bright moment for the Marine observation post on Target Hill. A freshly baked pie, apple, extralarge, was delivered by runner, compliments of T. Sgt. Roy A. BruBaker, thirty-three, of Louisville, Kentucky.

A couple of days after setting up his galley for the staff of the assistant division commander, BruBaker remembered the crew on the forward OP who had been stuck with spare rations. So he prepared a pie large enough to fit snugly into a combat pack. The pie was carried by runner through a mile of swamp and stiff slope. It was no longer hot, of course, by the time it reached us, but it was appetizing and appreciated.

The chief observer, Capt. Preston S. Parish, twenty-four, of Brewster, New York, an alumnus of Williams College, Guadalcanal veteran, and battalion operations officer, did his own good deed on the evenings when two Jap bombers made a regular appearance. No sooner did "Toe" and "Joe" show up for their late matinee performance, forcing all field phone watchkeepers into their dugouts, than Parish started his own on-the-air show, phonecasting a bomb-by-bomb, flak-by-flak description of the air raid to all his fans on the battalion circuit.

The Betty bombing on the night of December 30 blew off the arm of a leatherneck on the line, and while the raid was in progress, Sgt. James L. Maynor, twenty-six, of Mullens, West Virginia, rushed to him and applied a tourniquet with the sleeve of his jacket, saving the life of his squadmate. For his brave act the former coal miner was awarded a letter of commendation by Maj. Gen. William H. Rupertus, the Marine commander.

New Year's Eve was relatively quiet. We underwent the dusk bombing raid without loss despite the lethal spatter of daisy-cutters. I celebrated quietly that night at the command post phone with Platoon Sgt. James G. Toohy, thirty, of West Roxbury, Massachusetts, reminiscing about our college days—he at Boston College, I at Boston University—and about past New Year's Eves.

The New Year's Eve before, while I was still chafing in Noumea, he had been on a similar front line on Guadalcanal, where he had participated in seven battles in which his company had lost nineteen killed, twenty-three wounded, and forty evacuated for malaria.

We drank a toast of Adam's ale from our canteens to the New Year, and Jim rightly commented: "At least we won't have a hangover tomorrow."

The Jap soldiers had the nasty habit of infiltrating our

lines at night and bayoneting grunts sleeping in their fox-holes. Sgt. Vincent Jandenski, twenty-four, of Braddock, Pennsylvania, snapped up this night when he heard a rustle above his head. Afraid to shoot lest the rustler were a fellow Marine, Jandenski cried out:

"Halt! Who goes there!"

"What you say?" was the response.

It was the wrong response to that classic question.

"So I fired my tommy gun," explained the sergeant. The intruder was found dead, some yards from the foxhole, where he had crawled.

The critical battle of Target Hill took place on the eighth day after the Marines took the top. The Japs attacked at dawn, climbing up the curved finger of the crest through the forested draws, fighting with fury for two hours, and then with the doggedness of desperation for six hours more before retreating into the jungle, withdrawing their wounded and some of their dead but leaving some fifty slain comrades behind.

Hours later, we checked our casualty list, and it seemed incredible. Our own dead were three; our wounded hardly more than a dozen. And we learned to our amazement that a handful of Marines, perhaps thirty, had defended that finger-like ridge against ten times their number.

Preparing under the cover of night in the ravine below Target Hill, the Japs moved upward through thickly wooded draws defended by an understrength platoon and a single machine gun under 2nd Lt. Leo E. Lyons, twenty-four, of Buffalo, New York. The fledgling officer described the engagement:

"We first suspected that the Japs were up to something about 3:30 A.M., when we heard the movement of men in the ravine below, and the telltale tinkle of metallic objects. But we held our fire under strict orders to fire at night only when definitely attacked, in order not to give away our positions.

"The waiting was the toughest part of the battle. We could hear the muffled jabbering of the Japs, and once a loud voice shouting orders.

"Then, in the twilight that comes before dawn, a green

flare burst over the ridge—the Jap signal for attack. But it was also the signal for us to fire, for in the weird light of the flare we could see the chanting Japs clambering through our barbed wire, twenty yards below our foxholes.

"We literally poured our ammunition into them. We showered them with grenades as well, and our mortars from our rear burst among them with awesome destruction.

"Led by a major and four other officers—they were found among the dead—the Japs fought savagely and sought to blow us out of our positions with grenades and knee mortars and machine guns. But they never got more than a few feet beyond the barbed wire."

The victory of the little band of grunts was a glowing demonstration of fire control and discipline, the leathernecks being for the most part hardened Guadalcanal veterans. The bellowing voices of Platoon Sgt. John S. Owen, twenty-six, Anderson, North Carolina, and Pfc. Joseph M. Ziane, twenty-nine, Hudson, Massachusetts, encouraged the men while calming them, and the two inspired their platoonmates by example as well.

The boys grinned with elation as they heard the comforting clatter of "Eli's" machine gun singing a murderous tune and spraying the slope with deadly rounds. Only later did word get around that "Eli"—Pfc. Whitney P. Pierron, eighteen, of Houma, Louisiana—had kept on firing with his wounded assistant gunner raised between his knees. His buddy had been shot in the head, and Eli had propped him up to prevent his bleeding to death.

It wasn't until later, too, that they learned how a communications wire-layer took over and manned a wounded Marine's foxhole, laughed off two bullets that pierced his helmet, then was killed by a third. But in the few minutes before he died, the wireman had accounted for a dozen enemy with his tommy gun.

There was the problem of ammunition supply that night. The dump was uphill, about 300 yards away, and the crest was saturated with fire all the way. Nonetheless, all of a dozen round trips were made by Pfcs. Franklin H. Cunningham, twenty-one, of Bangor, Maine, and John A. Trotter,

twenty-six, of Chicago. Once, Cunningham's rifle was shot
from his hands, but he picked up another to get in his own
burst or two between ammo runs.

After the first two furious hours, the original defenders
were relieved, for only so many could defend the ridge at
any one time.

When the Japs pulled back and fled, we buried those they
left behind.

In eight days of hard fighting, the Marines on Cape
Gloucester gained not only Target Hill but also the two
airports.

I took advantage of a respite to dig up a score of stories.

No sooner did they hit the beach than a Marine company
racing toward the river a mile away ran into a strong Jap defense position. The captain, intent on his mission, called out
a wrecking crew to deal with the obstacle, while he by-
passed it and pressed his outfit forward to his assigned goal.

The brief encounter was ignited by Pfc. Mike Geraghty,
twenty-one, of Monticello, New York, who spotted the
camouflaged log-and-earthworks and caught the movement
of two Japs scurrying into the dugout. He tossed a grenade
into it. The enemy hurled two back at him, one a dud, but
Mike was not hurt.

At that point the column leader ordered Sgt. Lacey M.
Ward, twenty-three, of Wolcott, New York, to take Geraghty
and three other infantry men and take out the emplacement.
Ward quickly pointed at Pvt. Louis Beam Jr., of Brown-
wood, Texas; Pfc. Paul H. Eaton Jr., of Denver, Colorado;
and Pfc. Jesse W. Hamilton, of Dayton, Ohio, and with his
volunteer crew undertook the demolition project.

While two of the grunts covered the front access and two
the rear, Ward sneaked to the top, fired into the front opening, and followed up with a grenade. Two Japs made a break
for it but were slain by Beam and Eaton. A third Jap was
found hiding within the dugout and was finished off by
Ward and Hamilton.

The interruption took fifteen minutes. Ward and Co. then
rushed off to join their company.

A pack howitzer team, moving into the jungle from the

beach about an hour after the infantry, had started to set up when a Jap was seen crawling out of a hidden pillbox. The artillerymen, who had thought the area had been sanitized by the assault troops, took over the task.

Pfc. Charley "Moon" Mullins, twenty-one, of Dizney, Kentucky, quickly shot the Jap and killed him. Pfc. Robert L. Evans, twenty-one, of Tuscumbia, Alabama, heaved a grenade into the emplacement. Five dead were found inside, and Cpl. Bernard R. Jakalsky, thirty-one, of Chicago, in need of a cap, took one off the head of one of the Japs.

The following day, Pfc. Jack Wine, twenty-one, of Dayton, Ohio, passing by the dugout, ran into a leatherneck souvenir hunter who mentioned that he thought one of the dead Japs was still alive. Wine went into the hole to see for himself and determined that one of the dead was alive but seemingly unconscious, clutching a knife in his hands against his chest. Wine kicked the knife away, "just in case," and retained the blade as his own memento.

Taken to a field hospital, the unconscious Jap was determined by the medics to be playing possum, and Wine was credited with capturing the first live Jap on Cape Gloucester.

The prisoner—washed, fed, and given medical treatment—reacted like no other Japanese soldier I'd seen captured. He did not show guilt or shame for having been taken alive, and expressed his gratitude with toothy grins and garbled English. He liked to sing, and during six days at the field hospital frequently burst into song.

One of the corpsmen taught the prisoner a new tune, which the Jap took particular pleasure in humming. The Jap was never told the name of the song, nor the words: "God Bless America!"

I enjoyed writing we-won accounts, but I had to report the we-lost stories, too.

A Marine stretcher party—four wounded and six armed escorts—was ambushed behind our own lines by a Jap machine gunner who waylaid them as they were proceeding to the first-aid station.

All but two of the ten were shot up, and three killed.

Pfc. Arthur S. Davis, twenty-one, of Anderson, South

Carolina, escaped unscathed but severely shaken up, and he was still jittery when I talked with him at the station.

"God alone knows how I escaped getting hit. . . . We were so close to the machine gunner. . . . I couldn't see him in the bush . . . but I could feel the heat of the muzzle blast. . . .

"There were ten of us . . . one stretcher case . . . two walking wounded . . . one malaria case . . . and six carriers . . .

"Only a few minutes before . . . our company had engaged in a skirmish . . . and we were taking out the first wounded . . . down a trail leading from a small ridge . . . when we were caught head-on by the gun blast. . . .

"I instinctively dropped to the ground . . . lay like dead . . . trying to figure out if I'd been hit. I lay still for about five minutes . . . and managed to squirm out of my pack. . . .

"I whispered to our leader . . . asked if he'd been hurt. . . . 'Got it bad,' he said.

"Don't think I'm hurt," I said. "Want me to go for help?"

" 'If you can make it,' he said.

"I started to run uphill . . . shouting to Marines already running downhill to help us . . .

"One of the wounded men cried out for help . . . so I tried to pull him along with me . . . but the machine gun opened up on us and we fell to the ground . . . missed by the fire. . . . The Marines who saved us never found the machine gunner . . .

"It was a massacre. . . . We didn't have a chance."

Several leathernecks tipped me off to "Wild Bill Hickok," so called because he practiced shooting his tommy gun from the hip every chance he got. Soon after the landing, his platoon passed into enemy terrain, and "Wild Bill"— Private Melvin E. Caldwell, nineteen, of Alapha, Georgia— fired from the hip and killed a Jap who popped out of a bush, his rifle aimed at the platoon leader. His platoonmates still called him Wild Bill Hickok, but now with admiration.

Pfc. George O. White, twenty-two, of Fayettesville, Georgia, was a Sunday school teacher at the East Point First Baptist Church before he joined the Marine Corps "because men were dying and I felt that I must do my part in bringing the war to a quick end."

On the third day of his company's advance against opposition, plodding behind the tanks leading the attack, the offensive was pinned down by fire from a hidden emplacement on a ridge. White, by then an experienced scout, skirted the flank of the gunner, climbed stealthily to the crest, crawled within fifteen feet of the machine gun, killed two Japs, and scattered the others.

"They never even saw me," White said. "I'm a Christian, and I feel the Lord delivered them into my hands."

A couple of days before the New Year the Mitsubishis dropped not only bombs but leaflets as well. Brightly colored and with crude cartoons, some pornographic, the literature needled the Aussie soldiers, saying that while they were fighting and dying in New Guinea, the American troops were living it up in Australia, wooing their wives and sweethearts.

One leaflet I picked up depicted the Anzac diggers drowning in a sea of battle as President Roosevelt, in top hat and swimming trucks, made off with Australia. The text read: "While Aussies shed their precious blood, Ole Man Roosevelt finds his selfish aims going according to schedule."

Flung into the wrong battle zone, the crude circulars were good for a chuckle or two.

The next day, the mail arrived. Yes, we got mail on Cape Gloucester. Come rain or shine, come rain or monsoon, the mail came through. Mail day was sacred and raised the spirits of the homesick grunts—except for the few who received "Dear John" letters. And I got a warm letter from Bernice.

Most popular man of the day—that day—was Cpl. John S. Donohue, twenty-eight, of Brooklyn, New York, the mailman. He'd been wounded on Guadalcanal, where he'd delivered "mail" to the Japs with a machine-gun unit.

One envelope contained an ad that gave our platoon an old-fashioned horse laugh. It wasn't a bitter laugh, for living next to danger engenders a special sense of humor. It was rather a snickering, jeering *yuk-yuk*. The advertisement, from Hovey's Department Store, Boston, offered, at $2 a throw, "Foxhole pillows for your fighting man."

The pillow, 7.5 inches by 8, weighing only 4.5 ounces, the ad read, was what every serviceman on the front needed.

"Here's a practical gift that will help him relax or slumber: a pillow for his battlefield sleeping time, or to relieve his fatigue in a foxhole or trench or other awkward spot."

Such an awkward spot as during an enemy bayonet charge?

A platoonmate from New Waterville, Maine, received a November copy of his local newspaper carrying a home-town-hero story about him, and a front-page photo of the winter's snow-covered scenery. Just the right touch for our tropical, torrential New Year's Day.

I had been tipped off by a friend in Intelligence that a Marine amphibian tractor company had stormed the beachhead and controlling ridge with the Army's 112th Cavalry at Arawe on Cape Merkus, on the southwestern coast of New Britain, and then had been transported by sea in time to bolster the Marine landing on Cape Gloucester on the northwestern coast.

I tracked down Marine officers and crewmen who had taken part in the Army's Cape Merkus assault on December 15 and then had also provided punch for the Marine invasion of Cape Gloucester on December 26—a remarkable feat.

The leathernecks who participated in the double landings on New Britain already had two landings at Guadalcanal and Tulagi under their belts.

At Arawe, amtrac crews carried twenty-four GIs on their light, slow Alligators and the new, more powerful, armored Buffaloes five miles from the mother ship through the swells and a ring of coral spurs and shoots. The amphibians then hauled up supplies to the Army grunts for four days, in which the amtracs also shot down two enemy dive-bombers and led a charge against the entrenched foe with their .50-caliber machine guns.

The double-duty officers were 1st Lts. Robert N. Kitchin, twenty-nine, of Milwaukee, an engineer out of the

University of Wisconsin and Marquette; and Harold F. Harman, thirty, of Ada, Oklahoma, an accountant out of East Central State College.

Two of their crewmen were Corporals Amirault and Morris, the Boston University football team players whom I had met six months earlier with Coach "Pat" Hanley on Guadalcanal.

Corporal Amirault and Cpl. Ralph K. Marshall, nineteen, of Grand Rapids, Michigan, saw their Alligator sunk from under them after a leak from the ventilator system disabled their amtrac as it was plowing through the surf toward the shore.

"Unable to run the engine, we floated around for a couple of hours watching the show," Amirault said. "We were almost hit by a destroyer during the predawn haze, and later we looked on as a destroyer engaged in a duel with a Jap recon plane.

"We then managed to transfer our load of twenty-four GI troops to a minesweeper, and we were towing the Alligator when Jap dive-bombers attacked. Our ship made an abrupt spurt in its maneuvering, and the tractor took a nosedive into the sea. We had managed to get the troops' gear off, but Marshall and I lost everything we had. Except my toothbrush."

Later that D day at Arawe, Corporal Amirault and Cpl. Airkiel Cincone, twenty-three, of Somerville, Massachusetts—with three brothers in overseas service—manned a Buffalo to lead the Army's forward surge.

Corporal Morris, with his teammate, Sgt. John H. Burton, twenty-two, of Augusta, Georgia, took over the Buffalo's machine guns, and they were firing at an enemy Val when it simply came apart under the combined fire of several amphibian crews.

"I celebrated New Year's Eve on Cape Gloucester carrying the wounded off the lines," recounted Morris.

Another Alligator, foundering from a loosened pontoon plug, was saved when its crew split up the sailing, bailing, and flailing operations, after transferring its load of soldiers to other amphibians. With Platoon Sgt. John E. Rintallan, twenty-three, of Walled Lake, Michigan, driving and Cpl. Justin A. Bayne, twenty-six, of Niagara Falls, New York, scooping, and Sgt. Nathan M. Galvin, twenty-two, of Dunn, North Carolina, shooting at a dive-bomber, they salvaged the amtrac. When Rintallan's GIs were shifted to another amphibian, that one also broke down, and the GIs had to be spread all around among the remaining amtracs.

An overheated engine created a red-hot problem for Cpl. Samuel J. Alaimo, twenty-five, of New York City, and Cpl. Michael Hubiak, twenty-nine, of Herkimer, New York. When their Alligator was throbbing into the shoreline too fast, a Navy vessel nudged the amtrac as a warning, since a shouted alert could not have been heard over the noise of the churning Alligator.

Despite their difficulties getting ashore, the remaining Alligators and Buffaloes, commanded by Capt. Thomas N. Boler, twenty-three, of Toledo, Ohio, immediately went to work for the Army. Two of the Buffaloes, used like tanks, set up a W-crossfire from their four machine guns, to spearhead the three-mile drive that broke through the enemy perimeter, and secured the beachhead.

The Marine amtracs also utilized their machine guns for ground and antiaircraft defense during seven dive-bombing raids and were credited with two of the Aichis. And when called upon, the amtracs served as bulldozers, bowling over brush and brambles to clear fields of fire.

The amtracs could do many things, but, some critics noted, the amtracs couldn't fly.

CHAPTER 17

"Suicide Creek"

The four of us CCs and photogs had agreed to meet, if possible, as soon as there was a break after the first phase of the landing.

With Target Hill and the two airfields securely in the hands of the Marines, we gravitated back to the command post of Brig. Gen. Lemuel C. Shepherd Jr. and exchanged experiences and observations. Monte, it developed, had had the most dangerous venture among us.

Monte was moving along with the First Division units pressing out of the beachhead that first day, following the tanks toward enemy airstrips. He was happy with the action available for his camera, and pleased with the footage he got from the tank charge. But he felt he ought to take a shot inside a pillbox silenced by a tank. As he stuck his head into the emplacement, a startled Jap stuck *his* face out.

Monteverdi jumped back, grabbed for his carbine, and opened fire. Then, to make sure, he tossed a hand grenade into the hole and plumped facedown to watch it go off. Instead, the intact explosive came bouncing back out and blew up, showering Monte with shrapnel and wounding him slightly.

Thoroughly aroused, and no longer interested in taking pictures, Monte borrowed another pineapple, and this time counted after pulling the pin, then pitched it into the dugout. He smiled as he heard the thing explode.

Determined to get his shots, Monte again stuck his head in. When the smoke cleared, he saw another Jap. Monte ducked out to ponder his dilemma. Should he try the grenade ploy a third time, or should he give up the bizarre throwing contest and return to the tanks?

The cornered Jap solved the problem while Monte was arguing with himself. Another explosion shook the pillbox. The Jap had taken his own life.

O'Leary had, meanwhile, run into another problem. He had somehow uncovered a case of Filipino beer, good stuff, from a hidden Japanese cache. But what could he do with it and how could he possibly hide the case?

Jerry's quick mind came up with the answer. He spotted two Navajo comunicators—who relayed messages in Navajo so that the Japs couldn't understand the orders and reports even if they intercepted them—and made them an offer they could not refuse. If they would shuttle the brew and safely duck the case into a foxhole—which they would dig—he would give them four bottles. The thirsty Indians struck a quick deal.

O'Leary never did reveal his source for the suds, but he was soon passing it out among the grunts. Of course, he retained a few for him—and me.

We wished each other good luck and took off for our outfits because we learned at the CP that the next stage of the invasion was imminent.

Eight days after the landing on Cape Gloucester, Brig. Gen. Lemuel C. Shepherd Jr. ordered an attack on Hill 660, the key point dominating the Borgen Bay area.

The general determined on a powerful southeasterly sweep across our defensive perimeter aimed at dislodging the entrenched enemy and delousing the territory of Jap artillery that menaced our supply beaches.

The mission was assigned to the Third Battalion, Seventh Marine Regiment, commanded by Lt. Col. John E. Weber, twenty-seven, of Rochester, New York, with two companies in assault. Brenner and I went in with K Company, O'Leary with L Company. Monteverdi opted to circulate looking for photo opportunities.

The offensive was opened up at 10 A.M. of that January 2, with a hot sun glaring down at us during a lull in the incessant downpour, warming our rain-dampened spirits.

The two assault companies started out well enough, squeezing through the defensive barbed wire that had been hastily strung up the night before, and moving carefully into the thick jungle in combat file.

The scouts and pointmen cautiously probed the terrain ahead of them, looking for signs of the enemy the way a surgeon meticulously probes for a shrapnel fragment.

There was no bantering among the Marines, only acute alertness as they pushed their way through the jungle, examining the matted foliage of the bushes and trees for the hidden snipers, who opened up almost from the point of departure.

But the two columns, tempered on Guadalcanal, shook the snipers off and advanced at a slow, steady pace. By noon the Marines had progressed about 250 yards.

Communications crews trailed telephone wire immediately behind the assault teams so that the forward units could be in continuous touch with the command post to the rear. Reserve companies drew up behind the assault troops, the leathernecks standing by silently, their faces strained, ears focused on the cacophony of firing ahead of them.

By noon our forward echelon was within thirty yards of a stream, and the files held up while the scouts crept to the riverbank and stared at the other side, searching for enemy bunkers.

One scout reported he had spotted what looked like a camouflaged pillbox. A second caught a glimpse of eight enemy soldiers bathing downstream. Carefully backtracking, he reported his sighting, then slipped into the platoon line and picked off a sniper, his first, but was himself twice wounded across the arm.

The platoon of 2nd Lt. Arthur B. Gardner, twenty-three, of Long Island, New York, was dispatched to eliminate the suspected pillbox. What with enemy soldiers carelessly bathing in the river, it didn't appear to be a difficult undertaking.

Spreading out in skirmish formation, the platoon crept forward to the bank of the stream. For several minutes all that could be heard was the muted crackle of the grunts filtering through the brush. Then . . . then the earsplitting outburst of machine guns shattered the unnatural stillness, followed by the exultant shouts of the Japs and the anguished cries of downed men.

Instead of a single pillbox, eight machine-gun nests plastered the platoon with sweeping jets of shellfire.

Recoiling from the suddenness of the shock, the Marines engaged the enemy in a furious firefight as Lieutenant Gardner, only recently commissioned from the ranks, desperately tried to rally his stricken platoon even as he was cut down. Mortally wounded, he still shouted encouragement to his men.

Pharmacist's Mate 3rd Class Daniel Webster, nineteen, of Downey, California, saw Lieutenant Gardner go down and without hesitation the corpsman crept into the shoot-out to reach the fallen officer's side. But he, too, was hit, killed outright.

Then Pharmacist's Mate 2nd Class Dean L. Witters, twenty-three, of McCook, Nebraska, undeterred, charged into the firestorm. He rescued the platoon leader, but Lieutenant Gardner died within the hour.

Three Marines broke ranks, and I watched as they crawled into the kill zone to bring out Webster, the slain corpsman. Pfc. Edward E. Dalton, twenty-two, of Charles Town, West Virginia, and Pfc. Raymond P. Smith, twenty-one, of Rockingham, North Carolina, carried the dead medical aide, while Pfc. Roy L. Burton, twenty, of Shreveport, Louisiana, kept his tommy gun ablaze, covering the rescuers. They made it unharmed although a bullet drove through Burton's helmet.

Heartrending cries of "Corpsman!" "Corpsman!" rose brokenly above the clamor of the machine guns as the disciplined infantrymen, pinned down, held fast while the rescue teams—corpsmen and stretcher bearers—bellied up among the stricken to bring them back. A second corpsman, Pharmacist's Mate 3rd Class Jack W. Hoyt, gave up his own life in the heroic rescues, and two others were badly wounded

but were themselves lugged out to safety by their fellow
aides.

Some of the wounded were carried out on the backs of
their rescuers; some were carried out on their ponchos.
Some pulled themselves back to our line dragging gashed,
bleeding limbs.

An unnerved corporal staggered back from the ambush,
sobbing over and over again: "Frenchy's killed! Frenchy's
killed!" He sank to the ground, his chest heaving convul-
sively. A friend clapped him on the back, shouting words I
could not hear above the din. Tears welled up in the eyes of
some grunts, but they held their ground and kept on firing as
ordered by their NCOs.

The regimental surgeon, Lt. Cmdr. Vernon E. Martens,
USN, of University City, Missouri, looked down on two
dead Marines and softly murmured:

"They look just like two dirty little boys sleeping."

He was right.

After sixty minutes or so of battle, Platoon Sgt. Jack
Buckley, twenty-two, of Newark, New Jersey, could count
only nine other able-bodies of his original thirty-nine men.
In all, the two platoons suffered more than forty casualties.
But our riflemen and machine gunners exacted a high toll
from the ambushers until a half-trac gun carrier wheeled up
to the front and, with its 75mm cannon, blew up one pillbox.

Even as the Marines were ordered to dig in and scoop out
slit trenches with their stubby shovels, our mortar shells began exploding among the Japanese entrenchments. We were
so close to the enemy on the opposite bank of the stream
that shrapnel whistled through the air and fragments fell
among us.

One platoon which had started to cross the river—
afterward remembered as Suicide Creek—ran into withering fire from the other side, and found itself caught on a
narrow strip between the steep embankment and the stream.
The platoon was virtually wiped out by the surprise enfilade. But not all the men left on the riverbank for dead that
night were corpses.

Pfc. Kenneth L. Anderson, twenty-five, a former pie and pastry salesman from West Des Moines, Iowa, was alive, although his platoon had already listed him among the slain.

Following his rescue and revival, Anderson told me his living-death experience:

"I was on the right-flank squad when the platoon moved in skirmish formation over the rise of the riverbank. And just as we started down to the stream, about ten yards away, we were swept by a hail of fire.

"Reflexively, I hurled myself to the ground and lay there while the machine-gun bullets hummed all around.

"When the fire let up, I squirmed around enough to see that three of my squadmates had been hit, probably killed.

"I guess my movement caught the eye of a machine gunner across the stream, for he opened up on me, and I froze.... I was in an exposed position ... and the only thing I could do was lie as if dead and pray inwardly.

"From noon until dark, I lay there while our machine guns dueled with those of the Japs, while our own mortars as well as the Japs' shells fell around. A piece of shrapnel tore through my pack, and I lay there afraid to move.

"Toward dark, I took a chance and cried, 'Corpsman!' I wasn't wounded, but I hoped to attract attention from the other Marines, only twenty yards away.

"It turned out to be a suicidal ruse, for the Japs, to confuse and bring into the open the medical corpsmen ... who attempted to rescue the stricken members of the platoon ... had been shouting, 'Corpsman!' all during the afternoon ... and my call only drew fire from the Marines.

"Night came, but I was still afraid to move, for I knew what it would mean to attempt crawling toward our own lines—death at the hands of my own buddies, who would certainly take me for a Jap.

"God, how long the minutes were!

"I hoped that under the cover of night I could at least relax from the horrible tension, but again I guessed wrong. The Japs sneaked across the stream to rifle the bodies of our dead.

"I heard rather than saw them coming—the dirty jackals—and again I froze and prayed. I could hear them tearing the equipment off the bodies of my three buddies lying a couple of feet away. Then a Jap put his hand on my pack and, paralyzed, I awaited the blow of a rifle or the slash of a bayonet.

"Somehow, for some reason known only to God, the Jap released his grip on my pack and suddenly left me. I couldn't understand. I lost all sense of comprehension.

"Through the entire night—a terror nightmare it was—I lay aching with the pain that comes from taut immobility. I prayed all night long. I said every prayer I remembered, and I made up new ones.

"I did more than pray that night. I learned to pray.

"Dawn came, and I roused myself out of a semicoma. I fired my weapon at the Japs, again in the desperate hope that the Marines would recognize the sound of my BAR [Browning automatic rifle].

"Again my strategy backfired, for the Marines thought it was a Jap firing with our own weapon.

"By this time I was out of my wits, and would have made a break for it, but a few minutes later I saw a half-trac coming my way. It began to spray enemy positions, the cannister flying over my head.

"I guess I went out of my head. I must have cracked wide open. They tell me I jumped up screaming the name of my buddies and ran directly in the path of the trac. I must have been out of my head, because I had seen those buddies killed the day before.

"Neither the Japs nor the Marine guns must have seen me, for I stumbled into the half-trac. Somebody recognized me and hauled me aboard.

"I don't remember what happened after that . . . though they tell me I pointed out Jap pillboxes to the gunners.

"Maybe I did, I don't know . . . I didn't come to until two days later."

The Big Push for Hill 660 was stopped that first day on the edge of Suicide Creek. We had covered the length of little more than two regulation football fields.

We didn't get across Suicide Creek the second day, either, but we did clean out the eight pillboxes that had blocked our advance. We did it because of the raw courage of a small, skinny sergeant from Bell Vernon, Pennsylvania, and a squad of Marines, most of whom were themselves killed or wounded in annihilating the enemy strongpoint.

Led by twenty-four-year-old Sgt. Lloyd E. Crusan, the Marines charged those pillboxes. Crusan himself was an avenging fury, triggering more than a thousand rounds from his tommy gun and killing thirty Japs. Thirty more were accounted for by his squad. It took most of the afternoon to finish up the killing chore.

Meanwhile, the tanks—three of the new heavier and more powerful Shermans—were called up to smash through the stream and the Jap defenses on the other side, but the bank was too steep for them.

Engineers and Seabees of the 17th Regiment were rushed up with a bulldozer to improvise a ramp for the tanks, but that drew the immediate attention of the snipers and machine gunners on the other side, who stalled the operation by shooting up the tractor driver.

The leader of the crew, Staff Sgt. Keary Lane, of Perquiama County, Kentucky, hopped into the driver's seat and got the bulldozer going again, but had to give it up after being hit four times. He turned the machine over to another volunteer, walked back to the aid station, had the four slugs removed, and returned in time to take over again from the man who had succeeded him and had also been clipped by a sniper.

Lane completed the bulldozer's task, and the engineers followed up by throwing up a bridge solid enough for the tanks. The next day the Shermans crossed the stream and crushed the heart of the Japanese resistance, allowing us to capture the maze of Jap fortifications.

O'Leary, Brenner, and I had been in the middle of the turmoil and were thankful to have come through the three-day battle alive and unhurt. But we were all shaken up, especially O'Leary, who'd been with the platoon that was ambushed. It was Jerry's first combat and he was still reeling from the shock of the battle, which Bob and I had experienced on Guadalcanal and the New Georgias.

Bob and I had been caught in a mortar barrage the first day on the Big Push and a particle of hot shrapnel ricocheted off my helmet into Bob's hand. He had also waded into the river in order to get a better angle for his camera, and somehow got back to land without getting hit when caught in the ambush. The little guy was unfazed by his close call, but angry with himself for failing to get the shots he'd planned.

Once across the river, the drive forward eased long enough to allow us to regroup. Jerry and I decided it would be a good time to undertake a foray for souvenirs inside the abandoned Jap positions. Guessing they had been arranged for the comfort of Tojo's officers, we selected a set of caves dug into the hillside. We thought we might find prize items like sabers, hara-kiri knives, pistols, binoculars, and, oh yes, Rising Sun flags. I was still looking to bring home a Jap flag.

As we began to enter one of the caves, we noticed a flicker of light and shadow.

"Did you see something?" whispered Jerry.

"I did."

"Do you think it's a Jap?"

"I do."

Whereupon we spontaneously backed out of the lair to consider our next move. Investigating, we found another entry into the tunnel, substantiating our quickly formed opinion that the cave was U-shaped and that a Jap or two might be lurking within, concealed by the darkness.

"You go in, Jerry," I suggested. "I'll cover you from back here."

"You'll what!"

"I'll cover you," I replied. "Don't worry."

Well, the truth is Jerry was a little worried. He didn't like my idea at all. In fact, he went so far as to suggest that I go in while he covered me from the rear.

Our polite you-go-first offers abruptly ended when we simultaneously recalled Monte's cave-grenade caper. We each tossed one in, having the good sense to alert one another by calling, "Look out! Grenades!" then dropping to the ground.

Seconds later we looked up and discovered an entire platoon of Marines sprawled out behind us.

A reserve Marine unit, moving up the line, had heard us yell "Grenades!" and the wary platoon had hit the deck.

We never did find out whether Japs had been hiding inside that tunnel, because Jerry was too stubborn to go in while I backed him up. After all, I came up with the idea first.

Led by the Sherman tanks, the Marines forged through the jungle to reach their next immediate objective, a 150-foot-high hill. It took five hours of furious fighting for the leathernecks to take the top, but holding the heights against the counterattack turned out to be an even fiercer battle.

The Japs struck back five times during the first night in a ferocious attempt to recapture the ridge.

The counterattack was kicked off by a three-hour mortar barrage. One of the shells dropped into the battalion command post, injuring three Marines. Colonel Weber and 1st Lt. Maurice Keating, twenty-four, of Philadelphia (Villanova '42) were scrunched down alongside the wounded trio but escaped unhurt. A shell landed at the feet of Gunnery Sgt. Robert D. Christenbury, twenty-eight, of Catawba, North Carolina, but fortunately it was a dud.

Another fell close by Pfc. John L. Schluens Jr., of Somerville, Texas, and ripped the lid off his ammunition box, but the Texan refused to give up his machine-gun position, and collected dividends with the weapon later that night during the Jap attacks.

We hurled a few mortars of our own, but reserved our heaviest fire until about 3:30 A.M., when the Jap infantry—believed to be the victors at Bataan, the troops of the notorious General Homa—charged up at us from the jungle, yammering all the way. "They sound like cows and pigs in a mooing-squealing contest," remarked Sgt. William T. Burtyk, twenty-two, of Coverdale, Pennsylvania, a mortar section observer.

Then, as the Jap troops closed in, they mixed their English gibberish with cries of "Corpsman!" "Corpsman!" and "Hold your fire!", a ruse that didn't work for them that night. And then there were taunts like "What's a matta, you no shoot?"

Several Marines later said that Jap soldiers creeping to their foxholes shouted "Cigallet!" "Cigallet!" It sounded like they thought the word was some kind of slogan.

So intense was the fighting that Colonel Weber's battalion had only a few minutes of ammo left when the battle subsided at dawn. He had already told his men to save their ammunition and turn to their grenades and bayonets.

The order was enthusiastically carried out by Pvt. William E. York, of Penacook, New Hampshire. The former New Hampshire University hockey player, perched between two trees where the hill took a sharp drop, called for a gunnysack full of grenades and threw them down among the Jap soldiers trying to down him. When he wasn't emptying bags of grenades on them, he pointed his BAR downhill and sprayed the Japs with slugs.

Some of the enemy managed to infiltrate the American positions, and in the hand-to-hand fighting—with bayonets, rifle butts, knives—some were slain. As were some Marines.

Pfc. Francis J. DeGregario, nineteen, of Syracuse, New York, ran out of ammo and scurried back to the command post, fifteen yards away, to get more. The supply was so low at that point of the fighting that he had to borrow cartridges for his rifle from another leatherneck. He returned to his post to confront a Jap soldier running at him with pointed bayonet. DeGregario disposed of him with the borrowed ammunition.

One Jap sneaked through the forward position of the Marines and, although hidden in the brush, emerged and stood up in full view and committed hara-kiri with the traditional disemboweling ritual. All of us who witnessed that were astonished; we could understand fighting and dying for one's country, but could not understand that degree of self-sacrifice as the final expression of fealty to an emperor.

Many Japs were killed that night. We estimated, conservatively, 100. One enemy corpse was found dressed in a standard Marine combat outfit. Whatever trick he had planned had failed.

The machine-gun crews fired more ammunition that night than in any previous engagement. Outstanding was the crew of Sgt. S.C. Dixon, of Marion, Arkansas.

Colonel Weber was proud of the battalion's action that night, but he also turned to me and said, "My men are as fine fighters as you can find in the division, but we must say that the mortar and artillery men with their accurate firing saved the night for us."

The morning after, we named the 150-foot elevation "Morphine Hill," because the unflinching corpsmen had been so inextricably involved in our battles up and on the knoll. We, too, had suffered many casualties who were saved from death and- or relieved from agonizing pain by the Navy medics pressing up the hill and hanging on to their patients despite the counterattacks.

Within a few minutes of our drive up Hill 150, the first wounded Marine, a half-pint sergeant, limped to the first-aid station. "Only a flesh wound," he announced with an infectious grin. But as the sharp staccato of battle rose in volume, more of our boys were struck down, and the pharmacist's mates moved in quickly to help them, some themselves soon targeted and cut down.

Our stretcher bearers quickly began operating like an assembly line, at first smoothly, then feverishly as the pitch of battle rose. They knew—and we knew—that a quick shot of plasma could save a life, that a quick application of morphine would suppress otherwise horrible pain. The wounded, gently as possible under the circumstances, were moved to the rear first-aid station. The more seriously hurt were then taken to a field hospital farther in the rear for further treatment or evacuation.

But the most urgent task was the injection of plasma

to prevent severely lowered blood pressure and consequent shock. The wounded were, for the most part, stoic about their pain. They gritted their teeth and tried to choke down moans. But some of the stricken sobbed in pain, unable to restrain themselves. Some pleaded for water and help. Some spoke encouraging words to a buddy more severely wounded.

One grunt, critically hurt, was unable to control his spasms, and kept repeating over and over again: "I'm not yellow . . . but it hurts like hell." Quick fingers injected him with morphine, and quick hands carried him off to the rear.

Another infantryman, his head covered in bloody bandages, had to be physically restrained. "Tommy's still out there," he cried. "Let me go and get Tommy." But we knew that Tommy was dead, and the dead had to be left behind until the wounded were first brought out.

A young corpsman, still in his teens and in battle for the first time, frenziedly flew at his chief, who was coolly preparing a plasma injection.

"Quick! Quick!" gasped the first-timer. "The lieutenant is dying!"

"Nothing more we can do," responded his boss without interrupting the expert movement of his fingers.

"We've got to do something!" the corpsman screamed. "We can't just let him die!" He danced up and down hysterically.

The older pharmacist's mate halted his work just long enough to slap the first-timer across the face and spoke sharply:

"This is no time to start cracking up, bub. Cut out the crap and start pitching in!"

The slap and a loud cry for "Corpsman!" startled the corpsman out of his emotional shock, and he dashed off to respond.

It was excruciating to watch helplessly as the lieutenant died. He'd been given plasma four times, but a bullet had paralyzed his respiratory system and he was unconscious. We could tell he was dying by the changing color of his skin.

The lieutenant was only twenty-two. He had long fingers, like those of an artist, and, truth to tell, ambition to become a painter after the war, to go to Paris to study and train. Instead, that afternoon he had led his platoon against the enemy and his dream had abruptly ended.

The explosion of a Jap mortar shell on the hilltop froze us. We were, momentarily, terrified. Then we pulled three wounded into a bomb crater on a slope while the corpsmen continued to work their magic without letup. Shells burst around them, but in the crater, three aides still held their right arms aloft to allow the precious liquid to flow more easily through the injection tubes.

When the medics ran out of dressing, they collected our individual first-aid kits and our canteens for the stricken.

The Marines also ran out to rescue their wounded comrades. Pfc. John T. Owens, of Providence, Rhode Island, gave up his life trying to retrieve his buddy from the maelstrom of machine-gun fire. The LaSalle Academy all-around athlete and Guadalcanal vet was standing by with his mortar outfit to the rear when word came through that his pal had been wounded. "Happy" Owens and a batterymate, Pfc. John F. Carey, twenty-four, of Waterbury, Connecticut, immediately volunteered to bring out their friend and two other stricken Marines. Carey later told me, "We crawled up to the three wounded boys and managed to give two of them first aid, despite the Jap fire. Then we crawled back to bring up stretchers. We were creeping toward the wounded a second time, when Owens, in front of me, was killed by a machine-gun burst. Somehow, I was untouched."

Other grunts joined Carey in rescuing all three wounded men, including Owens's buddy.

Sometimes the rescue missions failed despite valiant effort. When they saw their leader go down under a hail of fire, Pfc. Harvey "Tommy Gun" Fisher, twenty-six, of Wilmington, North Carolina, and Sgt. Louis S. "Greek" Maravelas, twenty-seven, of Brooklyn, New York, wriggled into the entangled terrain while Pfc. Thomas H. "Citizen" Kane, twenty-two, of Springfield Gardens, New York, and Pvt.

Andy L. Solis, twenty-five, of Santa Paula, California, offered themselves as decoy targets. Behind them, on a flank from which he could oversee the entire scene, tensed Pfc. Forrest G. James, twenty-four, of Mankato, Minnesota, with his poised BAR. When the Japs opened up, so did James, with telling effect, although his canteen was punctured in the ensuing exchange. "Tommy Gun" and "Greek" reached their leader, only to find him dead.

The perilous effort had been made in vain—but it was for a comrade who might have been alive.

The bullet-riddled body of the sergeant was retrieved later and buried in the crude cemetery dug for the men who died in the battle for New Britain.

Among other hometown stories I sent back to HQ were these, in brief:

Pfc. Jeremiah J. "Ski" O'Shaughnessy, of Boston, Massachusetts, died by his blazing gun on Morphine Hill, according to his assistant gunner, Pfc. John Lichner, of Chicago, and his ammo carrier, Pvt. Robert D. Thornbury, of Ashland, Kentucky. Lichner said:

"Two of us were on watch at our gun emplacement, and Jerry was catching four winks in a foxhole nearby, when at about 4:30 in the morning the Japs started screaming and hollering and coming our way.

"I fired for a few minutes until Ski dropped in on the fly and took over. The Japs kept rushing us, but Ski never for an instant took his gun off the final protective line the Japs would have to cross to hit our defense.

"Some Japs got through and crept in around us. One got within a yard of Jerry, but one of the boys took care of that Jap.

"It must have been one of the Japs who got through that got Ski. I felt a thump on my helmet and saw Jerry keel over. I took over and Thornbury got a corpsman to help Ski, but he was dead. Died instantly. The thump on my helmet was a deflected bullet."

Pfc. Robert E. Pressler, twenty-one, of Huntington, Indiana, was happy to be released from his hospital bed in time to join his unit moving on Hill 150. Near the crest, he was nipped by a sniper. He yelled for a corpsman, and as he was given first aid, Pressler propped himself against a trunk and kept pumping lead at the suspect trees, blowing down two concealed Japs. He never was sure whether either of the two was the sniper who had nailed him.

A similar question faced Pfc. Vernon L. Schroder, twenty, of Peoria, Illinois. It was his first time in combat, and he shot at his first Jap from only six feet away, but at the same time a grenade burst near the Jap. Schroder could not in all honesty claim the dead foe for his own. Twenty minutes later, Schroder spotted a second Jap twenty feet away, ducking behind a tree. He waited patiently as the seconds dragged by. The Jap, less patient, made a break for it and Schroder cut him down. This time he was certain he had made his first kill.

A brother's gift saved the life of Sgt. William C. McCollum, twenty-four, of Cedar Bluff, Alabama. The sibling, Sgt. Warren Harvey McCollum, attached to an artillery outfit, had presented infantryman Bill with a pistol just before the Gloucester campaign. While creeping forward in the gloom with his unit, Bill found himself face-to-face with a rifle-armed Jap.

Bill swung out his tommy gun and fired, but heard only a click. That's when he realized that the magazine of his weapon had dropped out! The Jap, perhaps more surprised than Bill at the sudden meeting, failed to fire, giving Bill time to draw the gift from his shoulder holster and abruptly end the tête-à-tête with a single shot.

Bullets were flying thick when one tore the pistol from the hand of 2nd Lt. Otis P. Jenne, twenty-four, of Minneapolis, Minnesota. As the looey hit the deck, he felt the impact of another slug.

"My God! I've been hit!" he thought, but there was no sensation of pain. Even so, he could feel "something" oozing from the nape of his neck. He slowly probed for the wound and touched warm blood. He drew his hand back and examined the fingers—only to discover water. The bullet had struck the canteen hooked to the top of his pack.

As every jungle fighter quickly learns, you can't always

believe what you see in there. So when Pvt. John S. Henshaw Jr., eighteen, of Beverely Hills, California, reported to his commander that he had sighted a Marine ahead of the platoon, 2nd Lt. William W. Bailey, twenty-three, of Vinita, Oklahoma, became suspicious. His platoon was separated by a gorge from the other Marine units, but still, there *could* be a Marine scout or two out there.

Lieutenant Bailey held up his outfit for five minutes, moved forward, and carefully observed the helmeted form standing immobile fifteen yards to his front. The face of the guy in the Marine uniform was obscured by shadows, so the lieutenant challenged him, and was answered by four hand grenades and the rattle of machine guns as more Marine-clad Japs leaped into view.

The lieutenant had uncovered an ambush, and the platoon fought its way back to safe territory with but a single casualty.

In the damp, predawn darkness, Pfc. Joseph W. Seiberlich was on machine-gun watch. It was quiet, the noisy quiet of the jungle night, and so dark that all things took on fantastic shapes. His foxhole partner, Pvt. Robert G. Rowley, nineteen, of Buffalo, New York, whom he had relieved, was snoring softly, sleeping restlessly as soldiers do where danger is present.

Seiberlich's ears detected a rustle some fifteen feet away, and instinct told him that someone was creeping toward him. Joe tensed, his heart pounding like a trip-hammer.

"I said to myself," Joe later explained, "that maybe I could dispose of the Jap quietly with my knife.

"So I waited until the Jap crawled alongside my foxhole. Then I shot my arms out and caught him in a bear hug, pulled him into the foxhole, and jammed my knife into his neck.

"He still put up a fight, though, and we fell atop Rowley."

Rowley interposed. "Imagine how I felt to be awakened by two guys rolling over me? 'What the hell's going on?' I yelled."

"Got a Jap," Joe yelled back.

Rowley grabbed for his rifle in the pitch dark of the dugout.

"Tell me which is which?" Rowley demanded.

"Under me!" grunted Joe.

"So I hit the Jap over the head, and Joe stabbed him a couple more times."

Both insisted that they disposed of the intruder so quietly that their company didn't learn of the incident until morning. Other men of the company disagreed on that point.

Seventeen-year-old Pfc. Harold L. Barber, of Jacksonville, Florida, bloodied on Guadalcanal, was on scout patrol when he came upon eight enemy soldiers.

"We stared at each other for a couple of seconds, all of us dressed in jungle camouflage," recalled Barber, "and it was difficult to see who was who.

"But when I heard the officer say something, I knew what was what and I let go with a snap shot from the hip. The officer spun and fell. One of the Japs then shot at me, and though he missed me, I went down and played dead.

"They didn't bother to look at me closely, and when they left in a few minutes, I started to get up and saw another Jap coming at me out of the brush. I fired at him, and his helmet flew off.

"The other Japs came running back, but a buddy of mine appeared with a shotgun and mowed some down. The rest fled."

Pvt. Edward W. Seeley, twenty-one, of Stratton, Maine, was a woodsman who learned to love his Browning automatic with the passion he felt for his hunting rifle back home. He also learned to move swiftly and silently through the jungle as he had through the forest back home. When his outfit was blocked by a machine-gun nest, Seeley sprang from tree to tree dodging the rain of bullets that at one point knocked the BAR from his hands and clipped a bloody chunk from his neck. Nonetheless, the woodsman wormed his way above the Jap position and cut loose with his automatic weapon.

"The Jap never knew what hit him," Seeley said.

Asked about his bleeding neck wound, the Maine Marine said:

"I didn't even feel it. I guess I'm used to it. I was wounded three times on Guadalcanal."

First Lt. Stanley S. Hughes, twenty-five, of Tioga, Pennsylvania, underwent a unique and gruesome experience. He got trapped and trussed up in a Japanese snare contrived to set up the victim as an easy target.

"I crept up to a rise on a riverbank and spotted a Jap machine-gun emplacement. The Japs must have seen me at the same time, and their machine guns opened up. I spun around so as to fling myself to the ground below the bank, and stepped on a trip wire, which dropped a noose over me from a tree.

"The noose, luckily, failed to catch me square. If it had, I would have been thrown helpless in the air in full view of their guns. Instead, the noose caught my rifle, arm, and leg, twisted me upside down, and threw me on the ground away from the Jap fire. Somehow, I managed to get loose from the snare, although I could never tell you how I did it.

"I'd like to tell you my own machine guns wiped out the Japs, but we couldn't even try, for we were well pinned down. But the tanks, bless them, came along and did the job for us."

After Morphine Hill we had a short breathing spell and the triumphant, weary grunts gave vent to their feelings.

"If'n my old man ever again mentions the mud he saw in France in 1918, I'm a-goin' to bop him," burst out one grunt who had wallowed in the Gloucester muck—and rain—for days.

"And my mother told me before I left home never to forget my rubbers in the rain," another slogger chuckled.

"There's one good thing about getting good and wet, and that's you can't get wetter," someone cracked.

"It's lucky for us this is the dry season," chimed in another, oblivious to the monsoon weather.

Unfunny humor, crude humor, black humor were the secret weapons against the Japs that every Marine possessed in abundance.

My favorite among the quips: An Aichi dove out of the clouds and the boys lit into their foxholes. After several uncomfortable minutes, the fastest foxhole diver panted to the second-fastest sprawled on top of him: "Gee, Joe, I never realized you were so heavy." The second-fastest foxhole diver gasped to the fastest foxhole diver, below him. "You think I'm heavy? You ought to feel those two guys on top of me!"

CHAPTER 18

Hill 660

We were in high spirits—Jerry, Bob, and I—after the clutch of stories and photos we had culled in the offensive through Suicide Creek and Hill 150. We decided to catch up with other elements that had been assaulting Aogiri Ridge, another key enemy control point.

After getting directions from Intelligence, the three of us shoved off through the faint jungle track, which after three hours' plodding trickled into a labyrinth of indistinct trails. After another hour of trial and error, we had to admit we were lost. Of course, none of us had taken along a compass. However, we were more disconcerted than scared over our predicament . . . at least for the moment. We agreed our best course of action was to sit tight and listen for gunfire. That at least would give us a clue where the action was. We hunkered down in the bush, listening intensively for suspicious movement in the jungle around us while stretching our ears for the sound of guns in the distance.

After about two hours, our vigil was rewarded by the chatter of machine guns. We rose and, as quickly and quietly as we could, squirmed toward the sounds of the gunfire, all the while wondering whether we were safely to the rear of the Marines or had blundered our way behind the Jap lines. We kept our misgivings to ourselves, but we keenly understood the fix we were in. We'd find out soon enough whose perimeter was in front of us.

We proceeded carefully, very, very carefully until we suddenly heard the coughing staccato of nearby machine guns. We stopped short and eyed each other without uttering a word. I became aware that I was breathing too loudly, that my heart was palpitating, that I was sweating.

After an excruciatingly long wait, we nodded to each other and slipped Indian file along the blurred track that abruptly left the jungle and opened into tall, sawtooth kunai grass. We paused only for a moment, then snaked along a narrow rut, weapons at the ready.

Then, without warning, we popped into a patch of smashed-down kunai and and three dead Jap soldiers, their mangled and grotesque bodies seeping blood. The grisly scene overwhelmed us.

Bob was first to recover from our trance and snapped a shot of O'Leary and me staring incredulously at the riddled enemy corpses.

Before we could consider what to do, bursts of gunfire broke out near our left, and we could hear American voices and expressions of triumph.

We started hollering: "Don't shoot! We're lost Marines!" And kept on hollering over and over again!

The leathernecks heard us and—thankfully—withheld fire as we forced our way through the kunai toward them, our arms and weapons in the air. We later learned it was Jerry's thunderous voice that saved our skins. No Jap could possibly imitate O'Leary's roar when aroused.

We three never made it to Aogiri Ridge, which had been taken by the Marines after a furious battle. We missed that one, but immediately hooked up with the drive that was launched January 13 against Hill 660, the paramount prize of the Gloucester campaign.

Hill 660 rose steeply above the rim of Borgen Bay, and it was there that the core of the experienced Jap garrison defending Cape Gloucester had dug in for its last stand after eighteen days of battle.

From our lines, running inland from Silimata Point, where we had landed, Hill 660 towered as a formidable barricade along the path up the coast of New Britain. A strong, artillery-supported force entrenched on the dominating heights could command the terrain for miles around. The Marines could not afford to permit the enemy to retain control of 660 long enough to bring up their big guns and threaten our beachhead.

The leader chosen for the storming of Hill 660 was Lt. Col. Henry W. Buse Jr., a Naval Academy graduate out of Ridley Park, Pennsylvania, and at thirty-two recognized as a brilliant tactician. He had been laid up in a field hospital when the invasion chief, Maj. Gen. William H. Rupertus, deputy to General Vandergrift on Guadalcanal, picked Buse to carry out the assault with the Third Battalion, Seventh Marines, after its original commander had been seriously wounded.

Colonel Buse took over a tried, tough battalion of three infantry companies supported by heavy weapons and tanks.

The terrain facing the advance was a military crucible. On the left flank stretched the ocean and a hundred yards of tidal swamp. Hill 660 loomed forbiddingly across the center. The jungle hemmed in the right.

In preparing for the next morning's onslaught, Buse ordered all available artillery to harass the Jap sectors all night long to soften up their defenses and to give their soldiers the jitters. As soon as night fell, the first shells started screaming over our positioned infantry onto the Japanese. Then, at fifteen-minute intervals all through the night, artillery rounds swooped over our heads into enemy territory.

At dawn, the tempo of shelling crescendoed into an overture to the attack, lasting another quarter of an hour. Exactly at 8 A.M., our grunts plunged forward.

A heavy weapons company under Capt. Joseph E. Buckley, from Peabody, Massachusetts, ripped down the coastal road. He led his motorized column from the thinly armored platform of a half-trac gun carrier. His veteran Marines brushed aside an enemy roadblock to outflank Hill 660 on the seaward side, but were soon held up by Jap artillery.

The Marine infantry thrust into the jungle, halting at the base of the hill. The company of Capt. William J. King, twenty-seven, of Annapolis, Maryland, was then committed to scale the very steep face of 660 in the center of the advance. A second company, under Capt. James W. Shanley, twenty-five, of Plaindome, New Jersey, was assigned to climb the slope on King's right. Interspersed among the riflemen were the machine gunners and mortarmen of Maj. Hierome "Oakenwold" L. Opie, twenty-seven, Stanton, Virginia.

The grim, perspiring Marines advanced unopposed until the sun swung up overhead. The front was creepily still, so the leathernecks withheld fire. They were seeking the main force of the enemy and to avoid signaling their approach refrained from shooting at shadows.

At 10:30, King's vanguard reached a crevasse curling around the base of 660, which had not been spotted by our scouts. Confronted by the gorge, Lieutenant Colonel Buse ordered both forward companies to shift their interlocking lines to the right to bypass the ravine.

The companies executed the difficult maneuver without losing ground, and virtually without pause continued their slow, steady progress.

On their new tack, the two companies ascended nearly one-third of the way up the hill, still unopposed, only to be stopped short again, this time by a V-fissure that sliced vertically down the slope. At this juncture, King's men defiled up the left side of the cut, Shanley's up the right.

The earlier shift had divorced the infantry from direct contact with Captain Buckley's heavy weapons company on the beach road. And by that time the two companies were separated from each other.

Suddenly, invisible machine gunners poured broadsides into the leathernecks struggling up the forty-five-degree incline. And an enemy automatic cannon hurled explosive shells into the midst of the grunts, inflicting many casualties.

Our guys glued themselves to the slope, taking any available cover against an enemy they could not see. The Japs had burrowed into the hillside. King's men were pinned down; so were Shanley's.

After the initial shock, the battle-wise leathernecks hastily scooped out shallow foxholes with shovels, knives, bayonets, helmets.

On sizing up the peril to his men, Lieutenant Colonel Buse directed Captain Shanley, on the right, to withdraw and then effect a sweeping envelopment, while King's company held tight. To carry out the order, Shanley had to pull his men from under raking enemy fire. A platoon of reserves and two tanks were rushed up to shield Shanley's pullback, and in the ensuing action, two enemy pillboxes were knocked out. But it was 4 P.M. before Captain Shanley's company could be shifted. By then, there was no hope of taking 660 by dark that day.

That left the problem of extricating King's company before nightfall. It would be foolhardy for the unit to maintain its isolated position with the threat of an impending Jap night counterattack.

Lieutenant Colonel Buse decided the only way to get King out was with artillery—a risky decision because of the proximity of the opposing battle lines. If our shells were to rain on the Jap soldiers without hitting our troops, the artillery would have to fire with extraordinary accuracy.

The artillery observer, 1st Lt. Winchester D. Hardwick, of Pinehurst, North Carolina, deployed himself ten yards forward to call the shots. Then, inexorably, the Marine shells inched down the hillside, exploding among the Japs to within 100 yards of our own men. It was a neat exhibition of a creeping barrage in reverse, and King's company was able to withdraw to a more secure position without losing a man.

It was a remarkable tactic and operation!

Lieutenant Colonel Buse, in counsel with his captains, was determined to resume the attack the following morning. But next time the Marines would swing around to the western slope of 660, probe the Jap defenses, then punch through the first weak spot found.

Meanwhile, the battalion commander that first night issued orders that the galley crew below make certain that each of his men got a hot breakfast before the second day's assault. For some it would be their last meal. And for the night, men slept at the foot of the hill, too tired to think, too weary to worry.

At 9:15 A.M. on January 14, our mortarmen began to lob shells over 660 from the northwest to pound the rear slope, while other artillery pieces hammered away at the front incline. When the barrage ended fifteen minutes later, King's company fell back into reserve while the other two companies pushed ahead.

One platoon, skirting the extreme right, ran into a Jap bivouac area. Ignoring the snipers, the Marines went after the enemy machine gunners who barred their advance. Upward they struggled, slipping, sliding, holding on to vines to pull themselves up through the hail of enemy fire. Every few yards they had to halt long enough to rub out a machine-gun emplacement. In that battle, there was no surrender, it was kill or be killed!

The Japs, masters of camouflage, had the advantage of being the defense. To flush them out, the leathernecks had to expose themselves to deadly gunfire.

Fighting broke out all along the skirmish lines as our grunts drove deeper into the enemy perimeter. Just behind our assault troops, other Marines formed human chains to pull up and pass up ammo, as our ammo was quickly used up in the constant exchange of fire. Problem was, no man could climb up that rain-slick hill without using both hands.

Another unanticipated problem cropped up: Mud clogged our guns and no extras were available. Three leathernecks solved that one on their own initiative.

When Pfc. William B. Zoelle, twenty-one, of Mankato, Minnesota, discovered that his rifle had been gummed up, he tried to find a spare Garand. There was none to be found, but two sergeants, Wyatt A. Hooks Jr., twenty, of Atlanta, and Otha Nichols, twenty-eight, of Sprott, Alabama, grabbed the useless weapon and in the murk of their watery foxhole stripped the rifle down, washed off the mud, oiled the parts, and reassembled it in two shakes.

Zoelle then collected other jammed weapons—rifles, carbines, tommy guns, Browning automatics—and the nimble, well-trained fingers of the two sergeants restored them to action. All twenty of them.

Foot by foot, man by man, the hostilities persisted without letup through the afternoon. By 4 o'clock, we could see that the prospects of gaining the crest were dubious. Right then, Lieutenant Colonel Buse had to make another tough decision: Either abandon the plan to capture the hill that day and swing around the south base to form a junction with the weapons company on the beach, or take the bolder, more dangerous course of trying to seize the hill before darkness fell.

Lieutenant Colonel Buse chose the audacious alternative.

Like their commander, the Marines, fatigued as they were, were determined to sleep on 660 that night. In the accelerating pitch of battle and the resulting confusion of intermingled lines, the Marines were no longer fighting as companies or platoons, but as small units, each with the same purpose in mind: to get to the top, 250 yards up, before dark.

But to do so, the Marines had to overcome a number of obstacles. The angle of the slope was very high. The Japs had machine guns cunningly placed all over the ridgeline. And the leathernecks were dead tired after fighting for eighteen days. They had been pushed to their limits; they were going on raw nerves.

At that critical stage, the Marines rose spontaneously and, shouting defiance, charged up the near-vertical face of Hill 660, and drove the Japanese from their fortified positions. Surging over Jap defenses like wild breakers over a coral reef, the Marines took Hill 660 at 6 P.M., one hour before darkness.

The defenders ran before they could be completely encircled by Buckley's special weapons company, which had already cut off the escape route via the coastal road. They left behind their two-wheel automatic cannon, more than twenty Nambu light machine guns, and scores of small arms.

Exhausted though they were, the Marines automatically dug into defensive positions as the rain began to fall in a steady downpour.

They squatted among the unburied enemy dead and listlessly pecked at their cold rations, paying no attention to the green blowflies that were already depositing eggs in the open wounds of Jap corpses. The Marines drank the rainwater caught in their helmets. Even the trifling luxury of a cigarette was denied to them. There was no cheering, no boasting, no open sign of triumph.

When the tropical night descended over the pockmarked hill, half of the men rolled up in their rubber ponchos and dropped off into stuporous sleep, while the other half kept red-eyed watch against the expected counterattack.

January 15 dawned through a misty drizzle. With energy somewhat restored, the men set about consolidating and improving their positions. Marine cleanup details, sent out to bury the slain Japs in shallow graves, chewed and spit tobacco and covered their noses with handkerchiefs to decrease the stench. Green blowflies swarmed in clouds over the bloodied, rotting dead.

Meanwhile, Marine stretcher parties carefully picked their way down the slick slope, trying to avoid slipping and dropping the wounded, or their dead poncho-shrouded comrades. Other bands of leathernecks hauled up hot food, fresh water, and dry socks, which got wet as soon as they were pulled on in the heavy rain.

From the summit of Hill 660, the coast of southwestern New Britain could be seen for miles. Behind us we could see those bloody milestones Morphine Hill and Suicide Creek. Eight miles beyond lay the airstrips.

The Japs stayed out of sight January 15 and 16, and we took advantage of the respite to ready ourselves for the inevitable counterattack. By nightfall of the sixteenth, Hill 660 bristled with machine guns.

We were sure that the Japs would return in strength, because the troops we'd fought were no half-starved, sick enemy soldiers. They were the troops who had fought on Bataan and had been cited by the notorious Lt. Gen. Masaharu Homa, commander of the Imperial Philippine Army. They had proved they were fierce fighters.

The evening of the sixteenth, a duel broke out between their mortars and ours, with casualties on both sides, while the grunts, dug in, waited impatiently.

The Japs attacked at 3 A.M. on the seventeenth.

The enemy tried to cross us up by changing their customary tactic of heralding their attack with bloodcurdling screams. Instead, under cover of the moonless night, they approached silently up the southeast face. Not until they were within twenty yards of our line did the Japs start screaming, "Banzai! Banzai!" and "Maline you die!"

A decimating volley ripped into the closely packed ranks of the charging Japs. The Marines were now screaming too:

"C'mon! C'mon! C'mon and get it, damn your bloody souls!"

Only two—only two—of the Japs broke through our lines that night. They bayoneted a Marine machine gunner but were slain on the spot. The furious fighting continued until dawn. By daylight, the shooting had dwindled to sporadic fire.

As soon as the sun came up, Lieutenant Colonel Buse dispatched patrols down the corpse-littered slope, and they counted more than fifty enemy dead within fifty yards of our perimeter.

The patrols then made contact with the surviving Jap soldiers, about 200, who had retreated into the jungle. Buse hurriedly pulled back his patrols. The Japs, calling on an old trick, followed right on the heels of the scouts, so that we could not throw our mortars at them without hitting our own men.

Lieutenant Colonel Buse countered with an ingenious stroke. He issued an order, instantly obeyed, for all Marines to shout in unison: "Hit the deck!"

The returning scouts instantly flung themselves to the ground, and then our machine gunners poured hundreds of rounds over them. The Japs following behind were cut down.

In my mind's eye Little Jeezus was beaming beatifically in appreciation of so perfect an example of "Cover yer ass!"

Jap survivors of the bloodbath withdrew.

Lieutenant Colonel Buse allowed the enemy to retire about 100 yards, and then—there no longer being danger of hitting his own men—he blasted the remaining foe with mortar fire for three minutes, and in those three minutes the enemy was totally annihilated. Some 150 more Jap bodies testified to the effectiveness of Buse's coup.

But officers and enlisted alike were too worn out to celebrate. We simply hung on to our positions until relieved by reserves the next day—after twenty-three hellish days and nights of battle.

In a long, sinuous column, we weaved and bobbed down Hill 660, some of us staggering, slipping, and falling, but hanging on to our weapons.

We were trudging off the front line and we were glad, the grim tight-lipped gladness of grunts who had taken more than they could take and realized that for a few days at least they could ease up. They were hollow-eyed, staring, yet there was a contented air about them because they had beaten a fanatical foe.

The rain began to fall, lightly at first, and then in buckets, but the Marines were indifferent to it. Between the swamps and the monsoons, "wet" was now a part of them, as was the clayish mud that caked their helmets, packs, and bearded faces.

Some heads were covered with ocher-stained ponchos; some hooded by Jap rain capes. A few carried prized souvenirs—a saber used like a cane; a samurai sword clutched in a hand; a hara-kiri knife dangling from the cartridge belt; a Rising Sun silk flag worn as a neckerchief; a sniper's long-barreled rifle slung over the left shoulder; a stubby bugle blown erratically with irreverent toots.

That night they would surely get hot chow, but just then they were hungry, and so they munched K rations, or the beans and hash from the C rations—anything to eat, to chew on.

That night, maybe, but certainly by the next day, they would bathe their sore, tired, and dirty bodies in a stream, wash their filthy jungle clothes, dry their boots, and perhaps even shave. And they would sleep . . . and sleep . . . and when they had slept their fill, they'd sit around swapping experiences, lamenting the loss of comrades, and writing letters home. They'd rest for a few days . . . and grow restless . . . and gripe in their restlessness . . . and wonder aloud when they'd get into action again.

CHAPTER 19

Itni Patrol

When I lumbered down from 660, I bumped into Raymond Clapper, the highly regarded Scripps-Howard columnist, who was taking a look-see into the Pacific theater. He plied me with questions—the shoe was on the other foot—and I filled him in with the events of the battle and other encounters. He made nice mention of me in his nationally syndicated column—as I later learned from Stateside friends who sent me newspaper clippings.

I was eager to join a patrol being formed to penetrate jungle and mountains to the Itni River, but first I wanted to write about the artillery units that had played a key role in the taking and holding of Hill 660.

I chased down 1st Lt. James E. Stewart and his crew of thirteen gunners. The twenty-six-year-old Pittsburgher and his mortarmen had done the "impossible," a Marine descriptive term meaning "impossible to any but Marines."

The minimum safety range of the 60mm mortar is supposed to be 200 yards, but by turning the muzzles of their guns virtually straight up—at eighty-five-degree angles—the crew succeeded in lobbing their shells between 70 and 100 yards over the heads of our own infantrymen.

Lieutenant Stewart had followed the riflemen up the slope and found what he termed a "mortarman's paradise"—a defile shelf of 660, scooped out of a landslide-created draw and only twenty-five yards from the peak. He sent for his gang, who pulled up their guns and ammo, helped along by the willing arms of the grunts along the way.

The lieutenant and his observer, Sgt. Henry J. Abbott, of

Philadelphia, together made an estimate of the situation and figured they could do the "impossible."

The officer then relayed firing orders to the section chief, Sgt. William T. Burtyk, of Coverdale, Pennsylvania, and the crew started firing and kept on firing until they ran out of shells, destroying five enemy gun emplacements in the meantime.

Complications had to be overcome. At one point a Jap machine gunner imperiled the mortarmen and had to be eliminated by Marine riflemen. At another the wind changed direction 100 degrees during the firing, and the mortars had to be meticulously reregistered. And through it all, Sergeant Abbott was an open target for the ever-ready Jap snipers.

The 81mm mortar platoon under 1st Lt. Peter McDonnell, of Chicago, also gave a notable performance on Hill 660. Operating with the speed and precision they had acquired on Guadalcanal, the crew hurled 800 heavy shells on Jap positions to initiate the drive up. The gunners first launched a sixty-round barrage in forty-seven seconds. That's so quick that forty-three of the projectiles were in the air before the first landed twenty-one seconds after discharge. That feat was accomplished with only three of their guns. The fourth, the "best one," the crew pointed out, was temporarily out of action.

I also wished to get the details from a trio of grunts who, during the night of the ferocious Jap counterattack, had provided Buse's battalion with first aid of a different kind, not only when the infantrymen ran out of ammo but also when their guns became inoperable because mud gummed them up.

After the battle of Hill 660, Jerry O'Leary and I filed several dispatches jointly and then reported on the many episodes in which we were individually involved. When we came up from our typewriters for air, we learned that several attacks were being planned by HQ against enemy garrisons along the northern coast of New Britain between Cape Gloucester and Rabaul. Jerry chose to get into those operations.

Bob and I decided, instead, to join the Itni Patrol, which had already taken off to probe the mountainous interior of Cape Gloucester, where General Matsuda was believed to be headquartered.

The three of us abrazoed and split.

I had picked the Itni Patrol because it was commanded by Col. "Chesty" Puller, whose exploits against the Nicaraguan and Haitian *bandidos* and *insurgentes* had made him a figure of heroic proportion in the Corps, even before he demonstrated his remarkable qualities of leadership—his acumen, prowess, resourcefulness—on Guadalcanal and Cape Gloucester. I had missed him on The Island, but saw him in action on Cape Gloucester.

Puller had taken over two battalions on The Island after their commanders were shot out of action, and had led the two outfits in continuing, successful operations. He had duplicated the rare two-battalion takeover on Cape Gloucester when the original battalion leaders were disabled in action.

On Guadalcanal, Puller had commanded the 2nd Battalion, Seventh Regiment; in the Cape Gloucester campaign he had been promoted to executive officer of the regiment, but he continued to insert himself into the battle lines along with, and often out in front of, the grunts. He took his command post with him, at times to the consternation of his higher command. In Puller's open opinion, there were too many officers on staffs and they were too far from the action to make quick, effective responses to the changing battle conditions. Puller made quick decisions based on his keen understanding of jungle fighting and tactics.

Tales of Colonel Puller's feats burgeoned with each telling, and while some of the anecdotes were apocryphal, many were true.

It was said that on Guadalcanal, after being twice wounded in the leg, "Chesty"' carried on without pause, and still bore the bullets in his body. That was true.

It was said that he had been shot in the ribs during his Nicaraguan hitch and as a result his chest had been braced from within by metal. That was false. His chest protruded because of his natural straight-back posture.

It was said that he spit nails while chewing up officers and grunts alike for minor infractions of discipline. That was half-true. He was rough on subordinate officers who failed to carry out commands or who were arrogant with their men, but Chesty was encouraging with his enlisted men even when giving them "Demn it, old man!" and a tongue-lashing. He demanded—and got—alertness to the dangers lurking in the jungle; he demanded—and got—quick response to orders.

It was said that he pocketed a copy of Caesar's *The Gallic Wars* wherever he went, and that was true. He never completed his education at VMI, but he immersed himself in military strategy and tactics. It was said he wrote home to his wife in Saluda, Virginia, every day. He wrote almost every day.

Chesty believed in discipline, training, and resourcefulness, the traditional criteria of the Marine Corps, and he demanded those attributes at 120 percent from himself and from his officers and men.

After being placed on inactive duty as a Reserve second lieutenant in 1919, Colonel Puller rejoined the Marines as an enlisted man to serve in the Banana Wars. Emotionally, he never left the grunts behind. On Guadalcanal, on Cape Gloucester, he ate the same meager meals his grunts ate, slept on the wet ground when the grunts had to, and refused comforts of any kind when his men had none.

As a result, the men who fought under Puller's command worshiped him, fought the harder knowing that Chesty was sticking his chest out—and his neck out—even as they were.

Col. Lewis Burwell Puller was forty-nine and had already earned three Navy Crosses for valor. His First Battalion, Seventh Marines, which he had inexorably trained and hardened for jungle fighting on Samoa, did not arrive on Guadalcanal until September 18, some five weeks after the initial landing, but they went into combat the very next day, and stayed in battle throughout the remainder of that long campaign.

Of slender build, standing five feet nine inches but appearing taller because of his ramrod stance, weighing only 155, Chesty was a Marine of extrordinary strength and endurance because he never let up on his own rigorous training. He was easily recognized by his jutting jaw, powerful chest, and the pipe clenched in his teeth—and, close up, by searching green eyes.

His peers called him "Lewie" and his men called him "Chesty." He in turn called all hands "Old Man," except when angry, at which time he addressed the subject of his ire by his proper title. Then his low voice transformed from a unique mixture of soft growl, Virginia drawl, and an outlandish Brooklynese into a blast of wrath that murdered the King's English and devastated the transgressor.

Later he might forgive those fallen from grace, even recommend them for promotion if they proved deserving in battle.

Chesty also raised his voice when barking an order in combat, or when reading off a citation for bravery for one of his men during a formal review. Then he would thrust his jaw out a notch or two more and bellow.

Puller couldn't sit still. He paced back and forth in his tent, or folli, pondering a problem, awaiting a report. He walked swiftly along the battalion perimeter, meticuously checking every position both day and night, once, twice, three times. . . .

Puller believed the best defense was the offense. Major General Rupertus, Cape Gloucester commanding officer, said: "I can depend on him to push the attack." But Chesty was also a master of jungle defense, as demonstrated that October night on Guadalcanal when his battalion, defending a mile-and-a-half line, repulsed a Jap counterattack and slew 1,400 of the enemy with small loss of our own.

The Itni Patrol was composed of three columns: one prong to push inland from the southwest coast of Cape Gloucester, two to press inland from the north and northwest. The three elements were to rendezvous near the center of the island at the village of Agulapella.

The first column, led by Capt. Preston Parish—the telephone broadcaster on Target Hill, you will recall—had already taken off four days earlier when, on January 28, Bob and I joined a detachment of mortarmen and machine gunners whipped up to reinforce the patrol. We boarded three landing craft at Cape Gloucester and motored twelve miles west and south down and around the coastal waters to Sag Sag. It was a breezy, sunny run, but the fumes of the engines and the roll of the shallow-draft boats combined to sicken most of us.

Captain Parish had also taken off inland from Sag Sag, and we were in a hurry because we knew that one of the columns had already made contact with the enemy. Our guns were needed for the impending battle. All three prongs were now racing to juncture.

Sag Sag had been the site of an Anglican mission set in a coconut grove, but the Japs had razed the church and hauled off the dismantled segments and all the furnishings into the interior to build a comfortable headquarters for General Matsuda.

After two hours of foreboding jungle coastline, Sag Sag's pleasant beach offered a welcome relief. The local Melanesians crowded around our boats, and we tried to speak to them with our bits of Pidgin English, but the amiable fuzzy-wuzzies merely displayed a toothy smile and responded: "No savvy."

Well, there was no time to make savvy. Guided by a waiting Marine scout, we immediately shoved off into an obscured trail in a long, winding file.

It was two miles over a gentle upgrade to our first leg, Naveilpur, a scattering of follis in a jungle clearing. There we rested briefly and exchanged information with the former Anglican priest for the Kalingi district. He had returned as an Australian Navy officer to serve as scout and interpreter with the Marines and to help in the liberation and repatriation of his displaced, dispersed flock.

The padre told us that some of his Kanaka boys had been lashed and manacled by the Japs to prevent them from running away. The Japs had forced the black fellows into heavy labor, neither paying them nor providing them with food. Since Matsuda's troops had seized or pillaged the folli gardens, their chief source of food, the natives had been forced to live off the jungle, which, though teeming with plants, offers little for human consumption.

Out of utter desperation, many of the Kalingi had fled with their families to seek refuge in caves or under overhanging cliffs, hidden from the marauders, coping with fear and hunger. The Allied shelling of the region, which at first terrorized the natives, proved to be a boon. They scavenged through the bombed areas to find the carcasses of wild pigs and cassowaries.

We left the padre and his village and soon crossed the swift, sparklingly clear Gima River over a single-log bridge spanning a twenty-foot-deep gorge. On the other side, we halted long enough to fill our canteens with cold, sweet water, and continued on. At that point a tropical shower overtook us, and as we trudged ever upward, the muddy slush slowed down our progress.

In about half an hour we heard shouting up ahead:

"Clear the trail for the wounded!"

We pulled aside into the bush.

Led by a native water-bearer and protected by Marine guards, a stretcher party stepped gingerly down the skiddy track. They held up at a signal from Dr. Frank A. Stewart, Lt. (j.g.), MC–USNR, who was marching with our reinforcement detail. He examined all the casualties to see that they were amply provided for until they could reach the base field hospital.

The Kalingi carried the patients with reverential care to avoid jostling them and, despite the rugged terrain, always held their stretchers level.

As Lieutenant Stewart passed among the wounded, offering comforting words as he went, those of us nearest offered them lit cigarettes.

One Marine, seriously injured, was muttering over and over again:

"I never even saw them . . . never ever saw them . . ."

It proved to be three miles from Naveilpur to Aipati, the upgrade steeper with each step. The mortarmen, weighed down by by seventy- to eighty-pound loads, had to fall back and set their own pace. They were a tired gang, having just come off the lines after twenty-three days and nights of intermittent skirmishes.

We pulled into Aipati, another raggedy village, late in the afternoon, catching up there with Captain Parish's column. Altogether it had been a four-hour, five-mile hike for the day.

More than 1,000 feet above sea level, Aipati had been occupied by Parish's patrol hard on the heels of the evacuating Japs. The village was girdled with pillboxes and trenches, but the Japs had chosen to flee rather than fight.

I learned that an unusual military court had been held in the Marine camp the night before our detachment had arrived, and it was still the chief topic of conversation among the grunts.

A four-member recon team, and a volunteer native guide, had run into an enemy ambush, and one scout, "Smitty," had been critically wounded. His mates—Gunnery Sgt. John M. Kozak, twenty-six, of Elmhurst, New York; Sgt. James Maynard, thirty, of Mullins, West Virginia; Pfc. Leonard Cole, of Binghamton, New York—brought him back to camp on a litter improvised from two dungaree jackets and two saplings, while fighting off a score of pursuing Japs. For all their efforts, Smitty, shot in the groin, died from internal hemorrhaging.

The volunteer guide was accused by other Kanaka boys of treachery, of having led the survey party into a Japanese trap. Captain Parish ordered a trial of the accused before the assembled Melanesians and Marines. The courtroom was set up on one end of the hut- and tree-ringed village, and the dilapidated porch of the Lului abode became the bar of justice. The captain served as judge.

There was no jury, but in the uneven semicircle around the justice, cross-legged and uneasy, the Kalingi, naked ebony torsos gleaming in the sun, and the nut-brown Marines, faces masked by beards and grime, sat on the hard-beaten clay ground, unmindful of the blazing equatorial sun that poked at them through the lush coconut palms and the taller, more graceful betel trees.

The decision was important to the natives, to the Marines, and to the commander, too. He needed the confidence of his men in the native guides, and the Kalingi had to be sure that they did not harbor a spy.

The testimony of each witness was translated into English or Pidgin English by two Australian officers attached to the column, who served as interpreters. All the people of New Britain speak and understand Pidgin English, the lingua franca in that part of the world.

Six Kalingi rose to take the stand against Karol, the accused.

The judge declared that each witness must tell the truth.

"Straight-im talk 'long me," repeated one of the interpreters.

The accusers listed their charges. Karol, they all pointed out, "belong long way place"—was a foreigner who came from one of the Admiralty Islands. He couldn't even speak their Kalingi dialect; instead he had to converse in Pidgin, like the white men. Karol was too jovial in manner, looked too well fed. Karol wore khaki shorts, instead of a lavalava. And so on—a litany of charges.

A more telling accusation was made. Karol had been seen several days before delivering food to the Japanese camp.

"Dis-fellow Kanaka-boy kitch-im Japan fellow-man kai-kai."

Karol volubly professed his loyalty, and indignantly sputtered denials. He too had been surprised by the ambush, and had been pinned down by the machine-gun fire, had lain for hours where he fell, out of fear of the Japs, and had returned to the Marine camp as soon as he dared get up.

"Me talk true long on top," Karol declared.

Only one among the Kalingi arose in defense of Karol. He was a Tul-tul, a respected village official who had volunteered as a food carrier. He declared it was not unusual during the long months of Japanese occupation for the natives to bring food to the Japanese invaders in order to escape the brutal treatment meted out to those islanders who refused to cooperate.

Now, ordinarily, the word of a Tul-tul carries much weight, but this witness, although a Kalingi, belonged to a distant village, and his defense of another outlander made little impression on the local Melanesians.

At that point Sergeant Kozak took the stand. The natives watched him attentively and drank in his testimony.

"If Karol led us into a trap," the sarge swore, "then he was just trying to commit suicide. For he was right in the middle of the machine-gun fire, just like the rest of us. There is no question in my mind as to Karol's loyalty. I will trust him anywhere, anytime."

The other two Marines from that patrol likewise expressed faith in Karol, but their testimony was anticlimactic. Karol's white teeth were already flashing. The sergeant's assertion had left no doubt as to the exoneration of Karol by the judge and the spectators.

Karol was acquitted and—ah, happy ending—promoted to batman (gofer) to the column commander. Karol thereafter followed Captain Parish everywhere he went, like Mary's little lamb.

More than 400 fuzzy-wuzzies solemnly marched into camp to place themselves under the protection of the Marines. Together with their "Marys" and "monkeys," they flocked into our bivouac from their jungle hideouts.

They were subdued and half-starved: the men gaunt and somber, the Marys stoic and flat-breasted, bearing up under the family possessions stowed in huge baskets poised on their heads; the monkeys crying like any frightened kids; and the mangy dogs snapping at the heels and having a barking good time.

All the locals were fed, and their sick were treated by our medical team. Then they all shook hands respectfully with the padre and were escorted by a Marine detail to their abandoned village, Gie, a few miles away. The ragtag but colorful parade was convoyed by a Marine guard under Platoon Sgt. Gerard J. Golden, twenty-five, of Scranton,

Pennsylvania, and Sgt. Conrad B. Packard, twenty-two, of Baltimore, Maryland. It was a happy homecoming, the two noncoms reported.

"The chief let us know that for the period of our stay, we should consider ourselves to be Lului, and after the women had cleaned up the huts—the women do all the work—he put us up with him.

"We were treated like princes. The grateful natives, eager to please, somehow found and brought us bananas, papayas, and taro—a kind of potato which the natives relished and tasted like glue. We ate the taro anyhow, because we didn't want to offend their hospitality.

"The march there was a gay, noisy affair, and when we eased up on a particularly hard stretch of the trail to make it easier going for the overloaded women, the men waved us on impatiently. The women and kids actually kept up with the men.

"Once we reached the village, everybody went about their business. The women went to work rebuilding the grass shacks and gardens, while the men milled around talking loudly and apparently making important civic decisions.

"We had a delightful fresh fruit supper, but not much of a night's sleep, for all night long the monkeys cried, the men prattled, and the dogs yapped.

"Came morning, and we were glad to turn the reins of government back to the native Lului."

Some 1,500 natives who had fled the Japanese sought and received refuge from the Itni patrol.

The following day, January 29, at about nine, Parish's reinforced column swung out of Aipati and, climbing continuously, we reached a trail juncture; two miles in two hours.

It rained all day, heavily, and our track was alternately a bog or a rivulet. At 1 P.M., soaked and chilled, we broke march for chow—the inevitable K ration—near the top of a mile-high saddle that ran between Mt. Talawe, 6,600 feet, and Mt. Tangi, 5,600 feet.

An hour's tramp later, we met with the second column (under Capt. George P. Hunt, of Long Island, New York), which had dug in. The day before, Hunt's leathernecks had fought the Japs in a sharp skirmish, but the enemy had been too firmly entrenched in its cliff defenses and was too large a force to be dislodged by a single column. Hunt had nonetheless attacked to slow down the enemy's withdrawal.

Hunt's outfit had had to cross three mountain ridges and was lightly armed, only two machine guns to back up his riflemen. Cpl. Robert T. Powell, of Rochester, New York, in charge of those two guns, had taken a cast off a wounded leg so he could participate in the patrol. Powell got hit again in scouting Jap positions, in the knee. Even so, when he saw another Marine wounded, he managed to drag him some fifty yards back to the Marine line. Then both were placed on improvised stretchers and sent back ten miles to Sag Sag.

Our two columns were combined to attempt another attack, while the third prong, under Capt. John A. Crown, of Decatur, Georgia, was hurrying to encircle the Japs. To give the men who had just completed the day's short but lung-searing climb a chance to rest up for the fight, the frontal assault was scheduled for the following morning.

We bivouacked in the bush, chopping out enough elbow room for our night's perimeter and shelters thrown together of saplings and leaves.

The Hunt column had reached our rendezvous point via a trail that rose over Mt. Langila, an active volcano. The members of that patrol said a sulfurous mist and lifeless trees ringed the forbidding peak when they passed through. Their route, southeast from the airport, had also taken them through the haunted valley "accursed by the Massulai"—the evil spirits, described in Pidgin as "thing belong claw."

I was beginning to notice that some of our fuzzie-wuzzie auxiliaries were dandies. Except for lavalava (kilt skirts), shorts, or loin cloths, the locals went about unclothed, but heedless of the drenching of the rest of their bodies, the dudes always hastened to cap their frizzy hair with an enormous leaf whenever it rained. Many had bored holes in their lobes and decorated their ears with shell jewelry. Others had emblazoned their names on their chests with bright juice, and made markings on their faces that were meaningless to us Marines but apparently were of especial charm to the opposite sex. A few fops decorated their oily mops of kinky hair with a bright floral sprig or two.

The Melanesians displayed teeth of three colors, depending on whether or not they had chewed the narcotic betel nut—and how soon after that they were seen. The abstainers' incisors gleamed white; the chewers' were hideously red-orange or repulsively black. But the betel nut didn't appear to harm them, and we got used to the odd-colored teeth.

Many of the Kanakas were joining our patrol as cargo carriers or stretcher bearers. The inducement to do so was compelling. We fed them well with their favorite food—rice and bully beef—and issued them a double ration of their beloved tobacco sticks, which smelled like stinkweed. They politely accepted name-brand American cigarettes but considered them poor substitutes for the reeking real thing.

We restored their families to their villages and arranged to feed them until they could resuscitate their ravaged vegetable plots. Our Australian allies brought them fresh seed for mango, papaya, lime, lemon, taro, beans, carrots, and Chinese cabbage, which looked like spinach and tasted like horseradish.

The Marines also paid the natives the standard modest wage for carriers set by the the Aussies under their New Guinea mandate.

However, in addition to those inducements, the Melanesians, though docile and peaceable, wanted to help drive out their Japanese oppressors. Because of their poor physical condition, however, the natives were limited to loads of thirty-five pounds, half the weight borne by our mortarmen, machine gunners, and radio and wire crews.

I got up January 30—a Sunday—feeling miserable, feeling that another siege of malaria was in the offing. It had been a wretched night for all of us, because nothing we could contrive for shelter was impermeable to the all-night downpour. It was cold as well, and I spent most of the night shivering. The raucous night jay and his nocturnal neighbors screamed their heads off, indicating they were unhappy too.

The mosquitoes ignored the rain; they were eager to get a taste of our blood. They ignored my head net and the insect repellant with which I had covered myself. I always had a suspicion that the potion lured them instead of fending them off.

My tin cup of woe filled to overflowing that dismal morning when, unable to find dry paper or other tinder, I had to drink my coffee cold, forgetting in my dumps that I could have ignited a small blaze with the Scat.

The Japs, dug in on the other side of the steep-banked river, must have suffered through a bad night too, because under cover of the pitch-black dark they had scrammed.

We discovered the withdrawal shortly after dawn when our columns enveloped the Jap position over the gulch. The Japs had taken off into the trackless jungle, where they would have to hack their way through. To pursue them would have been impractical. Many of them would die from starvation or disease before they could reach the main body of their armed forces still fighting on the north-central coast of Cape Gloucester.

Communication was giving us trouble. Due to the density of the jungle forest and the intervening peaks, our portable field radios were unable to make contact with our base at Cape Gloucester. Through the incredible labor and resourcefulness of a nine-member telephone crew, more than ten miles of wire had been strung from the airport over Mt. Talawe to our current position. The communicators had overcome a lack of line by the ingenuity of Cpl. Thomas S. Callaghan, twenty-three, of Long Island, New York, who contrived a means of connecting the single-strand U.S. wire with the Japanese double-strand. He did it, I was informed, by tying the different types of wiring to a couple of bayonets jammed into the ground. I didn't understand the explanation, but it worked.

However, it soon proved to be impossible to lay more wire, so we had to rely on ground-to-plane radio contact, and that ever-ready standby—the runner.

The problem of food was also nipping at our bellies. By

noon we had run out of of the iron rations in our backpacks, and we would have had to forgo evening chow had not the carriers trekked twelve miles to bring in additional Cs and Ks.

We broke camp at 11:30, moving south and east, on our next lap, to Niapaua, another muscle-aching five miles. Less than an hour later we came upon another river gorge, where the Japs made a stubborn stand. We later recovered the body of a Marine scout, victim of a sniper, and buried him where he had fallen, on a ledge overlooking a deep chasm. An intelligence corporal marked the grave's location on a map for later transfer.

The Navy physician murmured a prayer as we lowered the slain rifleman into the shallow grave. Then we quickly covered it with earth, improvised a cross over it, and glumly moved on.

A runner, meanwhile, had been sent back to bring up machine-gun ammo from the trail junction depot two miles from the skirmish scene. The messenger, Pfc. Willy "Poncho" Vila, twenty, of Tampa, Florida, was stricken with appendicitis en route. Nonetheless, Poncho insisted on guiding the ammo packers back to our engaged unit. A game guy, the runner collapsed within five hundred yards of the battle line. Native bearers littered him back eight miles overland to Sag Sag, and then he was taken twelve miles by sea to the field hospital at Cape Gloucester.

The march took us up more ridges, down more ravines, the moss forest gradually merging with the more open rain forest. We trudged by abandoned enemy foxholes, vandalized gardens, magnificent rubber trees, and wild banana trees.

Niapaua, like most native villages, sat on a tonsured hilltop. We camped there and made contact with the third patrol column, which had occupied Agulupella, less than half a mile away, the key junction in the jungle trail network.

The next morning—January 31—I sloshed in a cold, refreshing stream—my first bath on the patrol. These untamed, invigorating creeks were the jungle's one saving grace.

I then joined the queue in front of the sick bay to get a

"paint job"—fungicide for feet and body. Fungus thrived on the warm dampness of the boots, and on the combination of wet clothes and sweaty bodies. Fungal infestations plagued us throughout the journey. The fuzzy-wuzzy carriers lined up to the "dockaters" too. They had only minor problems, but they wore the gauze and adhesive tape like badges of honor.

The three columns joined forces at Agulupella the next day, February 1, to organize for a sweep to the Itni River, some twenty miles to the southeast. There Bob and I paid our respects to Colonel Puller. He commented that like other old-timers he had at first felt the combat correspondents would degrade the high standards of the Corps, but had changed his mind after seeing that the CCs were well trained and had pitched in on the battlefields of Guadalcanal and Cape Gloucester.

Bob and I gave Chesty a brief rundown of our own experiences on the line, and he gave us permission to take off with any of the scouting missions he was sending out to find and eliminate the enemy trying to retreat to Rabaul.

As soon as I could learn the objectives of the scouting missions, I chose an Intelligence patrol, a search of the fabled "Jungle City" of Lt. Gen. Iwao Matsuda, commander of the western New Britain forces.

We had heard reports of Matsuda's grand headquarters from the natives but hardly expected to find so comfortable a personal pad in the jungle. Apparently it had been abandoned only a few days before.

When we entered the general's residence, a phonograph was wheezing out an Oriental version of jive. A Marine platoon had seized the military headquarters the night before, and the grunts, at their ease, were enjoying the exotic music.

The Imperial commandant's residence was a three-story frame building, built some ten feet above above the damp soil to keep it cool and dry. The structure was a crazy quilt of lumber, saplings, bamboo, and galvanized tin. Some of the boards had been brought from the Philippines, but most of the lumber had been drawn from the Anglican and

Catholic missions the Japs had ripped apart. The furnishings had been stripped from the two missions and had been transported inland on the backs of the enslaved Melanesians.

Matsuda's HQ contained a prayer room with altar windows, a reception room with a wide wicker chair and a mahogany desk, a well-provided kitchen, a built-in shower, and a fancy indoor—mind you, indoor!—privy.

The most impressive appointment was a four-poster bed, double width, with an eight-inch-thick mattress that was soft and bouncy. The bed was situated in the brightest room on the top floor of the "chalet," which from its perch on the knoll top offered an inspiring scenic view. Netting protected the bed from the ubiquitous flies and mosquitoes; tall trees shaded the generalissimo's lodgings from the tropical sun and Allied spotter planes.

The regal sack had been occupied the night before by Lt. Edward S. Rust, of East Detroit, who commanded the small occupation unit.

"Best night's sleep I ever had," he commented.

I envied him.

The general apparently ate few of his army's monotonous iron rations. His menus—judging by the remains—were pleasant and variable: rice, barley, pickled fish heads, canned tangerines. The mountain stream gurgling below his arched window was clear and cold, and flickering with frolicking bass.

Matsuda had feasted on pigs pried from the native villages within his reach, and the wild hogs and cassowaries caught in the jungle, and even the cockatoo, which is tasty, I'm told, when prepared *just so*.

All gardens within his dominion were robbed of their fruits and vegetables for the general's pleasure, and after dinner, he nibbled sticks of sugarcane.

The general drank special green tea, and he had a choice of other beverages: Coca-Cola; beer brewed in Manila by the Miguel Co., "authorized bottler"; and the "dead soldiers" lying around disclosed that he had available ample sake to sip or swallow.

A deep, roomy air-raid shelter, reached by ladder from the

kitchen, was at the disposal of General Matsuda. The dugout was well stocked with canned heat, candles, rice bowls, and chopsticks, and gave evidence of much use.

Go, an intricate chesslike game, must have been all the rage at Matsuda's headquarters; many sets were found scattered around the "city," and Matsuda himself had a set carved from mother-of-pearl. There was no way of telling how good a game the general played, but it can be safely assumed that he won more than he lost.

The big man in the camp had neat sartorial habits. He made generous use of clothes hangers. He wore pressed khaki shorts and favored silk shirts. But when it came to toiletries, stationery items, and the like, the evidence indicated that Matsuda had a predilection for standard brands.

Artfully tucked into the natural camouflage of the jungle between the slopes of two hills, the cantonment comprised dozens of sturdy lumber-and-thatch huts, dormitories, mess halls, kitchens, offices, and a hospital. Log steps were cut into the hillsides, and a network of vine-trellised boardwalks crisscrossed the area. A supply road, corduroyed and bridged, ran seven miles from the HQ to Borgen Bay.

Matsuda's men had wrecked their radio station in parting, and a flatbed press was left behind, ruined. A smattering of reading materials was strewn around the grounds. I came across a book, printed in Japanese and English, titled *Spying in Russia*, by John Vidor.

Flushed with excitement, I sat down on the general's wicker chair at the general's mahogany desk and in longhand wrote, on blank pages torn from the Japanese paymaster's ledger, my news dispatch of Matsuda's lush jungle hideaway.

I returned to Agulupella in time to witness the first airdrop of food from five Piper Cubs, "Our Air Force," as we affectionately dubbed them.

We signaled to the relief fleet by forming a white arrow and cross in a jungle clearing. Because our patrol had not brought the standard white signal panels, we made the marker with native white lavalavas and Marine-issue skivvies.

Each of the tiny planes, making as much noise as a big

bomber, flew over our encampment each day, notwithstanding thick weather, made two runs, and dropped a case of K
rations.

Marines below ran for cover when Our Air Force showed
up, because the aim of the pilots was erratic, one case having made a direct hit on the hut of the patrol commander, Lt.
Col. Chesty Puller. No one complained, however, since the
Pipers were the principal source of food most days. The hut
of Cpl. Edwin E. Spears, twenty-four, of Scottsville, Kentucky, was clobbered by the "biscuit bombers" three times,
but he refused to move. Stubborn, he was.

After a monsoon night, I awakened to find four inches of
water in my foxhole. I was not oblivious to the water but,
since there was no recourse, I tried sleeping in it anyway.
It rained buckets most of the day, but in the early evening,
the Piper Cubs flew in with K rations and—would you
believe—mail. None for me, though. Few letters caught up
to me as I shifted from one outfit to another.

The Parish column struck out on a five-mile, three-hour
jaunt to Aragilupua the next day, February 4. The village
was distinguished by paintings of fish heads on the Luluis'
huts. The Japs had been there before us: the garden had been
despoiled. But the thankful villagers revealed to us a hidden
cache of biscuits and rice. It was a touch of justice, I
thought; the Japs had starved the natives, and now the Japs
were starving in the jungle.

February 5, I joined a scavenger hunt to nearby Moro, site
of a former Jap camp. Good thing, too, for that day a Flying
Fortress dropped some 100 cases of rations on Agulupella
smack in the center of the village, demolishing several
huts and and injuring three leathernecks, who had to be
evacuated.

Off on another side trip the next morning, February 6,
taking our first break at Ararou, a unique two-level affair,
and then on to the most scenic townlet I had yet to visit,
Asilimapula, an oasis in the jungle wilderness, encircled
with gardens—deflowered, of course, by the Japs. There we
halted for noon chow and refreshed ourselves with the local
cocktail: the juice of a luscious brown-shelled, pink-rinded

coconut flavored with lemon juice. The beverage had an exquisite bouquet.

Our guide, unquestionably a Beau Brummell, wore a brilliant red and green lavalava, and two bright cockatoo feathers garnished his curly shock of tar-black hair. Rings adorned his earlobes. He watched us take out salt tablets we needed to replace salt lost through perspiration, and he ogled us like a dog silently begging at the dinner table. Finally, we offered him a handful of the tablets and he gobbled them down. He then got very sick "in da bell."

I got a chance to chat with an Army noncom, the guardian of "Duke," a German police dog, who served as point for our patrol. Duke was a quiet beast who had seen much action in Lae and Finschhafen, the sergeant explained, and he never once uttered a bark.

I learned a few things about patrol dogs, the most important being that they could not distinguish between Jap or native or white man, but could detect the presence of a human as much as twenty yards ahead. Duke confirmed his master's account by flushing two frightened natives out of the bush.

Back in patrol camp I found that the first Jap prisoner had been taken, but he was sick with malaria and was being sent back by litter to the main base. The native carriers didn't take kindly to him and jostled their patient about considerably until they were reprimanded. The native carriers were visibly fattening up; they were getting plenty of *kai-kai*. They were also feeling better. That evening I heard them singing:

"From the Halls of Montezuma
To the shores of Tripoli . . ."

An Aussie guide had taught the Kanaka boys the first two lines of the Marine Corps Hymn. Those natives were "Popies" who could sing the Catholic hymns in Latin.

We were off at dawn on February 8 for a ten-hour march over ragged terrain to Turitei, thirteen miles away. So precipitous was the clifflike bank of the newly bridged stream that the engineers had to fix a line for us to clamber down to the span. We kept running into Jap stragglers, and there being no request from HQ for more prisoners, they were killed in the brief encounters.

We spent that night in Turitei, the site of three large Jap bivouac areas, which we searched and then put to flames, reminding me of Sherman's March through Georgia in *Gone with the Wind*. Before lighting the torches, we stripped the encampments of usable stores, turning over all foodstuff and blankets to our Melanesian carriers and guides.

Oh, there were plenty of souvenirs, and just about every man came up with a Japanese flag—every Marine but me. There was plenty for the taking: belts, cameras, pen and pencil sets, Jap weapons. I settled for an officer's goatskin pack, which I figured would make a fine overnight bag when I got back to the States.

The most important find, however, was a large store of Japanese unpolished rice, which, like olives, takes a little time to learn to appreciate. The rice gave us a chance to vary our dull diet with mixed Spam and rice, sugar and rice, rice au gratin, and chocolate rice pudding heated and stirred in our helmets over a flame.

From Turitei we pressed on to Gilnit, nine miles more but fairly easy going. At the four-mile mark we came up to the Itni River—broad, deep, crocodile-infested. It appeared to be sluggish, but the natives warned us there was a strong undercurrent. We pushed along the river for five miles, then broke for the night on the bank opposite Gilnit, situated on the confluence of the Itni and Potsaken Rivers.

Next day Captain Hunt took a recon team across the Itni to scout Gilnit. We had been told to expect 300 or more Japs holed up there; they were gone. Captain Hunt sent back word he was staying at Gilnit for the night, and Colonel Puller reacted like a kicked mine. He exploded and ordered Captain Hunt arrested for disobeying orders to return that same day. He dressed down the captain for all to hear.

(Colonel Puller later recommended Captain Hunt for the Navy Cross for heroism on Peleliu.)

I returned to Agulupella to write my stories while small patrols shot out in all directions.

One evening, as I chatted with returning scouts close by the command post, Colonel Puller burst out, followed by a hapless message bearer. The colonel was roaring for all to hear:

"I'm being called back to Washington to train the nigras! Me! Calling me back to train the nigras!"

"Chesty" stomped around in a rage, his chest and chin thrust out as far as they'd go. No one, no one among the officers or men dared utter a word while Colonel Puller stormed in fury. Only when he abruptly wheeled around and strode back into his CP was there a whispered reaction of disbelief.

Next morning, while I was sharing coffee with my fellow Marines, Colonel Puller bounced out of his quarters with a round smile on his face. He looked around at the coffee klatch and announced:

"I figured it out last night. . . . I figured it out. They're calling me back to train the nigras . . . because I'm the only SOB that can do it!"

(As it turned out, I learned later, there was some thought in Washington to bring Chesty back to the United States, where he later shared his knowledge of jungle tactics with the Army. At that time, too, under pressure from President Roosevelt, the Marine Corps was beginning to accept black Americans, and the senior command was combing its senior cadre for a southerner to train them for combat duty. The task was finally assigned to Col. Samuel A. Woods Jr., a southern-born veteran campaigner. African-American Marines first tasted combat in September 1944 in the Peleliu campaign.

(Colonel Puller led a Marine regiment into Peleliu in December 1944 and later, in 1955, the First Marine Division into Korea. He was literally forced to take medical retirement soon after as a lieutenant general, with five Navy Crosses and a knapsack full of medals and citations.

(To this day, Chesty Puller stands tallest among the icons of the Marine Corps, the epitome of its standards and esprit de corps.)

On February 16, the Itni patrol camp broke up for the three-day march back to Borgen Bay, but, my infected feet swollen, I rode back to Cape Gloucester on a supply boat.

All the twenty miles back I kept relishing the thought of a comfortable night's sleep on a cot in a dry tent. It was not to be.

Jap bombing raids forced me to dash madly from cot to foxhole three times during the night. And when the alerts subsided, it began to rain. Then I discovered the tent leaked . . . right on me.

CHAPTER 20

Hollandia

On returning to base from the Itni patrol, I learned that Al Haley, my colleague at the *Washington Post* who had joined the Air Force, had made a crash landing, after his P-38 was forced down in a patrol flight in the New Guinea area, but had survived.

I found climb-in space on a Mitchell courier plane, flew over the channel separating Gloucester from Cape Sudest, and sought out Captain Haley in the Fifth Air Force field hospital, where he was trussed up in a Mae West cast but still smiling through his Errol Flynn profile and mustache, notwithstanding a fractured spine. He was attended by an attractive Army nurse, 2nd Lt. Agnes "Rosie" Roesle, also from Washington, D.C.

"You ought to have seen the plane, though, if you think I look bad," he crowed.

I didn't see the plane, but I did see a photo of the scattered remains of the Lightning. Haley had made a crash landing when one motor conked out and the second caught fire. "And I got out on my own feet," Al bubbled.

Haley had flown 130 combat missions with the Headhunters squadron, of which he was operations officer. Al insisted he would fly again someday. "Flying gets in the blood like newspaper ink, only it's stronger," he explained. "Every flight exhilarates me."

Captain Haley made his first score in a sweep over Wewak.

"I saw a Zeke on the tail of a P-38, and I dived after him. I gave him the guns, and kept screaming: 'Blow up, you bastard, blow up!' The Jap never did see me."

His second kill was during the Bloody Tuesday Army bomber raid on Rabaul.

"We were escorting the Mitchells, about 100 of us fighter planes. The Japs were waiting for us, at least 200 of them in a double lane so that, coming in, our bombers had to run the gauntlet.

"I didn't have to pick out a fight. This was no man-to-man stuff. It was a free-for-all, Irish picnic style. Planes were whizzing around like Ferris wheels. The scrap lasted for forty-five minutes, until we ran out of gas, and every second of it was fighting time.

"I mixed it up with several Zekes, but the only one I got for sure was the leader of a flight trio that attacked a B-25. I got him in a dive, and came out of it to find a half dozen of the devils on my tail. I didn't like that at all. So, my gas low, I scrammed."

In that rumpus, November 2, 1943, our pilots knocked off sixty-seven Zekes for sure, with twenty-six more probables.

The "Japanese Sandman"—Haley's Lightning—garnered its third Rising Sun flag in a similar shindig over Wewak.

In all, at the time of my visit to the field hospital, the Headhunters had 177 enemy warplanes to their account.

I spent a day with Haley exchanging experiences and news of our colleagues, then left him in the care of Rosie the nurse.

Before parting, I confided to Haley my ambition to participate in an Army Air Force bombardment mission. He suggested I fly to the Nadzab, New Guinea, base, and apply my master's degree in wheedling. I had to have one, he thought; how else could I, a noncom Marine, have reached him hundreds of miles from Cape Gloucester?

He was right. I bummed a flight to Nadzab and I persuaded the Army Air Force to take me along as observer on one of their raids. I showed the powers that be a sheaf of newspaper clippings of stories I had dispatched about the Marines and Navy, and argued successfully that my news report of an Air Force bomber mission would be good for their service, too.

On March 30 the Army Air Force initiated a four-day assault on the three major Jap airfields at Hollandia, Dutch East Indies. I was given the okay to participate in the attack scheduled for April 3.

It was still gloomy before dawn when I checked in at the Air Force airbase signal tower for the briefing at which the fliers were given last-minute info and instructions. No one except me seemed to be very excited about the impending strike. It might have been routine for them, but it was an exhilarating prospect for me.

"Your chief headache will be the traffic coming home," cautioned the operations officer.

I was assigned to Consolidated Liberator #197. The B-24 was a member of the celebrated "Jolly Rogers" squadron— "the best damn heavy bomber outfit in the world."

On the runway I met the pilot, 1st Lt. Glen L. Craig, and his crew, veterans of twenty-five combat flights over Wewak, Hansa Bay, Kavieng, and the Admiralty Islands. They assumed that it would be my first bombing mission, and I thought it wisest not to divulge that I had already made my maiden bombing run with a Douglas Dauntless dive-bomber on Guadalcanal.

Lieutenant Craig, twenty-six, of Topeka, Kansas, farmer, father of a two-month-old boy he had yet to cuddle, a man who won his wings after first serving with the Army ground forces, introduced me to his crew:

Copilot: 1st Lt. John B. Stripling, twenty-two, of Selma, Alabama, former Alabama Polytech student and U.S. Civil Service employee, married.

Navigator: 1st Lt. McElroy Smith, twenty-seven, of Pittsburgh, Westminster College alumnus, Harvard grad student, with Carnegie Illinois Steel before joining up.

Bombardier: 2nd Lt. Edsel F. Kingsley, twenty-three, of Madison, Wisconsin, also commissioned from the ranks.

Radioman and belly gunner: Tech. Sgt. Fred F. Schnurr, twenty-one, of Cincinnati, former Wright Aeronautical employee.

Engineer and top turret gunner: Tech. Sgt. Leon S.

Ciesluk, twenty-eight, of South Hadley Falls,
Massachusetts, factory worker.

Left waist gunner: Staff Sgt. John E. Wyles, twenty-nine,
of St. Petersburg, Florida, store manager, married.

Right waist gunner: Staff Sgt. Lee R. Elder, twenty-two,
of Channelview, Texas, rancher, married.

Tail gunner: Staff Sgt. Leopold Yandl, twenty-seven, of
Allentown, Pennsylvania, cabdriver.

Nose gunner: Staff Sgt. Roy E. Hutchison, twenty-two,
of Jamestown, Missouri, miner.

"This is a beano trip," one of the gunners joked. "When
we get through, there'll be no target left." The way he said it
indicated he wasn't kidding.

We took off, circled the field, flying into formation, No.
197, I discovered, was the very last plane of the Jolly Rogers
squadron. To see the better, I was told then. Most likely to be
attacked by enemy fighters, I learned later.

It took about an hour for the aerial armada to fall in, and
then in symmetric V-formations the 300 bombers roared
north, some 600 miles up the Markham Valley and along the
Stanley Range, running easily, smoothly. The land below us
was dark green and dull, rugged and forbidding.

From the waist window I counted thirty-six Liberators to
the right and front of #197, and it felt safer to have them
alongside. Closest was *Baby*, whose shimmer seemed
to convulse the grinning skull-and-crossbones insignia on
its tail.

We suddenly came upon a vast icefield of clouds below
us, and in the distance a tremendous peak appeared to be
capped in snow. As suddenly, I grew cold. I first thought my
chill was psychological, but when I was informed that we
were now over 8,000 feet and climbing, I donned a leather
jacket and congratulated myself for having worn two pairs
of socks.

An hour or so out, our P-38 cover caught up with us, and,
weaving to and fro, morphed into a protective pattern overhead, the silvery double tails of the Lockheed Lightnings
glistening in the bright sunlight.

As we approached the vicinity of Wewak, about two-thirds of the distance to Hollandia, Gunner Wyles remarked for my benefit: "Last time up this way, we were jumped by two Zekes."

I instinctively braced, but no Zekes showed up.

Two hours out I got so cold, I had to climb through the bomb-bay catwalk up to the flight deck to warm up by the heat of an Aldis lamp, which was used in emergencies for signaling. Twenty minutes before target time, I started back to the waist. As I went by, the navigator, Smith, leaned over and gave me a bit of advice:

"If we have to bail out, delay opening the 'chute. Else you'll be a soft touch for the Jap interceptors."

I thanked the lieutenant, but deep down I had no intention of bailing out. That was all enemy territory down there. I promised myself I would jump only after the pilot jumped.

Back in the waist, I peered through the gun window and saw that our formation had tightened up. The bomb-bay doors flew open, and the rush of wind pelted and blinded us with dust.

We were high by then, over 10,000 feet, and through broken patches of cloud a great green valley spread out below, and, sparkling in it, Lake Sentani with its network of streams and rivers. It was Hollandia!

Over the interplane phone we got the word:

"Plenty of ack-ack ahead!"

I braced again, not knowing what to expect.

I looked over the left wing and gawked at the bursts of antiaircraft shells around us.

By then we were over our own pinpoint target—a concentration of antiaircraft guns on the Hollandia air base.

"Bombs away!" cried the bombardier, Kingsley. Our ship rocked.

I tried to follow the downward trace of our eight 100-pound bombs, but a puff of cloud obscured my view. Instead, I watched scores of bombs from companion warplanes fall, hit, and explode in columns of flame and smoke. The airport below was studded with grounded planes, some lined up wingtip to wingtip, but the heavy bombers ignored those sitting ducks. The medium Mitchells would take care of those targets.

"Give it to them!" someone screamed on the interphone.

Elder, the right waist gunner, was grinning. He pointed for me to see that right out there a Zeke was tangling with a Lightning. As the Jap interceptor made a pass by our fighter, it swung off, and poured down at #197. My eyes were riveted on the Zero. I was mesmerized by the imminent catastrophe.

But not Elder. Not Ciesluk, the top turret gunner. They strewed the Zeke's path with tracers and shells, and about 300 yards away the Jap plunged into a sharp vertical dive. The two gunners and I felt certain that the enemy plane was hit, but we were flying too fast for us to see if it was a certain kill.

"I thought it was coming right at me," Ciesluk said. So did I.

Up ahead, the squadron's lead plane was also giving it to them, and shot down two definites. Other interceptors made fainthearted passes at the Jolly Rogers, only to be driven off. As it turned out, ours was the only other heavy bomber attacked.

Off our left, two Zekes tagged along with #197 for a while and the left waist gunner, Wyles, literally begged them to attack, but they held off until scattered by P-38s. In the distance two fighter planes were scrapping it out, but #197 raced off before I could see the outcome.

After dropping our load, we veered and headed toward Humboldt Bay, about five miles east. We spotted a convoy of small ships and I hoped someone would go after them. Two heavies, unable to find their primary targets, did just that.

The Allied attack on Hollandia by more than 300 bombers dropped 350 tons of high explosive and parachute-controlled fragmentation bombs on the three Hollandia air bases and demolished scores of enemy planes, antiaircraft emplacements, installations, fuel dumps, stores, and equipment over a five-mile area.

The high-altitude Liberators were followed by the medium

bombers, B-25s and A-20s, some of which raced in at tree-top level and hit everything in sight.

The blanket bombing took some sixty minutes for all the bombers to carry out their missions, and I, from my observation post, caught perhaps five minutes of the action around the target area, minutes in which we flew through the enemy's barrage, fought off enemy planes, laid a neat pattern of exploding flames around the airfields, and then raced seaward to make way for the incoming ground-attack aircraft.

Ten minutes or so after the airfield strike, it was discovered that the fuel had run low on #197 and that it was impossible to transfer gas from the extra tanks because the pumps had failed. To save gas, and make the fastest time over the 600 miles back home, #197 broke formation and took off on its own. Some of the crew kept to the guns as the others tried to get the pump to work. I kept anxious eyes on the fuel gauge.

We breathed more easily when, gas almost gone, we bumped to a halt onto an emergency fighter strip and gassed up.

But half an hour later we began perspiring all over again, and with good reason. For when we reached Nadzab home base, the wheels of #197 refused to lower—for ten agonizing minutes. I was in no mood for a crash landing.

That night the preliminary report on the raid stated:

"Practically everything in the Hollandia area came under the guns and bombs of our planes. It was one of the most successful and damaging raids ever made."

Photos taken by the low-level bombers showed all three airfields laid waste, scores of planes destroyed, burning, broken. It was impossible, despite the explicit pictures, to estimate the full damage, but some 300 planes were demolished in the four days of bombing. Dozens of Zekes were shot down, four by Lt. Cyril F. Homer, of Sacramento, California, who by that time had fifteen to his credit.

I thanked the gang of #197 for the "nice ride," filed a news story, and hitched a flight back to Cape Gloucester.

There, the hot breath of rumor at Intelligence HQ left no

doubt in my mind that official orders for my recall to the United States to sell Liberty bonds were on the way. Although I was drained by bouts of malaria and other jungle diseases, I was in no hurry to return to the States to that kind of assignment.

With the Cape Gloucester airports secured, and Rabaul isolated at the eastern end of New Britain Island, the First Marine Division was due to be relieved by the Army and transferred to Pavuvu, Russell Islands, for rest, recreation, and recovery.

I wanted no part of Pavuvu. I'd already been there with the Third Raider Battalion for a month, and that was more than enough for me.

To delay my inevitable bond-selling fate, I caught on with A Company, First Marine Tank Battalion, which I had learned was to be loaned to the Sixth Army for its coming invasion of Hollandia, still a formidable stronghold on the ground.

Commanded by Capt. John M. Murphy, of Longmeadow, Massachusetts, A Company was a seasoned outfit that had pioneered effectively with the light Stuart tanks on Guadalcanal and had dominated the battle for Gloucester with the bigger, more powerful, better-armored Shermans. The crews loved a fight more than they disliked operating with the doggies.

I joined Murphy's company on Goodenough Island, where it had been attached to the Army's 24th Division. The 24th then made a dummy landing Easter Day on Taupota Bay, New Guinea, to test timing, positions, unloading, etc., but it seemed to me the rehearsal didn't come off well. Too many GIs were lolling in the shade.

Easter services were held during the dry run by an Army chaplain, 1st Lt. Oram O. Bishop, of Neubert, Kentucky, on a little knoll fronted by the beach and framed to the rear by a coconut grove. The clear morning sun filtered through the coco palms and the magnolialike leaves of the neighboring trees, creating the atmosphere of a cathedral for the makedo chapel.

Outside that circle, only a few feet away, tanks were tumbling by, heavy artillery guns were trundling by, troops were marching by in rehearsal. Within easy eye's view, all along the practice shore, LSTs were disgorging vehicles; vessels of all types were maneuvering in the harbor. And all around the beach enterprising fuzzy-wuzzies were hawking coconuts and Japanese-printed shillings.

In that unusual setting Chaplain Bishop led the assembled GIs, Marines, naval personnel, and Coast Guardsmen in hymns and prayers, and delivered a brief sermon.

We embarked on an LST jammed stem to stern, top deck to bottom hold, with troops, vehicles, artillery, and supplies, and for two weeks we were packed in close confinement while our ship shuffled around to rendezvous with the then-largest invasion convoy in the Southwest Pacific, heading for Netherlands East Indies on the northern side of the massive island of New Guinea.

The Green Dragon looked somewhat familiar to me, but I did not immediately realize that LST had carried me from New Caledonia to Brisbane months before. But the Coast Guard crew, and the skipper, Lt. Thomas M. Kelley, a seafarer from Nantucket, Massachusetts, recognized me. They gave me a hearty welcome and reminded me that I had promised to write a story about the ship and crew after they had undergone some war experience.

That Green Dragon had been constructed at Evansville, Indiana, floated down the Ohio River into the Mississippi, down to the Gulf of Mexico, through the Panama Canal, and across the Pacific, some 10,000 miles or more. In the previous six months, "The Asiatics," as they called themselves by then, had landed guns, supplies, and personnel on Finschhafen and Saidor (New Guinea), Los Negros (Admiralty Islands), and Cape Gloucester, and had then evacuated the wounded. At Gloucester, the officers' wardroom had been converted into a surgery for eleven emergency operations.

Ironically, it was while anchored in a quiet harbor that the LST suffered its only battle damage. A Betty streaked over and dropped a 500-pounder that exploded twenty-five feet off the port bow, leaving six of the Guardsmen with broken eardrums or shrapnel gashes.

I kept my promise and later filed a story carrying the names and hometowns of every one of the threescore and ten officers and crewmen.

The Hollandia invasion was adeptly planned and executed despite unforeseen landing problems. The enemy had been awaiting an assault on Wewak, a major base 200 miles south of Hollandia. Instead, the Army landed a blocking force at Aitape, between Wewak and Hollandia, and trapped some 50,000 enemy troops.

General MacArthur wanted—needed—the Hollandia airfields to press an air assault on his main objective, the Philippines, 800 miles away. With the bulk of the Jap army penned in Wewak, the largest Allied armed force in the Pacific was able to concentrate on the capture of the airfields.

Lt. Gen. Robert L. Eichelberger broke his Task Force Reckless into two echelons, the 42nd Infantry Division striking at Humboldt Bay, the 24th Division striking at Tanahmerah Bay, thirty miles apart on each side of Cyclops Mountain, behind which nestled the airfields off Sentani Lake.

Shelling from our warships drove the defenders away, so the landings on the rainy morning of April 22 were unopposed.

The 24th Division disembarked on Red Beach 2, Tanahmerah Bay, but the landing strip was so narrow and small, a mere strand jutting between ocean and swamp, that it quickly became clogged with machines, men, and supplies. So dense was the congestion, there was no space for movement or bivouac, and the landing ships were unable to discharge their cargoes. The photo planes had failed to detect the marshland.

The Marine tanks could not debark there and had to be unloaded two miles away on another slim sandbank surrounded by sea, swamp, and the Cyclops massif. We dug in until LCMs (landing craft, medium) were found to transport the Shermans to the village of Depapre, where we had to shovel new foxholes for the night.

We Marines got little sleep that night and on the three succeeding nights because the 24th grunts were green. They fired on or threw grenades at every jungle sound and shadow. Oh, yes, some targets were hit: one Jap, a couple of GIs, several pigs, goats, and chickens.

Jungle-wise, we Marines sustained no losses those nights because we pulled our necks and posteriors into the Shermans or the foxholes covered by our tanks.

The following day, a platoon of four Shermans made a gut-busting effort to move up the massif and into the Sentani flatland in order to clear the GI approach to the airfields twelve miles away.

Pushing and pulling, drawing and dragging, churning and straining, the tanks thrashed through the swamp and slowly inched up a sixty-degree mountain trail, barely the width of the Sherman, which spiraled up the slope. Its surface a mushy clay, the trail twined and twisted in acute angles.

Ahead of us, the Army engineers blasted away at the face of Cyclops Mountain as three bulldozers struggled to open a path for the tanks. Where the mud was too deep for the Shermans to pass, we Marines felled trees and patched together a short corduroy road. The tanks and bulldozers pushed and pulled, singly and in combination, to get the Shermans a few feet forward.

After eight hours of the longest, hardest mile in their lives, the Marines and Army engineers were forced to give up when, at about 3 P.M., a landslide smothered the trail with hundreds of tons of earth. The lead bulldozer was buried in the avalanche, but somehow the GI operator escaped. Unhappy, the Marines rolled their tanks down the precarious trail to the beach, where they set up their guns to strengthen the bay defense.

That was it for the tanks in the Hollandia invasion, but the leathernecks then helped form the long human pack train that passed food and ammo along to the Army infantry driving toward the Hollandia airfields, which they seized April 26.

Meanwhile, in the village of Depapre the natives reappeared from the jungle, where they had fled, offering to sell Japanese occupation scrip at the rate of one worthless scrap of paper for one good Australian shilling. Other fuzzy-wuzzies conducted a thriving barter of one freshly caught fish for one government-issue packet of cigarettes.

On May 4, A Company rolled onto a Green Dragon to join the First Division, which was resting at Pavuvu. I boarded another LST from Hollandia to Finschhafen, where I emplaned for Port Moresby, and then again by air to Guadalcanal. There my orders, misdirected along the way, were awaiting me. They had been months in reaching me, so that back in Washington headquarters, it was understood that I was boondock-wacky and had been dodging the call-back because I preferred the jungle life.

Fact is, by that time, I had had my fill of the jungle, and I was ready to return to the States. Until a new idea crept into my mind: I decided I would go AWOL and take a leisurely look-see of Australia before returning to America.

I flew to Port Moresby, caught a flight to Townsendville, hopped on a train, and stopped off at cities along the coast: Brisbane, Melbourne, and other stops. I had little money, but everywhere I was greeted as a hero—after all, the Aussies felt in their hearts that the Marines had saved them from the Japs—and none would let me pay. I was taken into homes for the night, I was feted, I was cheered wherever I went. I must admit, I liked being treated as a hero for a few weeks.

After a month of coddling, I turned myself into the cantonment in Ballarat, where I had first caught up with the First Marine Division but which was, at the time, occupied by the Army. There I was held in friendly custody by the puzzled authorities, who wondered what a Marine master technical sergeant with outdated oral orders from Intelligence was up to. At my urging, they radioed General Denig in Washington. He promptly radioed back:

"Send Sergeant Stavisky back to Washington by fastest means. We need him for the war bond drive."

CHAPTER 21

Finale

I flew back to Washington without a hitch and presented myself to Marine Corps HQ to be greeted effusively by General Denig. Neither he nor any of his subordinates raised questions about my taking so long to respond to the callback order, apparently because *all* messages between PR and the combat zones went snafu.

The general called a press conference to publicize my arrival and a half dozen or so reporters from the Washington media showed up. The general gave me a florid introduction and wound up by saying:

"And of course you remember Stavisky. You knew him when he was with the *Star*, and *Times*, and *News*."

Of course they remembered Stavisky—when he was with the *Post*, the only paper the general, bless him, didn't mention.

I was given leave, and rushed to Chelsea to embrace my parents and family. I was written up by the Chelsea *Record* and Boston papers—ironically, as a "hometown hero." I then flew to New York City for a reunion with Bernice, whom I had not seen in three years. She had been a beautiful girl when I had left for the Marines, and now she had become a beautiful woman. I was overcome.

First words I uttered on seeing Bernice again were:

"Oh, Bernice, how you have changed!"

I was dressed in a fresh Marine uniform that was too big for my shrunken frame. She didn't comment then, but later confided that when she first saw me that day in the McAlpin Hotel lobby, she had said to herself:

"Oh, Sam, how you have changed!"

I had collected a chunk of my back pay from Uncle Sam and took her to an elegant and expensive Fifth Avenue restaurant. We ordered cocktails. When Bernice stepped out to freshen up, the tall, elderly, dignified waiter bent over to me and said, "Listen to me, Marine! Dinner here will cost you a fortune. Pay for your drinks and get out before you get burned."

I said not to worry, that it was a big celebration for us, and I was ready to surrender a month's pay for the special evening. I did, too.

In New York City, I was invited to participate in "Report to the Nation," Columbia Broadcasting System's weekly radio program anchored by Quentin Reynolds, the prominent foreign correspondent. (Television had not yet arrived.)

The program, broadcast Wednesday, July 12, at 10:30 P.M., featured a paratrooper from the Italian campaign; two congressmen who got to London by shipping as seamen on a tanker; CBS correspondent Bill Downs, reporting on the American entry into Caen; Maj. Alexander P. DeSeversky, a Russian-expatriate aeronautical expert, discussing bombs falling on London; then Sgt. Sam Stavisky, Marine combat correspondent, describing bombs falling in the Solomons.

When the broadcast was over, I phoned my folks at home to get their reaction to their son's nationwide radio appearance. "Fine, fine," responded Mama, who was given to short comment. My aged father, hard of hearing, expressed perplexity. He liked my remarks, Papa said, but he didn't understand why I had spoken with a Russian accent.

I was sent out to join a Liberty Bond sales team made up of returned "heroes" of all the services. We toured several of the eastern cities, relating our experiences and inspiring the preening local politicos to patriotic oratory.

Back in the nation's capital, I spent more time at the Naval Hospital with outbreaks of malaria than at Public Relations offices with boring chores. I asked to be sent back into the field, and was officially informed that my return was barred by the bug, but I would be useful around the PR center editing copy submitted by CCs in the Pacific war.

I wanted out.

Just as it wasn't easy for me to get into the Marine Corps, I discovered that it wasn't easy for me to get out. I persisted, however, and on March 12, 1945, was given a discharge with 40 percent disability for my tropical diseases. That disability score gave me a top priority to purchase a hard-to-get new car.

I also made a deal with the supply sergeant. I argued that in the olden days, a soldier returning from war to civilian life was given a horse and a rifle, but I would settle for a typewriter. The sarge, in a moment of generosity, accepted my reasoning and issued me a new Hermes, which I use to this day.

I returned to the *Washington Post* to cover the return and problems of the servicemen, which swelled to a flood when the war in Europe ended May 7, 1945, and in the Pacific September 2, 1945.

On New Year's Eve of 1946, Bernice and I were married—attended by Al Lewis and George Juskalian as best men—and our new life began. But that's another exciting story.

Bibliography

History of Combat Correspondents, by Benis M. Frank, chief historian, USMC, retired, published on silver anniversary, 1967.

The Island War—The U.S. Marine Corps in the Pacific, by Maj. Frank O. Hough, USMCR. J. B. Lippincott Company, Philadelphia, 1947.

The Guadalcanal Campaign, by Maj. John L. Zimmerman, USMCR, Historical Division, Headquarters, U.S. Marine Corps, 1949.

Marines in the Central Solomons, by Maj. John N. Rentz, USMCR, Historical Branch, Headquarters, U.S. Marine Corps, 1952.

The Campaign on New Britain, by Lt. Col. Frank O. Hough, USMCR, and Maj. John A. Brown, USMCR, Historical Branch, Headquarters, U.S. Marine Corps, 1952.

From Makin to Bougainville: Marine Raiders in the Pacific War, by Maj. Jon Hoffman, USMCR, Marine Corps Historical Center, 1995.

Condition Red: Marine Defense Battalions in World War II, by Maj. Charles D. Melson, USMC (Ret.), Marine Corps Historical Center, 1996.

The Right to Fight: African-American Marines in World War II, by Bernard C. Nalty, Marine Corps Historical Center, 1995.

History of U.S. Naval Operations in World War II, by Rear Admiral Samuel Eliot Morison, Vols. 3-4-5-6, Little, Brown & Co., Boston, 1948–50.

Dictionary of American Naval Fighting Ships, U.S. Naval History Division.

Approach to the Philippines, by Robert R. Smith, U.S. Army, 1996.

Sources

Kenneth Smith-Christmas, curator, Matériel History, Marine Air-Ground Museum, Quantico, Virginia.

Robert V. Aquilina, Reference Section, History and Museum Division, Marine Corps, Washington, D.C.

Richard H. Rayburn, Naval Textual Reference Branch, National Archives, College Park, Maryland.

Still Pictures Branch, Marine Visual Materials, National Archives, College Park, Maryland.

Ships History Section, Navy Historical Center, Washington, D.C.

Index